'THE MOST UNPRETENDING OF PLACES'

A History of Dundonald, County Down

Peter Carr

'THE MOST UNPRETENDING OF PLACES'

A History of Dundonald, County Down

Peter Carr

First published 1987
by the White Row Press Ltd
135 Cumberland Road, Dundonald,
Belfast BT16 OBB

The publisher gratefully acknowledges the assistance of the Castlereagh Arts Committee in the publication of this book; and cordially thanks the Northern Bank for its help with the book's illustrations.

Jacket illustration: Dundonald from the Raven maps of 1625/6 (Bangor Heritage Centre); inset: Dundonald village from a postcard of c.1910.

British Library Cataloguing in Publication Data

Carr, P.A.
'The most unpretending of places'; a history of Dundonald, County Down.
1. Dundonald (Northern Ireland) – History
I. Title
941.6'53   DA995.D9/

ISBN 1 870132 00 9

Data conversion and typeset by Textflow Services Ltd. Belfast
Printed by the Universities Press Ltd. Belfast

Contents

1. 700,000,000 years in six pages.   9

2. Ice and the making of the landscape.   15
   The ice masses gather, the meltdown, the glacial legacy

3. The first Dundonalders   21

4. The first farmers.   27

5. Cairns, pots and stones – the Bronze Age.   33
   Standing stones

6. The Iron Age.   41

7. Chapel, rath and souterrain – the Early Christian Era.   45
   Saints and chapels, introducing Edirsgal, raths

8. The Norman manor.   55
   The 'Manor of Doundannald', the little manors, decline, 'The conquest limpeth'

9. The Irish recovery.   63

10. From plantation to rebellion.   69
    Eight important years, the 'Towne' of Dondonell, the unfought battle of Dondonell, the Kirk, 'That confused and reeling time', love and marriage, a population on the move, 1690 and all that, to be or not to be?, 'A village in the middle of nowhere en route to somewhere else', the protestant parish, the gentry, the soil, wind and water, 'We the Volunteers of Dundonald', the '98

11. The long nineteenth century.   107
    Pew and Preare book, the toll war, squire John, ...and squire Robert, 'An improved and improving country', God's river, enter the constabulary, the County Down burnings, the age of the train, school and 'hedge' school, the picture postcard parish, upstairs downstairs, three years of grace, polite society, the creme de la creme, the have-nots, the texture of the countryside I, the texture of the countryside II: a farming family, society I: dwindling Dundonald, society II: the bone and sinew, church and castle, hastening slowly.

12. Up to the present.   162
    'One of the loveliest valleys in Ulster', the War, 'The quaint little old-fashioned village of Dundonald', the big race, goodbye Gape Row goodbye, the housing boom, the Second World War, as you were, 'Mrs Hugh Edgar's budgie laid an egg last Saturday', 'Unconditional surrender to the builders', Tullycarnet and the 'been, ferment and change, troubles, Dundonald's Disneyland, 'The most objectionable people in Ireland'

Appendices   231

Notes   233

Bibliography   239

Index   244

Postscript: district map   252

Acknowledgements

This book is very much a team effort. Thanks to Allen Anderson, Roy Allen, John Barkley, Karen Bautenbeck, Archie Bell, Mrs Boyd, T.J. Boyd, Mrs Brackstone, Olive Brooks, Mr & Mrs Maurice Cairnduff, Jack and Eva Cathcart, Central Library staff, Mrs Chancellor, Mrs Cochrane, Jimmy Conkey, Andrew Coombes, Rev. Eric Crooks, David Cruise, Margaret Dawson, Alec Dempster, Nancy Dickson, Micky Donnelly, Mr & Mrs Eddie Ferguson, Mr & Mrs Roy Ferguson, Meta Ferguson, Mr & Mrs John Fisher, Jimmy Fitchie, Canon T. Frizelle, Billy Galbraith, Fred Galway, Norah Gardiner, Leslie Goldring, Mrs Gourley, Mr & Mrs Stanley Graham, Stanley Graham, Ada Grange, Mr Greer, Gordon Greeves, Molly Greeves, Ronald Greeves, Ted Griffith, Stanley Halliday, Meta Hunter, Mr & Mrs Jackson, Mr & Mrs David Jebb, Agnes Johnston, Mona Johnston, Victor Johnston, Mr & Mrs Jim Kennedy, Barry Kirkwood, Billy Kirkwood, Nancy Kyle, Agnes Lawrence, Ian Legg, John & Sandra Lennon, Sam Lindsay, Mr & Mrs Billy McCallum, Billy McClurg, Mr & Mrs Tom McCracken, Joe McCullough, Pearl McCullough, Norah McDowell, Mr & Mrs Thomas McDowell, Alan McKibbin, Lawrence and Kathleen McMillan, Jim Mallory, Mr Marshall, Addie Morrow, Crawford Morrow, Judith Morrow, Phyllis Morrow, Paul & Mr & Mrs Richard Morrow, Robin Morrow, Mrs Patterson, Mr & Mrs Jimmy Rainey, Mrs Margaret Reid, John Robb, Kathleen Robb, Billy Rose, Jack Scott, Jim Shannon, Sammy Stevenson, William Vance, Tommy Walker, Rabbie John Walker, Richard Warner, James Watson, Mr & Mrs Ken Wheeler, Agnes Whiteman, Betty Whiteman, Mr Whiteman, Ian Wilson, Joyce Wilson, Matty & Marcella Weir, Helen White and Desmond Wright, without whom this book would not have been possible.

Thanks also to the N.I.H.E., St. Elizabeth's Select Vestry, John Greene and the News Letter indexing project, the Ulster Museum, the Ulster Folk and Transport Museum, Armagh Museum, the Dept. of Historic Monuments, the I.S.P.O., the P.R.O.N.I., and the Linenhall, Central, Dundonald, Q.U.B. Geography, and Presbyterian Historical Society Libraries. Thanks to mum, dad, Ruth and Helen for proofing the text. Thanks to Hugh for PCW 8256. Apologies to anyone whose name should be here but is not, and particular thanks to John Barkley for reading chapter ten.

Preface

When I first considered writing this book, I looked around to see what was available on Dundonald's history, in the hope of perhaps stumbling on a few short cuts. I was astonished to see how little there was. Dundonald's history seemed to have got lost somehow. Its story was mostly to be found in footnotes to the histories of other places.

This struck me as wrong. It seemed important that some attempt, however faltering, should be made to speak for Dundonald and to put its history on record. This book, then, is intended as much as an archive as a narrative. Much is included because if it is not it may be lost. At times detail has been written in at the narrative's expense, but not, I hope, to the point where it becomes an imposition. Much has had to be researched from scratch, or thereabouts, so on the credit side almost every chapter includes a mass of new or unpublished material. On the debit side, this sometimes appears in a relatively raw form, and I am conscious that this book simply sketches out a territory which others will hopefully go on to explore more fully.

Perhaps the most significant thing about this history is its timing. Dundonald has lately turned a corner. The small farming village of forty years ago has given way to something larger and infinitely more complex. But all memory of 'the quaint, old-fashioned village' has not quite disappeared, and with the help of about sixty or so of our 'old residenters' I have made an attempt to capture something of its spirit. Without their help and encouragement this book would have been very much the poorer.

My hope is that this book will inform and be enjoyed, and perhaps make a few people curious enough to explore a little of Dundonald's history for themselves.

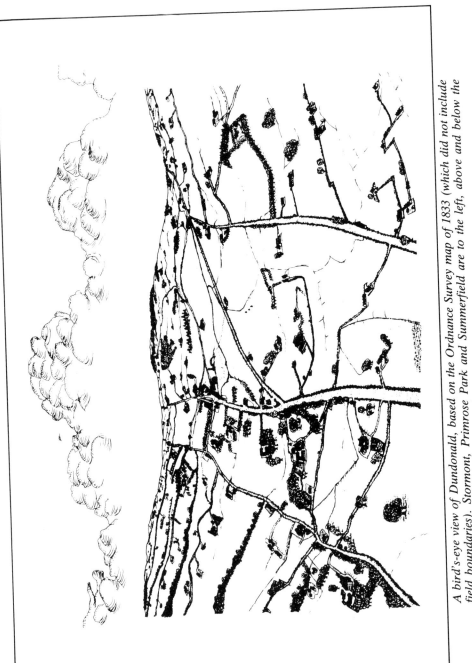

A bird's-eye view of Dundonald, based on the Ordnance Survey map of 1833 (which did not include field boundaries). Stormont, Primrose Park and Summerfield are to the left, above and below the now largely vanished 'King John' road.

1 700,000,000 years in six pages

Imagine you went up to the moat one afternoon, and found a time machine sitting there. Imagine you were to step inside, and travel back through the ages. What a journey you could have! If you survived the fall when, after a few seconds, the moat promptly vanished, and weren't injured when the hill beneath it did likewise a few minutes later; and assuming you weren't carried half-way to Cork by glaciers, weren't swallowed up by steaming mud swamps, or buried as a living fossil in sandstone; then without moving an inch you would voyage through hot baking desert, lush tropical forest, arctic waste, and just about everything in between.

It would be quite an afternoon! Many weird and wonderful creatures would nose against the window, not only mammals and reptiles, but fish and crustaceans, for the area we call Dundonald has spent as much time underwater as above it. Indeed, when we first glimpse it, Dundonald was an anonymous patch of mud and ooze on the bed of a great sea, which came into being some 700,000,000 years ago, and lasted for approximately 300 million years.

Modern Dundonald might be said to have begun between 530–440 million years ago, with the birth of the shales and greywackes that make up the western part of the Holywood and Castlereagh Hills. They began as fine grains of sand and gravel (parts of even older rock) which were swept onto the ocean floor by streams and rivers. As they built up, the seabed sagged, allowing more sediment to collect, until the weight of the later deposits pressed the early ones into rock, forming siltstones and mudstones. That their rock is fine grained suggests that Dundonald was then some distance offshore. The excellently preserved remains of tiny plants called grapholites which have been found hereabouts, imply deepish water and a quiet seabed.

The rock which makes up the eastern part of the Holywood Hills (the parts east of Stormont), and most of the Castlereagh Hills, was laid down between 430–400 million years ago, during the last phase in the life of this large and stable sea. However its calm was deceptive. About 410 million years ago the continental plate we are part of collided with another. The placid ocean was convulsed and Ireland was left high and dry.

The upheavals completely rearranged County Down. Its silts and mudstones were pressed into shales and greywackes and forced into tightly corrugated folds. Thin layers were cooked into graphite and chert. The county became a mountainous region of jagged ridges and plunging NW-SE tending gorges, which ran all the way to Longford. Amongst them, in the northern part of these highlands, lay the ancestors of the Holywood and Castlereagh Hills. These would have borne no resemblance to the low, round hills we know today. In places their strata sit almost vertically. These would have been wild, craggy, Himalayan peaks.

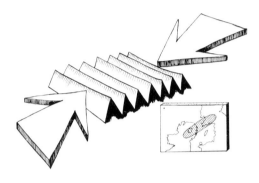

The violent creation of the Holywood and Castlereagh Hills some 410 million years ago. The present hills are the remains of these once towering peaks.

Another consequence of this complex adjustment was the appearance of cracks or fault lines. There are at least four running under Dundonald. The largest, known as the Newtownards fault, more or less created the Dundonald valley. It runs between parliament buildings and Stormont Castle, passes just above Dunlady House then continues in a fairly straight line through Carrowreagh, round the north of Newtownards, then down the west coast of Strangford Lough to Greyabbey. Countless tremors and earthquakes then pushed the land to the north of the fault two miles out of kilter with the land to the south. (The whole district was redesigned. Prior to the upheavals, for example, the land on which Stormont sits overlooked Quarry Corner.)

This invisible seam is perhaps the most significant fact in Dundonald's geography. Over the next 50 million years, the forces of erosion picked at it carving out the Mark One version of the valley. Our valley, then, is some 400 million years old, and thanks to the pattern of faulting, is of a piece with the Lagan valley and Strangford Lough.

This brings us to the first long gap in Dundonald's geological record, a gap of some 130 million years. But this does not mean that nothing was happening. On the contrary! Some 370 million years ago the valley is thought to have carried a large river, perhaps comparable in size to the Thames. It is believed to have risen in the Welsh mountains, and crossed the Ards peninsula between Portavogie and Kircubbin, deepening and broadening the Dundonald valley before emptying into the western sea; the shore of which ran from Lisburn to Holywood. Dundonald would then have been a pleasant, ferny river valley flanked by bare mountains, several miles from the coast.

About 345 million years ago, a warm tropical sea flooded Ireland. Coral grew plentifully in its waters, forming the limestone which underlies Castle Espie, near Comber, where there may have been a landlocked lagoon. Dundonald too probably bristled with coral reefs, and the valley may have received a coating of limestone, that has since been wiped off.

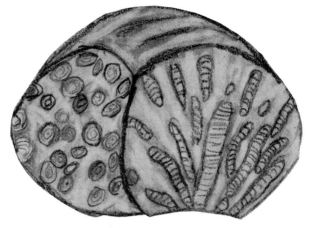

A piece of colonial coral found by Warren Rainey in the stream that runs through the Boy's High School. It is probably between 280-345 million years old.

On land luxuriant tropical swamp forests grew in long meandering deltas. Extravagantly tall trees, with long sausage-like leaves springing directly from their trunks, huddled together in the congenial mud. On the riverbanks large, clumsy amphibians pottered about on legs not far removed from fins, feeding on the pulpy vegetation. This balmy period came to a rude end some 280 million years ago, when another bout of upheavals left Ireland high and dry again.

In what looks very much like a re-run of events following the first upheavals and a desert-like climate established itself. It was punishingly hot by day and freezing cold by night. During the stormy season the desert became fleetingly glutted with water, and the upland debris was flushed into depressions, where marls and sandstones formed. Some of the deepest of these deposits, known as New Red Sandstone, were laid down in the Lagan-Strangford system. These run to a depth of some 200m under Dundonald.

Deep as these deposits are, we know from the red and purple staining of the Holywood and Castlereagh shales that the valley was once full to the brim with sandstone. But like a lot of the earlier infilling rock, the sandstone was softer than its shale surround. In the course of its long history the valley has been filled, scooped out and refilled several times.

These Triassic sandstones are the very stuff of the present valley. While they can be glimpsed in stream beds in Carrowreagh and Dunlady, they are best displayed in the disused quarries at Scrabo. Scrabo's 30m quarry face is a record of Triassic times. Its sun-cracks, rain pits and beds of hardened sand-dunes tell of an unsparing climate. However, the recent discovery here of fossilised footprints made by a reptile scuttling across soft mud, suggest that the district was not entirely devoid of life.

The hectic sandstone building came to an end about 190 million years ago when a warm sea advanced across the almost dead surface of the desert. Like an incoming tide, it drowned the valley, then crept up the Holywood and Castlereagh Hills, covering the whole of County Down except Slieve Croob, which remained an island for several million years longer. Its arrival ushered in the second great gap in Dundonald's geological record. The events of the next 125 million years are entirely unremarked on in the local rock strata. What makes this strange is that for most of this period Dundonald lay on the seabed, steadily accumulating deposits.

At first it lay beneath a stale, lifeless sea, rather like the Dead Sea. In time, however, this brackish annex was connected to the main sea, and its salty waters were dispersed. About 140 million years ago County Down came up for air, not for long, but long enough for most of its new deposits to be wiped off.

Artist's impression of life in the Dundonald village area some 120 million years ago. What is now the village would have been covered by a warm clear sea.

Then, like a summer bather, it went back under. For most of the next 60 million years the Dundonald valley would have been a shallow marine trench in a warm sea, full of life, about a hundred miles off the coast of a massive continental plain, which ran across Iceland to Canada.

These quiet spells never seem to last. This one came to a close about 64 million years ago when Britain and Ireland were unceremoniously thrown westwards, into roughly their present positions, and hoisted from the water yet again. The crust became punctured and tides of highly fluid lava spilt across the continental plain, turning the area between Belfast Lough and Greenland into a vast lava desert. Dundonald became caught between the devil and the deep blue sea. To the north the lava flow radiated ever outwards; to the south the ructions that were to form the Mourne mountains were underway. Even the Tourist Board would have had difficulty in making its situation sound attractive.

The valley was probably drowned in basalt, which has since been eroded. (That the Antrim plateau was then twice as thick as it is today will give some idea of the power of the erosive forces.) Lava also invaded it from below. At an undetermined date a large bulb of dolerite bullied its way through the sandstone towards the surface. It didn't quite make it, however, and it had to be content with hardening below ground, where it too was intruded into, with equal ruthlessness, leading to the formation of an elaborate system of sills and dykes – the largest of its kind in the British Isles.

Erosion has since exposed its upper reaches at Ballybeen/Ballyhanwood, where Praeger records that its ferocious heat baked the underlying sandstone into a yellow quartzite; and at Ballyoran/Ballyrainey/Greengraves Ballyalton/ Scrabo, where a much larger mass lies, like an iceberg, with just its tips peeking above the surface of the sandstone sea. A boring at Ballyalton showed the sill there to be over 150m thick, so the exposure is still in its infancy.

Minerals from the disintegrating dolerite have enriched the surrounding soils to the extent that some of the finest (and most highly-priced) farmland in Ireland lies on Scrabo's eastern slopes. The intrusions also condensed and

The geology of the Dundonald valley.

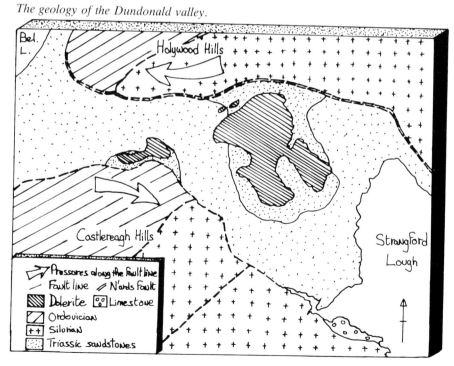

strengthened the nearby sandstones, making them tougher and more suitable for building. They had the further effect of inflating the landscape between Dundonald and Newtownards. Had they never occurred, Dundonald, not Newtownards might have stood at the head of Strangford Lough!

The lava was weathered into fresh fertile soils and tropical forests grew. In the centre of Ulster a depression (the forerunner of Lough Neagh) came into being and filled with water. Forests crowded from its shores through the Dundonald valley into what is now Strangford Lough. Some 25 million years ago, however, the temperature began to drop and the woodlands were replaced by grasses. As the downward spiral continued even these began to find life difficult. The grassland became patchy and about two million years ago conditions of unprecedented cold established themselves. The Ice Age had begun.

2 Ice and the making of the landscape

It would seem that nothing can be taken for granted. Not even the ground beneath one's feet. And especially not if that ground is in northern County Down. For as many people will long have suspected, this part of the county is not entirely Irish. Nor is it fully Scots. It is something in between; being made of stone and till introduced by both Scottish and Irish glaciers in the course of a long struggle between competing masses of ice. (However, in case anyone is getting carried away, the idea of a pure Scots-Irish race farming racially sound Scots-Irish soil does not stand up to scrutiny; particularly not around Dublin where the earth is just as Scottish!)

But let's start at the beginning. Though conditions of severe cold settled on Europe two million years ago, it was not until maybe 200,000 years ago that the first Irish and Scottish ice masses formed. Even then the ice came and went perhaps three times, and the intervals could be warm and long-lasting. For most of the time, however, Ireland appears to have been a frozen waste not unlike arctic Canada today. And, just as the climate alternated between warm and cold, it swung between dryness and a kind of damp that was conducive to the formation of ice.

The Ice Masses Gather

The most recent ice masses are thought to have formed about 26,000 years ago, when glaciers from the Donegal mountains trundled across Tyrone and Derry into the frozen Lough Neagh basin. Around the same time a number of powerful glaciers from the Scottish highlands found their way to the channel separating Scotland and Ireland. We can imagine them as a long cliff of ice dozens of metres high, poised on the coast, here and there extending into the shallows, then slowly advancing into a sea rolling with pack-ice and icebergs.

The temperature dropped further, the build-up intensified. Huge columns of Scottish or North Channel ice advanced into Antrim and Down and, not for the last time, Scottish and Irish elements confronted one-another. At first the Scottish ice seems to have had it very much its own way. It came in from the north and north-east (that is to say from the Craigavad/Bangor direction),

 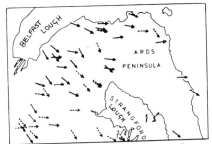

Local striations and drumlin debris associated with the first (l) and second ice flows.

gnashing its way over the Holywood Hills, then hardly acknowledging the valley, it proceeded over Castlereagh, grinding up the hill tops and casting them over central County Down.

Dundonald became covered by perhaps a mile of ice. Carried in it were thousands of tons of grit and debris, including blue-speckled Ailsa Craig microgranite, pieces of which have been found in local gravel pits and can be picked up from the plough-soil. Like a bad set of teeth, the ice was also riddled with cracks and cavities, through which ran a slurry of water and debris, which eventually became tailored into the low slouching hills known as drumlins, arranged along the line of flow.

Just as the Scottish transgression seemed complete, however, the Irish ice asserted itself, apparently displacing the overextended Scottish glaciers from large areas. For a time Ulster became something of a rough-house, a confused, brawling scrummage of ice. Eventually, however, a new flow pattern emerged.

During this second and more formative phase the ice appears to have crossed Dundonald from the north-west, that is to say from the direction of Stormont. The new flow seems to have powered down the valley, decapitating its newly formed drumlins then bulldozing Scrabo, which it scattered as powder over Strangford Lough. Instead of Ailsa Craig microgranite this flow carried with it sandstone gathered in the Lagan valley (or perhaps even Ballyregan/Dunlady). Some of this was released a few miles later, in what became the gravel pits of Unicarval and Ballyrainey; some was carried into Strangford.

So far so good. However, while the general evidence tends to suggest a north-west to south-east ice flow, the local detail is highly confused. Why, for example, do the striations on the Holywood Hills run uniformly NNE-SSW, when those in the Castlereagh Hills run in every direction but this? Did two ice

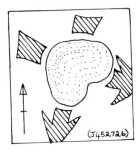

Dazed and confused. Sow's Hill, Ballymagreehan, showing how its drumlin was formed by a north-south, and re-modelled by a west-east ice flow.

flows meet here? We can only guess. The more closely the local glaciation is studied, the more mysterious it becomes.

The Meltdown

About 15,000 years ago the temperature rose and the glaciers came to rest. Melting began and slowly the Castlereagh and Holywood Hills became visible again. The Scottish ice shrank towards its source, taking up position just off the coast, and the county became ice free.

The most active phase in the landscaping process now began. All around the valley streams and rivers reappeared. Tumultuous and full of sediment (which gave them a sharp cutting edge) they cut deep gorges into the hillside, creating Dundonald's five glens. Each covered its corner of the valley floor with a blanket of fertile alluvium.

In the Lagan valley the story was the same, with one important difference. Here, a section of the Scottish ice sheet blocked the entrance to Belfast Lough, whereon the meltwater is thought to have drowned the valley, forming 'Lake Belfast', an infertile and unstable entity twelve or fifteen miles long and some

Lake Belfast, showing the decaying remains of the ice sheet (top right), and the overflow channel which ran through the Dundonald valley into Strangford Lough.

four miles wide, with a shoreline around Ballyhackamore. Its shivering waters drained through gaps at Bloomfield and Ballymagan, emptying into Strangford Lough via the Dundonald valley. The overflow may have taken the form of a river, however its sands and gravels are poorly sorted, suggesting that the water may have spilled out in freezing sheets, which towards Dundonald took the form of a braided river, active and quiet by turns.

After this, in spite of the occasional plunge in temperature, it was all downhill. The Scottish ice shrank whence it came, unplugging and emptying Lake Belfast. County Down became ice free. Abundant plant and animal life returned, and some 13,000 years ago elks, bears and hyenas roamed the north Down grasslands. (During the last century the skeleton of an elk was recovered from a dried lake bed between Quarry Corner and Newtownards, possibly Lough Maroney.) Between 10,500–10,000 years ago the climate again deteriorated, however no ice formed, and after this final flourish the 'Ice Age' came to an end.

The Glacial Legacy

The glaciation gave the landscape its finish, smoothing down the hills and filling the valley with till, over which the meltwater spread low gravel mounds and a veneer of rich alluvium. Well-shafts have shown this infill to be anything from several centimetres to over 35m thick. It is far from being an undifferentiated sludge. Borings have revealed that, like a disorderly lasagne, it is made up of layers of sand, gravel, till and alluvium, arranged in sequences that have yet to be decoded. (It can be colourful too. When H.B. Muff examined the local gravel pits and cuttings in 1904 he found streaks of yellow, orange, purple and red.)

The ice also cobbled the valley with drumlins. They are everywhere. The Ulster Hospital and nurses homes sit on one, or rather in it, for its natural shape has largely been erased. The Knock Golf Course is laid out around another. The Cumberland estate sits on the tail of a third. Culross Drive runs along two more, and so on. Ballybeen, rather like ancient Rome (and here the similarity ends) is built on seven drumlins, or more accurately, on their remains. In the west, where the valley is broader and the rock softer, or the infill deeper, they tend to take the form of low, unyeasted mounds. To the east of the village, however, where the valley narrows, they billow into a full blown drumlin landscape.

Its complexity is staggering. Almost half a dozen scholarly papers have been written on the drumlins of northern County Down, and still they are not fully understood. Alan Hill, author of the most detailed and most persuasive study, suggests that Dundonald lies between two quite different sets of drumlins. To

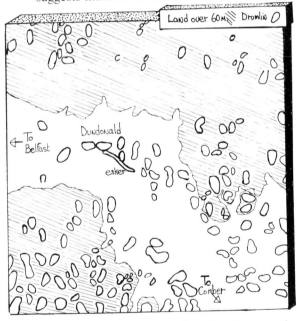

The drumlin landscape, showing the confusion of the local drumlin field. Dundonald's geography is the product of two contrary tendencies: the unifying effect of the valley, offset by the splintering effect of the drumlin swarm.

the north lie NE-SW tending drumlins, made largely of 'Scottish' till. To the south, beyond Comber, lies a much bigger NW-SE tending swarm, largely composed of 'Irish' till. Dundonald's drumlins are made of both tills, which leads Hill to see the valley as part of a sort of transitional zone, in which the Scottish drumlins were refashioned into grotesque, fantastical shapes by the second ice flow.

Two of the biggest and fattest of the local drumlins are Ferguson's Hill(r) and Boyd's Hill, seen here from the Ballyrainey Road.

Snags on the rock floor have added to the confusion. In the townland of Greengraves, for example, the ice seems to have been thrown off course by a hard shelf of dolerite. Here, the rules governing drumlin formation have been flouted in spectacular fashion. Where you expect to see more closed hillocks, the landscape opens and the drumlins form a kind of amphitheatre. (This effect can be seen very well from the dual carriageway, about a mile beyond Quarry Corner.)

This landscape, in all its magnificent diversity, is perhaps best seen along and from the Ballyrainey and Greengraves Roads, where the effervescence scenery and the effortlessness of modern travel make it easy to forget that drumlins often meant bad roads and poor drainage. (Imagine that you were a horse pulling a cartload of vegetables along either of these roads!) It is a landscape that tends to divide and splinter, and as we shall see, it has had a powerful influence on the district's history.

One of the glaciation's most interesting gifts is (or rather was) the esker known as 'the Rank'. This ran from Cooper's Corner to what is now the Rank Road Methodist church, where, though it got a little lost in a complex arrangement of debris involving drumlins, it continued as a flat-topped ridge, ceasing near Dundonald's most celebrated piece of glacial landscaping, the hill that has had its top scooped up to make the motte. This half mile long bank is thought to chart the course of a stream that once ran under the ice. From the early 17th c. until its destruction in the 1960s it was one of the lynch pins of the valley's road network; indeed it had probably served as a routeway since prehistoric times. The scraggy sandhill beside the Moat Park playground is another glacial hangover. It may be a rarish feature known as a kame, which would have been created when the ice was stationary.

The drift has not only been of value to geographers. Salted away in it are huge caches of sand and gravel; bright clean gravels which when freshly cut (as during the building of Wellworth's supermarket) stand sheer like Byzantine mosaics, or frescos stolen from some Renaissance palace. These gravels have long been commercially extracted, and their fate, rather a sad one for such beautiful stones, has been to be used by contractors in the making of concrete, most notably perhaps in the building of Stormont.

Sand has long been extracted too. It has been used in building and iron moulding, and was much in demand during World War Two, when a large slice of the Whinney Hill (now Cumberland) was packed into sandbags, leaving a 100x5m exposure, now crumbled and overgrown. Dundonald's other main sandpits lay behind the village, where there was a crisp 5m face complete with nesting sandmartins; and at Peartreehill, where most of another sandhill was removed. Both sandfaces have now disappeared: one under brambles, and the other, more characteristically, under houses.

3 The first Dundonalders

Ireland was first settled about 9,000 years ago. For many years it was believed that its first people might have come from Scotland, perhaps along a land bridge from the Mull of Kintyre. However, this view has recently had to be abandoned (Ireland was apparently settled first); and while a convincing new settlement theory may lie just around the corner, it is presently thought that the first settlers came from the rolling plain that then existed around the Isle of Man, and that one of the first areas to be settled was Ireland's most easterly county, Down.

It is not clear what brought them, but the quantity of material found on the Isle of Man and around the base of the Pennines suggests that the spur to cross may have been pressure on resources, plus the fact that, like Atlantis, the Manx peninsula was slowly being drowned by the sea.

Hence, perhaps, the drift westward. The journey would not have been difficult. Summer trips to Ireland may have been a routine part of foraging long before the country was settled.

When we look at what they would have found we might wonder that they did not go straight back again, for Ireland was then covered by forest almost to its

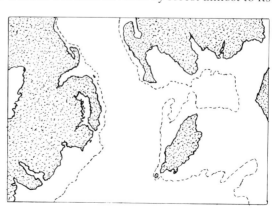

The modern shoreline and the possible shoreline around 7,000 b.c. (after Woodman). North eastern Ireland and western Britain would then have been relatively close.

shoreline, not the nicely groomed plantations weaned by the Forestry Commission, but a dense tangle, inhabited not only by cute and cuddly species, but wild cats, wolves and bears. However this was what they were used to. Their world was forest and water, and they were probably expert at living off both.

Strangford Lough, shallow, sheltered and teeming with fish and wildfowl must have seemed like paradise to the first settlers, and it would not be too far fetched, perhaps, to see it as one of the cradles of man in Ireland. Mesolithic debris has been found at Mahee Island, Reagh Island, Ringneill, Gaws Wall, White Pillar, Cunningburn, and at Temple Midden near Mountstewart House,

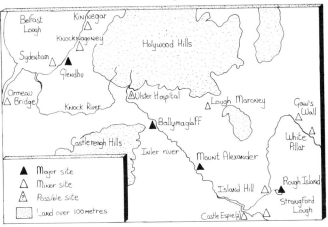

Local mesolithic sites. Mesolithic flints are regularly turned up near the Inler river: last year a core was found near the Longstone, and a core and five blades were discovered in Castlebeg.

where an oyster midden was discovered in the course of farmwork. There have also been valuable finds along the estuary of the Inler River. On the south side, several dozen cores, a Bann flake, a slug knife, two scrapers, and a range of narrow blades were turned up near Castle Espie. The most remarkable finds, however, were on the north side at Island Hill and Rough Island.

In 1934 a posse from Harvard University descended on Rough Island and more or less took it apart. They uncovered a midden over 2m high (a shell altar, which may have been charged in the minds of its makers with some food attracting power), and an abundance of core and flake axes, microliths, Bann flakes, cores, blades, and bladlets, including five blades finished in a style 'unknown in the rest of Ireland', making Rough Island one of the richest sites of its kind in the country.

The clear waters of the River Lagan, and its broad marshy floodplain, with their large population of salmon, trout, shellfish and game, would have been similarly inviting to them, and their remains have been found along the Lagan, and Connswater estuaries. The southern shore of Belfast Lough is dotted with their settlements. A shell midden was found in Ormeau Park, near the Ormeau Bridge at the end of the last century; it had become exposed and its contents were found spilling over the embankment. A cockle and oyster midden, and the possible foundations of a 6,000 year old house have been discovered by the old shore in the townland of Knocknagoney. In 1892 a hearth surrounded by burnt flint and bones, including the remains of wild boar (spiked perhaps, after a *Lord of the Flies* style chase through the undergrowth) were found under what is now the Harbour Airport.

One of the most melancholy remains to perhaps have come down from this remote age was the unfinished canoe found in 3m of mud near the Albert Bridge in 1894. This crude half boat, half tree-trunk (the end of which was still forked) seems to have been thought very little of; it could not be dated, and its fate is unknown.

The overland route between these two giant larders, and on to the Bann, and the Antrim coast, was of course through the Dundonald valley, then a long, furry gutter, with thick forest, running down to a pondy, marshy floor. Stray flint tools have been found all along the Inler, suggesting that this path was much favoured by the itinerant communities of the time.

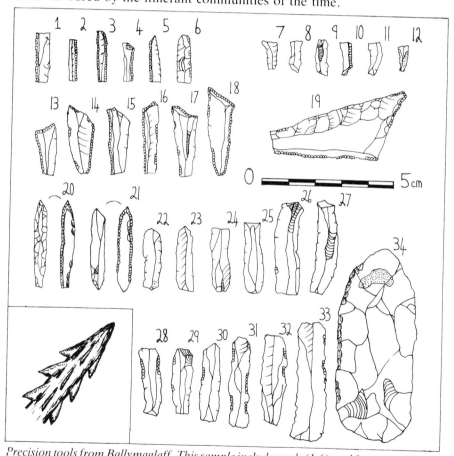

Precision tools from Ballymaglaff. This sample includes rods (1-6), rod fragments (7-12), scalene triangles (13-18), an unusually massive scalene triangle or oblique arrowhead (19), needle points (20,21), bladelets (22-27), retouched blades (28-33) and an axe (34). All are 8,000-9,000 years old. The inset showns how triangles may have been fitted to weapons.

But the valley was more than just a staging-post. It was attractive in itself, and the proof of this can be found in the townland of Ballymaglaff, on the southern edge of the Ballybeen estate. The very first 'village' of Dundonald stood here, on a gravelly ridge by the Inler, 8,000–9,000 years ago. More than 1800 pieces of struck flint connected with it have been found so far.

This is a most exciting site. It would seem to have been a hive of activity. Flakes from every stage of the manufacturing process have been turned up: crude wedges of outer skin, waste flakes, axe re-sharpening flakes, finely chiselled cores, scalene triangles, rods, nail-like points, blade-end scrapers, core axes, and hundreds of keen-edged blades and bladelets, most of them broken, but some of them perfect and almost sharp enough to shave with. Charcoal, burnt bone, oyster shells and burnt blades were also found. In places the plough had turned up rills of black living-debris embedded in gravel, suggesting that people lived here before the ridge acquired its soil. This is distressing, for it means that part of the site has been destroyed. Ballymaglaff urgently needs excavation, before any more damage is done.

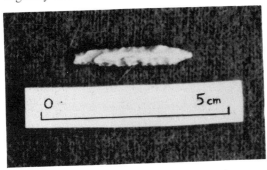

Needle point from Ballymaglaff. Note the extraordinary delicacy of the workmanship.

Another promising Early Mesolithic[1] site has recently come to light in the townland of Mount Alexander, near Comber. Like Ballymaglaff, this site lies on a low ridge by the river, within a small reserve of natural flint. The land upstream was marsh until quite recently, and Mr Ted Griffith of Newtownards has suggested that during the Mesolithic this may have been the exit point of a small lake. 220 pieces of worked flint have been found here, including blades (simple and retouched), bladelets, flake axes, blade-end scrapers, waste flakes and cores, plus two slightly unusual oblique arrowheads, and someone's trusty pick.

This settlement is very different in character to Ballymaglaff. It is much smaller and more casual, yet it is just as intriguing, for its remains seem to belong to two distinct technologies. There may even have been two camps here, separated from one another by hundreds of years. Strangest of all, neither seems to have been related to Ballymaglaff, for both Mount Alexander's sets of flints seem to be the fruits of different industries.

It is unlikely that these were their only way-stations. There are many unexplored places along the Inler that might have been attractive to them, some of which share the outward characteristics of Mount Alexander and Ballymaglaff. Four former lakes also offer possibilities. The mire behind the

Quarry Inn (which is said to have swallowed 600 cows) would then have been a small lake, well stocked with fish and birdlife. Likewise the mires just north east of Quarry Corner and at Dun Rogan. The best candidate of all, however, is the former Lough Maroney, now a sticky mudhole. In the last century flints from the Later Mesolithic were found here by Hugh (Anti Que) Kirk, a local antiquarian, or one of his swarm of juvenile field workers, whom he rewarded with 'as much as a shilling for a good point.' These are now in the National Museum, Dublin.

The hummocky land to the west of Dundonald village has as yet yielded nothing, and its possible sites are much less obvious. Mesolithic material reportedly gathered in the vicinity of the Ulster Hospital (*Archaeological Survey of County Down* p10) cannot now be traced, and the 'Tardenoisian' flints found in the Castlereagh Hills, (the subject of a learned article in the 1938 *Ulster Journal of Archaeology*) have since been found to be natural.

Artist's impression of life at Ballymaglaff.

What sort of people were these first Dundonalders? It is clear from their flint work that they were fine craftsmen. To survive they would also have to have been skilled hunters, fishers and woodsmen, well versed in the ways of the forest. Ballymaglaff was probably the home of an extended family group. As life expectancy was low, this would largely have been a society of children and teenagers; living in a climate comparable to that of the present day south of France.

Their diet varied with the season, and according to what was in ready supply. Our crowd might have spent the spring on the shores of Belfast or Strangford Lough catching shellfish, birds and eggs, and, when they could, wrasse, mullet, flatfish, sealpups and young cod. (Anything that moved had a spear jabbed at it.) Towards summer they might have moved up the Dundonald valley, hunting in the margins and fishing in the small lakes, where bream and rudd shoaled unsuspecting. As summer turned to autumn they would have trapped eels and salmon, harvested nuts, roots, raspberries and crab apples, and hunted pigs and deer. They may have wintered inland at Ballymaglaff, and we can imagine them, light-footed, bows and arrows at the ready, stalking boar through what are now the streets of Ballybeen.

4 The first farmers

While Ireland hunted, fished and gathered, the peoples of the middle east began to farm, husband animals, weave and make pots. The new skills seem to have reached Ireland around 3,700 b.c., for at about that date pottery was being made in the vicinity of the country's oldest 'semi', at Ballynagilly, Co. Tyrone. The discovery of the remains of a domesticated ox (dated to around 3,500 b.c.) at Ringneill on Strangford Lough, suggests that they probably filtered into County Down at around the same time.

Though there is some doubt as to how the new lifestyle took root here, let's for the moment go along with the idea of settlers, and imagine we were natives, watching their arrival in County Down. We would have found them highly peculiar. Not only did they keep skinny animals and grow things, they would probably have looked, spoken and dressed differently. They would have used sophisticated tools and weapons, and probably looked to different gods. Altogether, their arrival would have been a rude shock.

How did the locals react? Were there centuries of guerilla warfare? Or was there bartering, and a polite exchange of gifts? We can only guess. Eventually, however, some sort of marriage of the two traditions seems to have taken place, and by degrees people exchanged the insecurities of hunting and fishing for the lengthier uncertainties of farming.

Unlike today's farmers, who nurse and care for their fields, Dundonald's first agriculturalists had a hunter's approach to farming. Good land was cropped to exhaustion, and when it stopped yielding the farmer moved on, leaving a waste that would eventually be reclaimed by the forest. These farmers tilled the lighter soils. They had no ploughs or spades, and are thought to have opened the ground using stakes, which would have been unequal to medium and heavy soils, meaning most of County Down was useless to them. Large tracts of marsh further restricted the cultivable area. In these circumstances places like the Dundonald valley, with its rich light soils, would have stood out like welcoming islands.

Their hit and run tactics were almost certainly practiced here, and their flint tools have been found in dribs and drabs throughout the district. The biggest

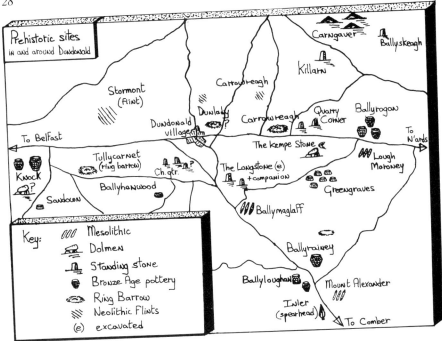

Prehistoric sites in the Dundonald area.

cache consists of 71 Neolithic (and Bronze Age) flints mostly found near Stormont between 1887–9 by the antiquarian William Patterson. Their most spectacular remains, however, are the big stone mausoleums known as court cairns, passage graves and dolmens.

There are three dolmens left in north Down.[1] The finest of these, known as the Kempe Stone, stands just under a mile and a half east of Dundonald village in the townland of Greengraves; which was formerly known as Ballycloughto-gal, 'the town of the raised stone' (from tochar, which can also mean a causeway, in this case a causeway to an afterlife.)

The origin of the name is uncertain. It may derive from the Norse kampsten or big stone, but then again, Kempe means warrior in Anglo-Saxon, and according to local legend the dolmen is the grave of a giant slain by one of his rivals. (In one impoverished version of the tale the giant is said to have been called Green, hence Greengraves.) The name Greengraves may come from Grainne gaireah, 'Grainne's grave, or bed', as the eloping lovers Dairmid and Grainne are said to have spent a night here on their way to Scotland.

More recent visitors have been content with inspection, and it has excited considerable admiration. The correspondent from the *Dublin Penny Journal* (1834) described it as having 'a grand and majestic appearance, especially when we contemplate its antiquity and the probable state of the arts at that time.' In 1846 *The Parliamentary Gazetteer of Ireland* called it 'a remarkable monument of a very striking appearance'. One of its most discerning 19th c. visitors, the Belfast historian George Benn, thought it 'an amazing work . . . one of those which the ancient Irish denominated "eternal houses".' Estyn Evans called it 'The best surviving example of a single-chambered grave in the county'.

Facing east on a gentle rise, about 80m above sea level, the site needs only a nearby brook to make it a classic dolmen setting. It is built of glacially deposited basalt, abundant in the local clay, and its builders probably found all the stone they needed within a few hundred metres of the site. It is thought to have been raised in the late Neolithic (c. 2,250–2,000 b.c.), and was probably built seasonally, with the bulk of the work being done in the summer when things were slack.

From a distance it is hard to see what all the fuss is about. But the stone deceives the eye, and as you approach it the small homely tumble gradually reveals itself to be quite large, and elaborate. Its constituent parts have been exceptionally well chosen, and the whole thing has been composed with great delicacy and skill. Several of its stones look almost hewn or sculpted.

Unlike a sculpture, however, it was not built to be seen. Originally, it would have been secreted beneath a long cairn, the rump of which can be seen at its base. This cairn may have been massive, the area around the dolmen is thick with stones, which the distinguished 19th c. antiquarian William Grey called a

The Kempe Stone.

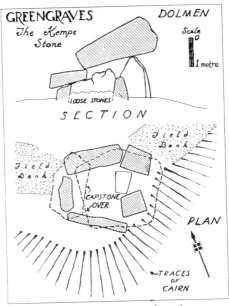

Kempe Stone plan and section

'dismantled megalithic monument of very considerable importance'. What we see today, then, is the essence of a much larger structure.

It represents a considerable outlay of energy. The return may have taken various forms, for it is unlikely that this was purely a mausoleum. It has also been suggested that dolmens were also talismans or votive offerings, built to secure big harvests and fat cattle. They may have been gathering points, or religious centres. They may have been expressions of dynastic power; or a way of letting the neighbours know that you were a force to be reckoned with. In a more egalitarian society, they may have had something to do with strengthening the community's sense of itself.

The site is associated with some interesting material. Borlase writes that 'The interior of the cist was excavated . . . about 1830 . . . when human bones were found.' It has also produced a massive Sandhills pot rim, decorated in an original style. 'Five or six' food vessels, found in Greengraves, have also been attributed to the stone. However, none of this pottery is likely to belong to the monument's builders. The food vessels, in particular, were probably made about 500 hundred years later. If they came from the stone, (and there is some doubt about this) it would suggest that the cairn remained sacred and largely undisturbed for some centuries. Eventually, however, its magic waned, and its stones were carted off for use in field walls, without even fear of bad luck to follow.

When is a dolmen not a dolmen? These stones sit on a hilltop in Ballyrogan. Though they look very like a collapsed dolmen, they are probably a natural arrangement and may have begun as a single stone, left here when the glaciers melted.

What does all this tell us about Dundonald? Quite a lot, for only a group living comfortably above subsistence level could have contemplated such a project. Only an organised people could have executed it. That the Kempe Stone observes the conventions governing dolmen building throughout western Britain and Ireland, suggests that Dundonald's was not an isolated community, but part of a network of like-thinking peoples.

However the stone throws up as many mysteries as it answers. What sort of society would have built it? This of course depends on what it is. But if we accept that it was primarily a mausoleum, then we are forced inexorably to the conclusion that it was built to the glory of some great family, like its modern counterpart in Dundonald churchyard; and that it was probably built by a hierarchical society, in which wealth was concentrated in few hands. The evidence from elsewhere tends to confirm this view, and the recent discovery of a Neolithic hill fort on Donegore Hill, Co. Antrim, probably scotches the idea of the Neolithic as a sort of happy hour in Ireland's history, when the country was inhabited by a 'free-holding bourgeoisie' who used their sophisticated flint weapons for hunting. Such fragmentary evidence as there is suggests that the Neolithic was a time of great social and economic stresses, and an era that encompasses a succession of cultures.

In its particulars, however, our history is lost to us. Given the attractiveness of its soils, it is surprising that such a relatively small amount of flint has been

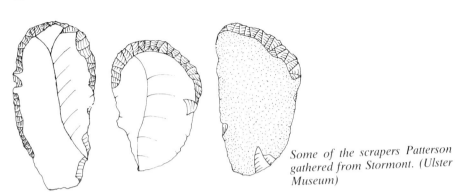

Some of the scrapers Patterson gathered from Stormont. (Ulster Museum)

found here, and that no major neolithic site has been found in, for example, the Holywood Hills. But then in some ways it is early days. Our understanding of this period in Dundonald may yet prove to be in its infancy.

5 Cairns, pots and stones — the Bronze Age

The Cairn Hill, the Everest of the Holywood Hills and the site of an Early Bronze Age necropolis. The two mounds on its eastern slopes (r) are said to be unopened cairns.

If prehistoric Dundonald can be said to have had a golden age then this is probably it, for the area in and around the valley is, or rather was once rich in remains from the early and middle Bronze Age. The loftiest and most exalted of these would have been the now badly mutilated Early Bronze Age cemetery on the summit of the Cairn Hill, the highest point in northern County Down. This is where the rulers of north Down buried their dead some 3,500–4,000 years ago.

There were originally three big cairns on the hill, forming what would have been a haunting and majestic funereal landscape. This would have been our suitably humble equivalent of the pyramids of Giza. Unfortunately only one cairn, Carngaver, remains and it is in a very sorry condition. When Estyn Evans surveyed it for the *Preliminary Survey* in the late 1930s the cairn was 30m in diameter and 3m high, but it is now just over half this size. At its centre would have been a stone chest or cist containing a burial, but this has been emptied, possibly by treasure hunters, who seem to have reached it by quarrying away the cairn's western side. All that now remains is a sad looking, 'C' shaped heap of stones, formerly used for cock fights, and now a cattle feeding pen.

Some 120m to the south, on a small eminence, Evans noted 'The remains of an unrecorded cairn, from the base of which 4 stones emerge, 3 of which may be part of a cist. The fourth stands 4 yards away.' The third stood about thirty yards to the west of Carngaver. The upstanding remains of its cist (including a 'roof stone') were blown up in the early 1960s. Templeton, who mentioned Carngaver in 1804, makes no reference to adjoining cairns, however the dynamited cairn appears on the 6 inch O.S. map of 1859. Its stones are said to have been used in drains: thus are the mighty fallen.

Each cairn could itself have been a small cemetery. Templeton writes that when a similar, smaller cairn at Mountstewart was dismantled during 'improvements' in 1776, 'a sort of stone chest' was found. It contained an urn which was 'soon torn to pieces by the men on the supposition that it contained hidden treasure.' When work resumed between sixty and seventy attendant cists were discovered in the southern part of the cairn. 'Several other chests and urns shared the same fate', writes Templeton, 'but when (the men) found they did not contain anything but a spoonful of blackish granulated earth, they desisted and preserved some of the urns.' (This is not a isolated example, in 1937 nineteen cists were discovered in a mound at Comber.)

Did the Cairn Hill cairns each house a similar array? Was each a single, compact cemetery? If so it might explain why Carngaver's western side was removed, en masse at so much trouble. Though it is less pleasing to the eye, in terms of its unrivalled situation and above all, its suggestive power, this ruined cemetery is a monument to rival the Kempe Stone.

This period saw the beginning of the slow change from a stone to a copper then a bronze based technology. In a sense this may have worked to Dundonald's favour, for some of the richest copper deposits in north-eastern Ireland lie a few miles to the north east at Conlig, and these would seem to have been fully exploited. The coincidence of copper deposits and light, fertile soils is likely to have made the region attractive.

Early Bronze Age pottery: (l-r) Pigmy cup from Ballyhanwood, urns from Knock and Ballyrainey, food vessels from Sandown and Neill's Hill.

Something certainly did, for the valley has yielded an impressive concentration of Bronze Age pottery; all of it funereal and some of it of high quality. Food vessels have been found at 'Sandown', and Neill's Hill. A cordoned urn containing over a pound weight of burnt bone was found with flints in a field at Knock. A pigmy cup containing cremated bone was found in Ballyhanwood in 1837. Two 'urns' were found in Ballyloghan in 1885, in a field by the Comber Road. Cremated bone and fragments of a large cordoned urn have been

The Greengraves food vessel.

unearthed at Ballyrainey. (Whoever owned this got their money's worth, for the vessel was apparently used as a cooking pot before being spruced up to receive the ashes.) As ever, these would have held the remains of persons of quality: the ordinary farmer could not manage or would not presume to this class of interrment.

The most spectacular local find took place 'about the year 1830' at Greengraves. Workmen were removing stones from a field where it was 'thought urns might be found' when they stumbled on five or six food vessels. According to the tantalisingly brief account later published in the *Ulster Journal of Archaeology* 'when lifted out (they) were quite soft, but all were perfect.' All have since disappeared, save one, which found its way by a a circuitous route to the Armagh Museum.

While it is possible that the bowls came from the Kempe Stone, they are rather more likely to have come from what seems to have been a huge urnfield in the adjoining townland of Ballyrogan. Templeton (1804) described this as follows:

these tumuli do not consist of a number of stone chests but of a number of little caves of a round and elliptical shape and each is covered with a very large flag and the whole covered with earth resembling the Barrows in England.

In this assemblage of tumuli I have seen some stone boxes, at least one resembling those in Mount Stewart. I an informed, that in some of these very large urns were found, of the size and shape of a common bee hive . . . These, when found were full of fragments of burnt bones.

This remarkable 'assemblage of tumuli' seems to have been well on its way to ruin by Templeton's time, and all knowledge of it has now gone.

It is when we try to give this wealth of pottery a social context that the problems really begin. However, it might not be too far off the mark to picture the valley as marsh and forest, within which sat a belt of scattered farmsteads, around which might have been ranged a few barley or corn fields, for it is thought that the kinetic farmers we met at the beginning of the last chapter came to rest towards the end of the Bronze Age, shifting their cultivation around a fixed point. Their houses would have been made of wood or mud and thatch, and accidental fires seem to have been the bane of these dwellings. One house on Scrabo was apparently destroyed by a fire so fierce that it partially baked the mud walls.

Artist's impression of the Dundonald valley some 3,000 years ago. The valley may then have been a region of small mixed farms, each with its handful of fields hard won from the forest.

In the uplands the pattern was different. Cultivation was on a garden scale. The emphasis was on ranching. Houses were built in small groups: there was society. The Bronze Age 'village' on Scrabo hill is a fine example of this kind of settlement. Tucked in between clumps of scrub and heather are the remains of at least twelve huts, a granary, paddocks, lean-to's, and a roughly cobbled footpath, together with some older and less easily explicable features. Though nothing to look at these remains comprise one of the most extensive Late Bronze Age settlements in the north of Ireland. That anyone should build their home on this inhospitable redoubt implies a people who had to look as much to their defence as their comfort, and the number of bronze weapons recovered from its vicinity suggests that the settlement may have been a military centre. We can only guess at the relationship between it and the valley.

Standing stones
We could not leave this era without mentioning standing stones, the simplest and most obscure of our megalithic remains. These have been variously interpreted as phalluses, cattle scratching posts, tomb markers, time-pieces, boundary posts, way pointers, altars and astronomical indices. North Down,

with eight stones between Dundonald and Donaghadee, is particularly well provided for. (This unusual conjunction has prompted the idea, currently out of favour, that they mark an early trade route, a view ostensibly supported by finds of bronze implements along its supposed path.) Three lie within the parish of Dundonald and two just outside it in the townlands of Greengraves and Killarn.

The most celebrated of these is the Longstone, some two tons of basalt standing on a natural terrace by the flood plain of the Inler river. (Its point of origin is unknown, it may be a glacial erratic, but then it may come from a

The Longstone, no longer very long, pictured during its excavation. (Photo: Jim Mallory)

dolerite outcrop some 400m to the west.) When the young George Benn visited the stone in the early 1820s he found:

a pillar about ten feet in height, formed of one rough stone, supposed by credulous people to cover a treasure of the most precious of all metals, and to turn around every midnight at crowing of the cock.

(Benn seems to have found the people of Dundonald rather superstitious, his only other reference to them is equally disparaging.) O'Laverty confirmed Benn in 1880 when he recorded 'a pillar stone ten feet high', which together with other local antiquities might he thought 'indicate the site of an ancient village'.

Clearly it was a stone of some stature. How it shrank to its present 2m (if it did) is not clear, but may be explained in terms of natural weakness. Traces of fractures can be seen in the stone. Over the last hundred years, particularly over the last twenty the stone has become convenient to large numbers of people, and as well as being sketched and admired, it has been stoned, picked at and painted, much accelerating the process of decay. We can only hope that when the Ballybeen estate is extended its new neighbours will see it comes to no harm.

The Ballyskeagh standing stone. This splendid fang-like stone was once whitewashed annually along with the gate piers. Unfortunately its antiquity is doubtful, as is that of its equally magnificent companion in Killarn.

As older residents may remember, up until the 1930s the Longstone had a companion stone, slightly smaller, but roughly the same size and shape as the present stone, which stood on a similar platform 200m to the east. Children played around it and cattle used it to scratch on. In contrast to the Longstone's death by a thousand cuts, this stone seems to have been swiftly and unceremoniously despatched. After falling over it lay for some time, then was dragged to the edge of the field by farmer James Kennedy, using a tractor and a chain, and the field was planted with corn. The stone was later broken up.

When the Longstone was excavated by a team from Queen's University in the summer of 1983, they uncovered not a crock of gold but an Edward VII ha'penny, in very poor condition. A short line of stones was discovered immediately north of the the main stone, but whether they were part of a more elaborate version of the monument, or something else again, is not clear. With the exception of one lucky find, which we shall come to shortly, the results were disappointing, and they throw little light on the purpose of the stone.

Less well known, but no less interesting is the pair of standing stones near Quarry Corner. As is perhaps appropriate for stones whose purpose was possibly fertility related, theirs is a private landscape. Invisible from either road, the stones rest on almost level ground just south of a small lakey marsh. Curiously, they have only just begun to appear on maps; and either they escaped the attentions of 19th century commentators or were thought too trifling, for there are no early mentions of them. When we consider that they are one of only three sets of paired stones in County Down this indifference becomes odder still.

The larger Quarry Corner stone.

As for the stones themselves, the smaller is about 1m high and hunch-backed like a chessboard bishop: the other is over 2m high and stands about 120m to the east. Between them lie some large recumbent boulders, including an oval stone 1½m in length. The disparity in size is common to 'cock and hen' stones, with the larger stone apparently representing the male and the smaller the female. Animals were said to become more fecund if driven between them. It is likely they were also thought to influence human fertility, and for a period of centuries people from miles around may have brought their troubles to the stones.

The other missing stones stood off the Comber Road, near the East Link Road and close to the railway embankment; probably too close for their own good. They are shown on the 1834 6 inch O.S. map as part of the border between Ballybeen and Church Quarter. When the map was revised in the 1850s, however, the stones were either omitted or had gone. The interval saw the building of the Belfast & County Down Railway, and there is a local tradition that the stones were a casualty of its construction. As the disappearance of the Longstone's sister stone shows, collapsed stones could be removed with very little fuss.

Stone raising ceased around 1,200 b.c., for reasons that are far from clear. Classy funeral pottery also stopped being made, and from this point on our knowledge of prehistory depends entirely on chance finds. One such quietly

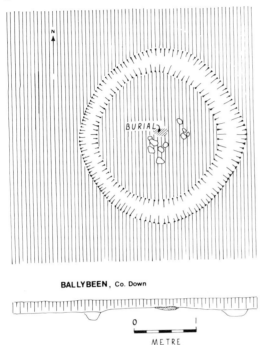

BALLYBEEN, Co. Down

0   1

METRE

The grave and ashes of the earliest known inhabitant of Ballybeen. The remains lay under a field track and had almost been pounded to dust. Identification of age, sex, etc. proved impossible.

sensational find occurred during the excavation of the Longstone. A small cremation burial was found in a ring ditch about 50m east of the stone. It was dated to c.900–775 b.c., making it one of only four Late Bronze Age burials known in Ireland.

And that is it. But before going on, let us for a moment go back to a few hundred years b.c. and the last phase in the life of this mysterious society, and picture again the great forest, patchier now, and regularly interrupted by farmsteads, each with its small bevy of fields, the whole overseen, perhaps, by some aristocratic military court. Meanwhile, deep in central Europe, the great celtic expansion had begun. This settled order was about to receive a very rude shock.

6 The Iron Age

The invasion, when it came, may not have been the deluge suggested at the end of the last chapter. Nor might it have been 'celtic'. Indeed there may not even have been an invasion. Ireland's first iron-using people appear to have come from the Iberian peninsula, or possibly France, and they may have arrived as early as the 5th century b.c. Going for the jugular they apparently succeeded in carving a place for themselves in the heart of the country's most affluent Late Bronze Age society, that of north Munster.

At first these developments are unlikely to have affected life in County Down, but here too, several generations later, it is possible to detect evidence of unease. At the end of the Bronze Age there was a sizeable open plan settlement on Cathedral Hill, Downpatrick. Sometime around the 4th century b.c. however, the era of open plan living came to an end, and the hilltop was fortified with formidable trench and palisade defences.

Just who was defending themselves from whom is not clear. Nor is it known whether the defences were successful, however, after a few years the political climate seems to have become more relaxed, for the defences were apparently allowed to moulder. This was a mistake. Soon afterwards there was great activity on the hill, which its excavators took to indicate its conquest and resettlement. The defences were overhauled: a new palisade was put up, and the ditch was planted with a welcoming carpet of stakes.

The stakes provide a possible clue to the identity of the new occupants, for these were a favourite device of the continental Halstatt peoples and their descendants, and their appearance at Cathedral Hill may mark the presence of iron-using, celtic speaking people in County Down. Unfortunately we have only the most shadowy picture of their impact on north-eastern society. Nothing that can be unequivocally attributed to them has been recovered from County Down.

Nor are stray implement finds much help. Our acidic soils dissolve iron (bogs are kinder to iron, but Dundonald's had disappeared by about 1800), and while some iron slag has been discovered on Scrabo, all the Early Iron Age metalwork known from County Down is made of bronze. However, since there are only five known items, this may not be significant!

The only survival which tells us much about the state of the county at the time is a 2½m beaten bronze trumpet, recovered perfect from a bog at Ardbrin, near Annaclone, in 1809. As the bog was alomst certainly a lake two thousand years ago, the semi-circular trumpet's last journey was probably through its dark, peaty waters at the height of some great ceremony. It is a masterly piece of craftsmanship, indicative of a wealthy, settled court.

The rest of the county has as yet produced nothing to match this. Three locally made horse bits, and part of a rather miserable looking bronze plated brooch have been turned up, but of this small and uninspiring collection little

The Carrowreagh ring barrow. Several other soil marks have been discovered in the field, so this may once have been the centrepiece of a much larger cemetery.

can be said. The horse bits are the nearest the county comes to corroborating the existance of the lethal battle chariots of Cuchulainn and King Conochobar, which in Estyn Evans' view 'closely resembled dung carts', though no strong evidence has been produced for either vehicle.

Until recently Dundonald had two outstanding antiquities from this age of shoguns. It now has one: the Carrowreagh ring barrow, known locally as 'the fairy ring'. (J438742) This is a marvellously discreet monument, massive but unobtrusive, and though its edges have been smoothed by regular ploughing, it is well defined and otherwise apparently intact. Though it may be earlier, in which case it may be a smaller version of the Giant's Ring (we will not know until it is excavated), this is most likely to be the grave of a member of our Iron Age aristocracy, one of the hard drinking braggadocios of the tales of the Ulster Cycle. (Such remains are extremely rare in north eastern Ireland. The nearest comparable structure, at Loughbrickland, is said to be the grave of the great 1st century warlord, Bricru.)

The other, 'the fairy mound' in Tullycarnet (which was covered in bungalows in the early 1960s), may also have been a ring barrow. It took the form of a low, hilltop mound, within a shallow ditch, and an outlying bank some 10m away, part of which had been destroyed. When it was illicitly 'excavated' in the 1950s charcoal and burnt bone were found. The 1858 Ordnance Survey map identifies it as the 'ring of (a) fort', suggesting that other sites with this designation may also be barrows.

The 'fairy's graveyard' on McCullough's farm in Ballyrainey (J448724) may have been something similar, but this is less certain. It took the form of a hilltop ditch 4–5m in diameter, which was clearly recognisable in Peter McCullough's father's time, indeed when he was a boy Peter remembers their servant girl taking him there at dusk 'to see the fairies dancing', but the two of them got frightened and ran home. Ballyregan's small 'fairy ring' (now built over) may

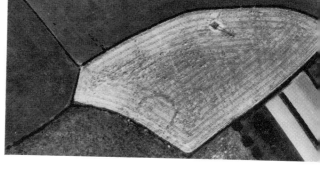

The Ballyrainey fairy ring from the air. Aerial photography shows the valley to be thick with the remains of forgotten boundarys and enclosures, all completely invisible from the ground.

have been something similar.

The Roman occupation of Britain also had its effect, not least in leaving the district with a curious piece of folklore. There is a tradition that the Roman army recruited near the Longstone, a story which, to spoil a good yarn, probably owes more to the reputed find of Roman coins here than to anything military. Tacitus tells us that Agricola spoke 'frequently' about taking Ireland, a job which he seems to have regarded as little more than a formality. And if Bricru and his fellows fancied their chances against the legions, then the arrival

This fairy thorn tree stands in the middle of a field in Ballyhanwood. Look carefully and you will see where the trunk has been partially severed. Field thorns such as this are now rare here.

of refugees like the southern Englishwoman who was buried near Donaghadee (along with her favourite knicknacs), bringing with them news of the slaughter of the Icenci, will surely have encouraged them to take a friendlier line. Following the Roman evacuation the situation was reversed and elements from eastern Ulster won substantial territories in western Scotland.

It is when we try to find out what happened in between that things get difficult. In the words of one commentator, 'The story of Ireland in (these) centuries is not very clear.' This is putting it mildly. As for Dundonald, until its barrow is excavated its history will remain completely obscure. However there are several developments we should note before passing. This period saw a drift away from light soils. By the Late Bronze Age middle weight soils were not only cultivable, but could out-produce light upland soils. As the habitable area expanded old settled districts like Dundonald lost some of their prominence.

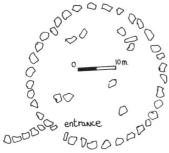

This circle of giant boulders (which the 19th century antiquarians called 'Cyclopian masonry') overlooked the Ice Bowl. This fascinating structure may be a cashel, but then again it may be a compound of hut circles. Its entrance is shown above. The remains of what may be another enclosure lie hard by. Structures such as this are extremely rare.

If in passing, we attempted to sketch a picture of Dundonald in the first centuries a.d., we could do worse than imagine a valley dotted with patches of forest, marsh and pasture, in which lived a quiet farming/ranching community of perhaps a dozen or so ranches. Each would have supported a warrior/rancher, his family and their slaves (the unfree, who according to MacFirbis, included the remains of Ireland's pre-celtic peoples). All would probably have been related, and would have owed allegiance and paid their dues to the wealthy, aristocratic family, which seems to have at one point held court here.

We now approach the crossover into history. From the 4th century on our knowledge of the past begins to come as much from written sources as archaeological finds. This has had an important bearing on how we think about the past. The society which emerges from the mists of prehistory is of course celtic in speech and culture, and may have been so since the Late Bronze Age or before. It springs into being fully formed, comfortable in itself, at home with the land and its traditions. By contrast the pre-celtic societies do not seem fully real. Writing creates an artificial horizon beyond which all seems hazy and obscure.

Had Irish society begun documenting itself around the same time as, say, the Egyptians then 'ancient Ireland' would have become synonymous with a very different type of society; this might also have had the useful effect of exploding the idea that the island belongs to any single sort of society or set of people. Had the records been kept earlier we would no doubt have heard much about the unwelcome arrival of the celts. Celtic misdeeds and outrages would no doubt have been chronicled in grisly detail. We would watch as the native language was displaced, perhaps for reasons not unlike those which eventually led the gaelic tongue to become eclipsed by English.

But all this, fascinating as it is, would not be satisfactory. It would only push back the horizon and discriminate against the mesolithic element which, it has been suggested, in spite of neolithic, celtic, viking, Norman, Scots, Welsh and English overlays, may constitute the main genetic element in Irish society even today.

7 Chapel, rath and souterrain – the Early Christian Era

Saints and chapels

Christianity came early to our district. The 'monastery of Cummer' and the church of Gortgrib can both claim to have been founded by St. Patrick, who is said to have trodden the valley on journeys to Comber; travelling via the esker, Millmount and Solitude, on a track that has since disappeared.

En route he may have refreshed himself at Gortgrib, but this is by no means certain. Gortgrib's association with the saint is tenuous, resting on a fragment of a sentence in the 7th century *Tripartite Life* which records that he founded many churches in Dal-Araidhe, including 'Raith-Epscuip-Fhindich (the place of bishop Fhindich) in the country of the Hui-Dearca-Chein.' O'Laverty has suggested that this was Gortgrib, arguing that the little townland of Gortgrib was once part of its larger neighbour Gilnahirk, or Cille na h Earca, the church of the Earca, alias the Hui-Dearca-Chein of the *Tripartite Life*. The theory is ingenious, but inconclusive, for even if Gortgrib is the church of the Earca, it does not follow that it was necessarily founded by St. Patrick.

The church can be identified far more clearly with another early saint, Molioba of Gort-chirp or Gortcirb. If, as seems likely, these are Gortgrib, then the church is 8th century or earlier. As for Molioba, the *Martyrology of Donegal* commemorates him on August 5th, and the Martyrologies of Leinster and Tallagh honour him on August 6th. Nothing else is known about him; however St Molua's church at Summerhill keeps his name alive in the district.

There is an interesting footnote to the story of Gortgrib. When playing fields were being laid in the grounds of St. Patrick's College in 1970, the clear pattern of graves and ditches could be picked out from the top of the nearby hill. Bones were apparently found, poking through the topsoil. Work stopped and two archaeologists were called in to investigate. They reported that:

No traces of the church or of any medieval structure were found; but remains of a cemetery were uncovered some distance away, and it is probable that the site of the church lay under some adjacent houses. (Kingsway Park) However a complex of ditches and of intersecting gulleys were revealed which proved to be of Later Iron Age date –

*Excavating Gortgrib. Children
from St. Patrick's were brought
along to see what they could find.*

one ditch produced a vessel of 'Souterrain Ware' (10th-12th c. pottery) and several
further sherds of this were found

This tallys with Carmody's mention of a field here called 'the graveyard', where
human bones were found.[1]

    There is another obscure church sites at Chapel Hill in Carrowreagh (first
lane on the right, off the Carrowreagh Road). The church is said to have been
in the field just below the lane (the Chapel Field), and the cemetery was
reportedly in the field above it.

    This is a puzzling site. There is a strong local tradition of there having been a
church here, but no documentary evidence of one. O'Laverty has suggested
that it may be the site of a 6th century convent, which fell out of use before the
coming of the Normans. He backs his claim with a characteristically fiendish
piece of linguistic detective work:

In several of the Inquisitions regarding the Montgomery property a townland named
Carrowcallyduff (The Quarter-land of the Black Nuns) occurs between the townlands of
Killarn and Greengraves (in the inventory), which exactly corresponds with Carrowreagh. In the Inquisition of 1623, a townland called Carrowkilnevagh occurs between
"Carrowreagh" and "Ballyorane". Perhaps this is the site of the Convent, which,
according to an ancient Life of St Finnian of Moville published by Colgan, that saint
erected for his sister St. Quarriar, at some distance from his own monastery.

It is a good try, however Quarriar, or Corcoria, now appears to have had no
connection with County Down. And perhaps it is just as well. According to
Colgan's 17th c. biography anyone who disturbs her grave will be struck blind,
birds passing overhead will drop dead, etc, such is the sanctity of her tomb.

    This leaves us with a mystery, for the names Carrowcallyduff, and Carrow-
kilnevagh, ('the church of the ravens': a reasonable enough synonym for black
nuns, apparently preserve the memory of a religious foundation of some kind.
The fact that it was built on the edge of the Carrowreagh barrow cemetery is
another strong hint that it may have been early; and the recent discovery of
trenches of dark topsoil in a nearby field not previously associated with the
chapel suggests that the site is bigger than had hitherto been thought.

Pulling up the stone lined graves in Castlebeg.

The little townland of Castlebeg contains another of these elusive church sites. O'Laverty writes:

This church seems, like many of the ancient Irish churches to have been surrounded by a circular entrenchment faced with stone called a cashel; thence, probably, the name of the townland cashel-beg (the little cashel). The site of the cashel is still observable, and is called the Fairy Ring.

A large number of well made, stone-lined graves were uncovered here around 1830 in a field known as the Fairy Field. Until the 1950s the traditional church

This single sycamore tree (on the left of the Comber Road about half a mile before Comber) reputedly marks the site of the thousand year old "Capella de Castelbeg".

site was marked by a ring of boulders (called 'the Fairy Ring', as fairies were said to dance here); and in a remarkable persistence of tradition the site is today marked by a sycamore tree.

This federation of small, semi-independent chapelries provided the framework for the district's religious life during the centuries after St. Patrick. There may have been others: there is a church site of uncertain age in Killarn, 'the church of the sloes', a name suggestive of an Early Christian date. Drawings of the time show these churches as tiny steep roofed structures, of about the size of a small garage. Inside they would have been gloomy and intensely atmospheric.

Dundonald may have had other 'churches'. Paganism, as we dismissively call it was 'splendid and far flung'. The church's battle with the old gods was hard won, and it would not be too far fetched to see the very first church at Carrowreagh as something of a revolutionary cell, abeit one in fairly friendly territory. The next phase was the monastic movement, which led to the setting up of most of north Down's great religious houses. Dundonald became almost surrounded by monasteries. This may have raised the tone somewhat, it would certainly have increased the options of the gentry, and if extensive lands close to Dundonald's borders came under church control, this might have helped make for a quiet life – occasional viking raids not withstanding!

Introducing Edirsgal
Politically, Early Christian Ulster was quite a complex entity. It consisted of 2½ counties, divided into three kingdoms, ruled by two distinct ethnic groups. One kingdom, Dalaradia, had a Cruthinic aristocracy; the others, Dal Riata and the kingdom of the Dal Fiatach, had gaelic aristocracies. All had hybrid populations, which contemporary chroniclers commonly identified using the name of the most recently displaced aristocracy. It this scheme the population of Dalaradia can be described as Cruthinic, and the populations of Dal Fiatach and Dal Riata as gaelic.

In the 5th c. Dundonald seems to have fallen within Dalaradia. However the balance of power shifted, and at the time of the viking wars it seems to have lain within the under-kingdom of the Hy-Blathmac[2], as did the parishes of Holy-

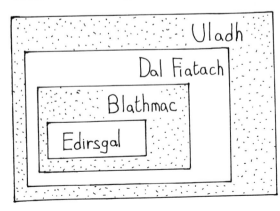

From the 8th century on Dundonald seems to have been part of a district called Edirsgal. The diagram shows how it might have fitted into the political system of the time.

wood, Comber, Killinchy, Tullynakill and Kilmood, and substantial parts of Newtownards, Bangor, and Knockbreda (O'Laverty). Blathmac was part of the kingdom of the Dal Fiatach.

Under-kingdoms such as Blathmac acknowledged the king of Uladh's authority by accepting his gifts. the *Book of Rights* written around 1000 a.d., records rather wishfully that:

> The stipend of the king of Ui-Blathmaic is
> Eight large handsome bondsmen;
> Eight steeds not driven from the mountains (i.e. not untrained)
> with bridles of old silver

In return our tributary district, Breadach, was obliged to furnish the king with:

> A hundred cows and a hundred cloaks
> and a hundred wethers and a hundred hogs

a hefty tribute.

Can we say more than that Dundonald lay within Blathmac? Not with certainty. However an Inquisition of 1333 names the district between Bally-oran and Holywood as Edrescall. If, as seems likely, Edrescall is a Norman attempt at the Irish 'Edirsgal', then the name is much older. Reeves provides a fascinating clue as to its possible origin. Quoting the 17th c. geneologist MacFirbis he associates Edrescall with Edirsgal, a scion of the princely Dal Fiatach family, and the founder of the 'Kinel Edirsgal' in the 7th or 8th c. If Reeves is correct the Clan Edirsgal would have inhabited the north of the parish from the 8th century on.

Raths

While nothing is known about the Kinel Edirsgal, quite a lot is known about some of the places they may have lived in, the generally circular bank and ditch earthworks known as raths (from the Irish for digging), ringforts or more coloquially 'forths'; misleading names, because raths were not usually forts, they were corrals, or enclosed farmsteads, the centres of busy farms or ranches. When lived in they contained a huddle of clay/wooden buildings, the home of the cattle baron cum gentleman farmer, his family, and their servants and slaves. To and from them may have trooped a travelling circus of tradesmen, poets, wandering priests and entertainers.

The rancher's house usually stood near the middle of the yard. Houses were less houses than enclosed campfires, and the most striking thing about them may have been the smell, for our forebears seem to have had a wonderful indifference to domestic squalor. Waste littered the floor being picked over by fowl and flies. When it got uncomfortable a new clay carpet was laid and the cycle began again.

In or near enclosures stone-lined tunnels known as souterrains are sometimes found. These are thought to have been hidey-holes: their entrances are small and anonymous and their interiors are sometimes laced with ingenious feints and traps. If the rath was attacked the souterrain was often all that

Exploring the Moat Park souterrain.

stood between the farmer's family and slavery.

There are only three raths in Dundonald. Each is of a different type. The most stately and orthodox is Galway's Fort in Ballymiscaw.[3] Superbly sited at the angle of the valley, 170m above sea level, it commands fine views towards Belfast and Comber and is so archetypal it could almost have been made from a textbook. The interior is some 35m in diameter, and close to the centre there is a circular raised area about 6m across where the house may have stood. Though the rath took a mauling in 1984, when the eastern part was removed to make way for a silo, it is otherwise in fairly good shape, and is at its best near the entrance where the bank and ditch form a massive bulwark. Over half the ditch survives within a counterscarp bank made by dredging.

Wheras Ballymiscaw is almost classical in its form and setting, the rath in neighbouring Dunlady is an oddity, and the more you look at it the odder it gets. Even its setting is unusual. Tucked away in the glen between Dunlady and Carrowreagh, it seems to have been made by scarping the slopes of a small promontory that was then severed from the hillside by the digging of a trench. A small floodwater stream was then apparently diverted to run through the gap, creating an oval platform some 15x30m in extent. Though its surface is even it has a marked gradient and loses about 1½m on the long axis, a reminder that despite all, it is still of a piece with the hillside. The rectangular 3 × 5m raised area may be a house site.

Could this be the fortress or 'dun' that gave its name to Dunlady? Hardly, it is too small and timorously sited. Where then might this great dun have been? We can only guess. The translation of Dunlady as 'the fort at the fork of the rivers' offers a promising clue, for on the other side of the townland, where the valley is steep and plunging two streams join, and the land between forms a hillock known as Kildownie Moat. But this is also too small to be a candidate.

There is one more tantalising possibility. The 1859 OS map shows a faint semi-circular contour, eaten into by field boundarys, about 100m north of Kildownie. Could this indicate the remains of a rath, and if so might it have given its name to the adjacent glen, 'the wood of the fort', remembered in the modern corruption Kildownie? Possibly, however its position is even worse than the first rath's. No good candidate emerges.

Uncertainty also surrounds the dun that gave its name to Dundonald. It sat on the Moat hill, apparently on the site of St. Elizabeth's church. But was it made of earth or stone? Marshall (1929) in quite definite:

Galway's fort, Ballymiscaw, when in use.

Adjoining the moat is a rath or dun on which stands the Episcopal church and burying ground . . . A portion of the dun's encircling trench can still be seen in the adjoining field on the south side of the churchyard.

A section of this can still be seen near the church gates. Behind it stood some stone tumble. Lawlor, writing in the usually reliable *Preliminary Survey* seizes on the tumble and states that the church was 'formerly surrounded by a stone cashel now entirely gone.'[4]

Dundonald translates as 'the fort of Domnall'. Who Domnall was 'history and tradition are alike silent' (Marshall). He may simply have been the fort's last occupant before the coming of the Normans. Domnall or Domhnall, latinised as Domnaldus, was then a common christian name, borne by kings and high kings as well as our aristocrat. Its modern form is Donal, and it is notable that the earliest spelling of Dundonald (c.1185) is 'Dudoenald', with an 'e' in the second syllable, a phonetically accurate rendering of the Irish.[5]

Marshall adds that, 'Many years ago the sexton, when digging up a grave discovered a souterrain on the north side of the dun'; from which, perhaps, the tradition of a tunnel linking the moat and church grew up. There is another souterrain behind the Moat Inn, and though it is more likely to have been used to protect property than to embezzle it, it is said to be a smuggler's tunnel.

The third rath can be found in Ballyoran, set on a drumlin and encircled by beech trees. It is of a kind known as a platform rath and is about 20m in diameter and 1–1½m high, with no trace of a ditch. A closed souterrain is reputed to run beneath the nearby cottage; and in case the rath is ever excavated, scholars of Early Christian husbandry should note that it has lately served as a cemetery for its owner's son' pets. In 1900 R.L. Praeger wrote that it had:

a hedge of Beech, much beloved of the fairies, for the occupier has told us how certain cows of his broke through the hedge, where upon they sickened and one of them died. But the hasty replanting of the injured part of the hedge appeased the fairies, who removed the ban, and the other cows quickly recovered.

Not everything that looks like a rath is one, and we now turn to the pretenders, the most shameless of which lies adjacent to Parliament Buildings at Stormont. This tree/bush ring was planted for the Clelands in the mid 19th c., when there was a vogue for ornamenting parkland with 'fairy forts'. It was the largest of four, the others having been removed on the building of Stormont. Then there is the mysterious, overgrown mound off Fort Road. It has recently baffled three visiting archaeologists. Whatever it is, it is unlikely to be a rath, and the presence of several massive boulders gives it an almost megalithic aspect.

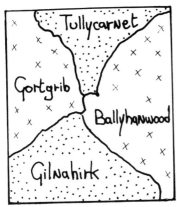

A puzzle. This mysterious bump in the border of Ballyhanwood occurs where four townlands meet. Might it have been a gathering point in Early Christian times?

Now for the casualties. It has been a bad century or so for our earthworks. Building, mechanisation (which made levelling a rath the work of an afternoon), and the decline in belief in the fairies, a decline which has yet to be offset by respect for the Historic Monuments Office, have all contributed to their decimation. Two raths in the townland of Killarn have gone, as has another in adjacent Ballybarnes, two in Ballymaglaff, one in Ballyhanwood, two in Ballyrussell, and another in Ballystockart. Gortgrib may also have lost two raths. When it was cultivated a big, circular cropmark is said to have appeared on the hill near where St. Patrick's now stands. Its well known mound may be the truncated remains of another.

The southerly Killarn rath is the only local rath to have been excavated. This took place in 1958, by which time so much of it had been destroyed that it was decided to let trainee archaeologists loose on the remainder. The dig turned up two fire pits, three bits of souterrain ware, part of a jet bracelet and a jigsaw of post holes, that were adventurously interpreted as (possible) scaffolding for a roof that may once have have covered the entire living space. Only three such roofs are known in Ulster.

Killarn's more northerly rath has entered the last eerie phase of its existence. Though faint almost to invisibility, the ring of the ditch can be made out as a slight depression in the field. Traces of another rath can be picked out in Ballylisbredan, behind Bellavista, where a curious, semi-circular kink in the field boundary, highlighted by trees, preserves what looks like the outline of a sizeable platform rath. The platform is extant to a height of 1½m to the NW, and invisible to the SE, where it has been combed back into the field. Could this be the place commemorated in the 17th century townland name Ballylisdrum-bradan, 'the town of the rath of the ridge of the salmon'?

Most of the district's souterrains have also gone. Until recently there seem to have been two in Greengraves, on the hill to the east of Craiglea. The possible keel of one was removed in 1979. Its remains were about 6m long with a

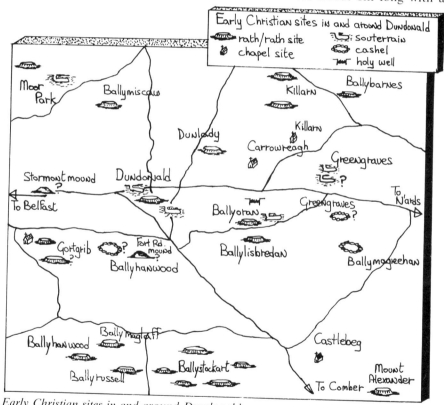

Early Christian sites in and around Dundonald.

regularly flagged northern wall ½-1m high, made up of three courses of stones, and a smaller but clearly discernable companion line 1m away. These are said to have once formed 'a passage, like Newgrange.' The other, known locally as a burial chamber, cannot now be precisely located but is said to lie near the top of the hill.

This is typical, for Dundonald's souterrains have been not so much lost as misplaced. None of them can now be pinpointed. The 1937 R.A.C. *N.I. Gazetteer* (p33) mentions a souterrain 'traditionally used by smugglers' in Cave Glen, Moor Park farm, Ballymiscaw, but its whereabouts are also unknown.

Given the likelihood that at one time most of our raths belonged to a single extended family, they would probably have seen much to-ing and fro-ing, not to mention much music, feasting and dancing. Their main common interest, however, was security. The rath network acted as defence in depth. For example if some youngblood from the Ards had set on Ballyoran, the kinfolk in Killarn or Ballyrussell would hopefully have come galloping to the rescue.

The *Annals of Ulster* and elsewhere make no mention of any place that is recognisable as Dundonald, and this, considering their generally lurid content, is maybe no bad thing. The Hy-Blathmac make one belated and not very inspiring appearance in 1172, when a party of them killed the abbot of Bangor. The murder was swiftly avenged by the king of Uladh at the battle of Derry-Ceite, at which many men from Blathmac died. By then, of course, it was academic. The Anglo-Normans had established themselves in Meath, and around 1175 Henry II of England half jokingly offered the lands of Ulster, if he could take them, to a young knight called de Courcy.

8 The Norman manor

The 'Manor of Doundannald'

On the morning of February 1st 1177, after three days march through difficult passes, John de Courcy's tiny expeditionary force drew up to the seat of the kings of Ulster at Down. His sudden appearance threw the court into confusion. The king, Rory MacDonlevy, fled returning with two great levies, but both were bloodily defeated and the power of the province broken.

To secure and administer his gains de Courcy built a network of motte 'castles', and introduced a version of the manorial system. Dundonald found itself elevated in the most spectacular fashion. It became an important military, fiscal and administrative centre and the hub of a huge manor, the territories of which, on paper, included the baronies of Lower Castlereagh, the Ards and Dufferin – three shattered celtic petty kingdoms. But before we explore the manor and its workings lets take a closer look at the magnificent motte castle it was organised around.

The motte at Dundonald is one of the biggest in Ulster. It is over twice the size of the average Ulster motte, and it was clearly built to impress. Like the motte at Knock, or the obliterated motte at Ballymagan, it belongs to the earliest phase of the conquest. It was probably built by Irish serfs or prisoners in the late 1170s, and in all likelihood was commissioned by de Courcy himself, who may well have stayed here on occasion.

Marshall writes that it was built beside the celtic dun, which he suggests was employed as a bailey or defended courtyard, creating what might loosely be described as a downmarket sand and gravel version of Carrickfergus Castle. If building beside an older fort sounds odd, it was not. The Normans shrewdly exploited existing power centres. Nor is the absence of a purpose-built bailey remarkable. Only threatened frontier stations were usually equipped with them and Dundonald quickly became part of the principality's largely untroubled interior; whereon the invaders, with a nice sense of irony, built a chapel in the dun.

To 12th century eyes the motte castle must have seemed impregnable. Imagine a vast tract of marsh, out of which rears a steep drumlin, on top of which sits the ditched motte, surmounted by a stout palisade, and perhaps archer's pits (the medieval equivalent of machine gun posts) and a look-out tower. It would have been enough to demoralise any would-be attacker, and the psychological impact is important, for the motte's natural defences are largely illusory. Though almost surrounded by marsh, the castle can be approached from behind at little disadvantage.

When conditions settled the tower might have been replaced by a house or hall (turning it into the district's most desirable residence), but this is guesswork, and as the moat's habitation layer (the thin circuit of information buried

Approaching the motte. The motte occupies a fine site on a large drumlin, which had the advantage of facing the frontier and tailing off in the direction of the securely held "Nova Villa de Blathwic' (Newtownards). It commanded the valley, the coastal route to Down and the main approach to the Ards.

in its top) has been erased, we shall never know for sure: the great mound is archaeologically dead. The surrounding ditch (extant in 1837) has also vanished, as has the great platform all sat on. It was smoothed down when the graveyard was extended. The moat itself might easily have gone the same way: O'Donovan (1833) recalls a colleague remarking that 'if this were his property he would level it.'

Benn (1823) mentions it occasioning 'many absurd stories amongst the vulgar', and thankfully, there are still some around. According to one it is a giant's grave, and is the shape it is because the giant was buried sitting, so it had to be built high to cover his knees. According to others it is hollow, and contains an arsenal, or is full of fairies. Tunnels are supposed to connect it to the parish church, the Moat Inn and Dunlady House.

But let us return to the early years of the manor. Its first lord seems to have been Richard de Dundonald, a French speaking knight, whose name along with that of his brother Reinard, appears on a de Courcy charter of c.1185: 'Ric. de Dundoenald, Reinero fratre suo'. Little is known about Richard, however the charter is full of clues as to his standing. Its date suggests that he may have been one of the disgruntled members of the Dublin garrison who travelled north with de Courcy in 1177. That he took his name from his new fief suggests he was not highborn (nobles brought their surnames with them). That his name appears well down the list suggests that he was probably a dependable middle-ranker, a veteran of Down and a staunch de Courcy man owing everything to his lord.

This would seem to have been his undoing. When de Courcy was replaced by de Lacy in 1204–5 the lordship of Dundonald apparently changed hands, for when de Lacy in turn fell foul of King John in 1210, he numbered Dundonald among his personal posessions.

John has the distinction of being the only reigning English monarch to visit Dundonald. In the summer of 1210 he came to Ireland to winkle out his opponents, and on July 30th the king and the flower of English chivalry passed through Dundonald.[1] They came in from Sanctus Boscus (Holywood) along the Stoney Road (which Marshall says became known as the King's Road), then down Church Road, and along through Comber to Ballymorran, near Killinchy, where John spent the evening gaming with the Earl of Winchester, losing 2d.

John confiscated de Lacy's estates, including Dundonald, and entrusted their running to his steward Roger Pippard. The Pipe Roll (or ledger) for the year 1211–2, which has by good luck survived, shows the crown investing heavily in its new estate:

And for a new bridge at Dondonald and a new grange and a new pigsty there 41s 4d.
And for the purchace of supplies there 9s.
And for salt and iron for 3 plough teams there 25s.
And for mowing the meadows and reaping the corn 24s.5½d.
And for estover for the servants and oxherds there £6.12 10d.
And for clothes for the constable for 2 years 40s.
And for wages for the above mentioned servants and oxherds £7.
And for the purchace of 22 oxen and two bulls there £6.16s.
And for the purchace of 80 pigs 42s.
And for the purchace of 50 sheep there 78s.

As well as being a manor Dundonald was a big working farm or 'vill', comprising three ploughlands or carucates (a unit roughly comparable with a townland.) The ledger brings the medieval farm fleetingly into focus. The estate was overseen by a constable, who gets two new robes, a generous allowance, that points up the importance of his office. (The constable of Dundrum castle received only 20/-.) The new bridge may have been a motte bridge, suggesting that the castle was still in use. The grange would have been a smallish granary. Their replacement may have had to do with with the troubles

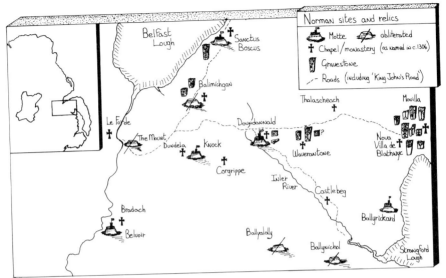

Norman sites in north Down.

of 1210, but it is more likely that the old ones were collapsing, the Normans used unseasoned wood and nothing lasted.

As well as renewing the outbuildings, the new management built up the herds. Perhaps some of the livestock had been slaughtered to feed John's army on its way south. The plough teams were rekitted and supplied with large teams of oxen (implying heavy ploughs used on big, open fields.) The sums paid in wages and estover (food and clothing) suggest maybe a dozen servants, with the same again being taken on for the harvest. Most if not all of these would have been Irish.

What might the 13th c. visitor to Dundonald have seen as he arrived, say, to pay his taxes? Following the track up to the motte, he would probably have seen a cluster of thatched wooden buildings: the big beamed manor house, just visible above the motte's rough palisade, the small church and graveyard, the granary, ratty peasant's cottages, lichened wood and turf stacks, hens scratching for food and children playing. Having seen it all before, however, he would probably just have paid his dues (which he no doubt thought excessive), and maybe had a yarn and gone home.

The little manors
The manorial farm was surrounded by a plethora of little manors ('minutis maneriis'), all functioning separately from it, and owing its lord no allegiance. By far the biggest of these was Wauerantone (Ballyoran), waueran being the Norman attempt at 'huaran' or cold spring. We can chart its rise. The 20/- spent on a new mill in 1211–2 will have removed its dependence on the manorial mill. By 1306 it had its own church, valued at 6 marks (£4), the same as the manorial church. (Its site is now unknown, however it is said to have stood in the 'Chapel field' near Rockfield.) On the eve of the Scots invasion it extended over 5½

carucates and was valued at £5.10/-, making it the richest estate in the district.[2]

In the early 13th century it was one of five estates held by Roger of Chester, a former de Courcy constable.[3] However, when he died in 1218 the king's unscrupulous justiciar de Marisco snatched four of these and gave them to his supporters. Roger's son John protested and an inquiry was called, but the outcome is not known. In 1333 Wauerantone was held by the Earl of Ulster.

The other 'little manors' were Dunleth (Dunlady), Castelbeg, and Edrescall. Dunleth is mentioned in 1333 as '1 carucate, formerly worth £1.13.4d. but now

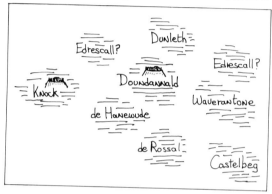

Knightly estates in and around Dundonald, c. 1200.

nothing'. Castelbeg, which will have included the parish's most southerly townland Castlebeg, is described in the same document as '1½ carucates worth £1 formerly, now nothing'. Edrescall, perhaps the heartland of the old Cinel Edirsgal, is described in the 1333 Inquisition as '2 carucates in demesne, formerly worth £1.6.8d, but now nothing'.

Lawlor mentions Edrescall as being near Comber, but this seems unlikely, and its site cannot now be pinpointed. Its derisory valuation is no help. This may indicate unprofitable uplands, but it could easily mean its owner sat on the tax commission and wangled himself low rates. In 1210 Edrescall was the fiefdom of Robert de Weldebuef, a de Lacy man captured in the seige of Carrickfergus. De Weldebuef forfeited his estate to the crown, however, in a gesture which gives a misleadingly generous impression of King John, he was regranted it in 1216 (on payment of a fine).

There may also have been vills in Ballyhanwood and Ballyrussell, which may have been held by a branch of the De Rossal/Russel family of Lecale. Ballyhanwood has been identified with John de Hanewude, who was granted Duncrue near Carrickfergus, in return for his support in 1210. However life did not go smoothly for the de Hanewude family. The story has a familiar ring. On de Hanewude's death in 1219, Geoffrey de Marisco siezed Duncrue, dispossessing de Hanewude's widow Eve (who, appropriately enough, is the first woman we can associate with Dundonald) and her son John, referred to in the sources as John FitzJohn de Hanwood. But de Marisco's plan backfired. John petitioned Edward III, and the king in a somewhat impatient reply directed de Marisco to 'allow them to hold the vill in peace.'

All that remains of these estates are a few place names,[4] and a handful of gravestones. Two were found near Quarry Corner around 1812, when a road was being cut into the Glen Hill. These are likely to have come from Killarn graveyard; and were used to ornament the garden at Cooper Hill, before being given (intact) to the Ulster Museum. A third stone is said to have been built into nearby Glencovitt, but it cannot now be traced.

Two fragments from Dundonald's medieval church were turned up in 1896. They were discovered ten feet underground during the building of a new chancel. (If this seems a great depth, remember that the church sits on a centuries old mound of its debris.) The most beautiful was a section of graveslab decorated with an eight spoked cross, fringed with *fleur-de-lis* nibs that clearly recall the French connection. The most illuminating was an angular fragment of window tracery. This suggests that the manor had a stone chapel,

The finely sculpted gravestone found in 1896. It has since been built into the wall of St. Elizabeth's. (U.J.A., 1902)

and raises the intriguing possibility that the church shown as roofless in the 1625 Raven maps may be the shell of the manorial chapel.

The finds caused great excitement. Writing them up for the *Ulster Journal of Archaeology* in 1902, the antiquarian Francis Bigger declared:

This proves that Dundonald was of much more importance than is generally supposed . . . All other traces of its former greatness have, however, passed away. Doubtless much of it is buried beneath the present modern church and well used burial ground.

That much seems certain: we may not have heard the last of the manor of Dundonald.

Decline

With several traumatic exceptions the century or so after the conquest was peaceful and prosperous. Dundonald flourished. We next hear of it in 1221, when de Marisco was finally removed from office. It and Ballymagan appear on a list of twelve royal castles transferred to the incoming justiciar. As was customary, de Marisco sent two knights to Westminister to surrender them on his behalf. Dundonald probably remained crown property until 1226–7 when Hugh de Lacy bruised his way back into the position of Earl of Ulster. De Lacy took charge of Dundonald, and on his death in 1243 it passed to his widow Emeline de Ridelsford.

Emeline drew a large, regular income from Dundonald. On her death in 1276 the six-monthly receipts from the manor totalled a hefty £20.14s. It was highly profitable. However, reading through the lines one gets a sense of the manor sinking in status.

For fifty or so years after the invasion Dundonald was a key component of the Norman settlement in Ulster, enjoying an importance it had not had for centuries. The reasons it dwindled are unclear. One handicap was that, for most of the century, it had no resident lord. Moreover, its agricultural production would soon have reached its natural ceiling. To keep growing it would have needed to attract a fair, a religious house, or even a borough charter. But this was impossible, for reasons which touch on the very nature of the settlement in Ulster, which set clear limits on the the extent to which an inland site could develop.

Furthermore, by 1276 Dundonald's glory, the motte castle, had become something of a white elephant. With its fortress obsolete and unlikely to be replaced by a stone castle (never built inland), Dundonald ceased to be an important military base. It lost out in other ways. Nova Villa replaced it as an administrative centre. (The manorial court may have continued to sit here, but it would probably have been taken by the county sheriff riding in from Nova Villa. Dundonald lost its position as a regional centre.

The larger Quarry Corner gravestone. The steps at the bottom are believed to represent Calvary, and the shears show that it was made for a woman. (Ulster Museum)

After 1276 Dundonald was again administered by royal agents. Around 1280, however, it passed into the hands of the young Richard de Burgh, lord of Connacht and newly appointed Earl of Ulster. He not only contained 'the great Irishry', pent into the unconquered north west, but encroached into north Derry and Inishowen; and in a remarkable illustration of the strength of the Earldom, sent large levies to Scotland to help the crown in its war against the Scots.

'The Conquest limpeth'

Anxious to undermine the English position in Ireland a large Scottish army landed near Larne in 1315. Three years of intermittent warfare followed, during which Dundonald was devastated. As the 1333 Inquisition records:

In this manor there are no buildings, but there was a castle which is now prostrate and destroyed by the War of the Scots.

At the site of the Manor there are 7 acres of land and pasture which used to be let to farm for 4s., but are now worth nothing on account of the destruction of war and want of tenants.

A water mill at Dondannald which used to be worth £2:13:4 in the Earl's time now only £1:6:8 on account of the war, etc.

At Doundonnald 3 carucates in demesne, formerly worth £4 in time of peace, now waste.

The estates at Castlebeg, Dunlady, Edrescall and Wauerantone were similarly wasted, with only Wauerantone (now 'let to tenants') yielding a taxable income.

Even so, it would probably be a mistake to write the district off as a wilderness. Though a profound shock, the war was also a great excuse for getting the rates lowered. The estates may have ticked over at a disguisable profit, however nobody wanted to pay the crown more than they had to, and it was in everyone's interest to paint the blackest possible picture.

The Inquisition is our last contact with Norman Dundonald. It is unlikely, though, that it marks the end of the manor. Under Robert Savage the Earldom's frontiers remained largely stable until 1360, and this could not have happened without a strong economic recovery. Thereafter, though patently incapable of looking after its own defence, the enfeebled Earldom struggled on until the 15th century, propped up by justiciary expeditions from Dublin. Dundonald became insecure march land, its people living 'daly in drede' of having their lands spoiled by the renascent O'Neills.

Sir Samuel Ferguson made a stab at capturing this turmoil in a story based on the murder of Hugh MacGilmore in 1407/8, and a battle fought between the O'Neills and the Norman Savages at Cave Hill in 1468. It follows an ill-fated romance between MacGilmore and an imaginary daughter of the Norman lord of Dundonald. Gory killings, muttered oaths and thwarted passions abound, however, though completely over the top (i.e. 'It is a brave burning', admitted MacGilmore, 'but I will make a brighter blaze of Dundonald castle', he said with a ghastly smile.'), the tale does to an extent capture (though it might be more accurate to say caricature) the unsettled feeling of the times.

In 1449, in one of the last acts taken specifically to preserve the settlement in north Down, the Great Council provided for the walling of Newtownards. By the late 15th century, as far as Dundonald was concerned the struggle was over, and three centuries after de Courcy, the gaels of the Clan Aedh Buidhe, an O'Neill sept, became firmly established in north Down.

9 The Irish recovery

The arrival of the Clan Aedh Buidhe has had a mixed reception from local commentators. On one extreme there is the *County Down Handbook*, which speaks in grieving tones of 'two centuries of regression, stagnation and comparative anarchy'. O'Laverty, on the other hand, can hardly contain his delight: 'after the tyranny of the Anglo-Normans', he writes, the Irish of County Down 'hailed . . . their clansmen from Tyrone and Derry as deliverers.'

Neither view has much substance behind it. Indeed, one could go further and say that no view can have much substance behind it, for almost nothing is known about life in north Down at this time.

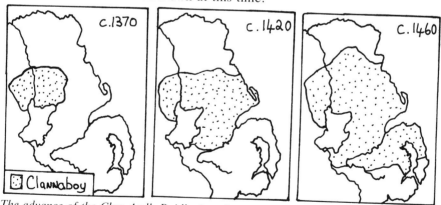

The advance of the Clan Aedh Buidhe into Down.

In contrast, the dynastic affairs of Dundonald's new overlords, the O'Neills, are quite well recorded. Aedh Buidhe O'Neill, who gave his name to the Clan Aedh Buidhe, who in turn gave theirs to Clannaboy or Clandeboy, was a 13th century king of Cenel Eoghain. Ironically for someone whose successors would almost extinguish it, Aedh was an ardent admirer of the Earldom. The Clan Aedh Buidhe first appear in the annals in 1319. By 1344 they had carved a territory for themselves to the north of Lough Neagh, and by 1370, they occupied a large tract of land on the Earldom's border.

A heated dispute over who was to become rector of Breda in 1442 shows us that the clan had by then arrived in County Down. The primate decided that Nellanus McMalwawg should get the job and called on Aedh Buidhe II to enforce his decision, should the need arise. Evidently the O'Neills were the power in the land. Their territory seems to have reached its fullest extent in the early 1500s. After 1537 no single leader retained control, and by the 1560's their vast, rambling dominion had become divided in two.

For most of the 16th century Dundonald was ruled from Castle Reagh (caislean-riabhac, the gray castle), which tradition rather over-enthusiastically dates to the reign of Edward III (d.1377). O'Laverty implies that the castle, or more properly tower house, may have been built in the 15th c., but Reeves identifies its earliest occupant as Brian Feghartach, the ruler of Clannaboy from 1537–48. It is first mentioned in 1552 when the Lord Chancellor, Cusacke, wrote that Brian Feghartach's successor Hugh had two castles, one at Bealefarst:

The other, called Castelrioughe is fower miles from Bealefarst, and standeth uppone the playne in the midst of the woodes of the Dufferin.

Writing in 1907, Matthews talked of an 'ancient paved road' between the castles, which could be seen 'down to the last century'. It apparently crossed the Connswater via the pack-horse bridge, however there is no trace of it today.

Belfast's vulnerability (it had been razed in 1476, 1489 and 1503, and occupied in 1512), coupled with the division of Clannaboy and the contraction of their power may have prompted the O'Neills to build out of the way at Castlereagh.[1] While no descriptions of their tower house survive, if it followed

Castle Reagh in 1895, by J. Carey. (From R.M. Young, Historical Notices of Old Belfast)

the standard design it would have been three or four stories high and square or rectangular in plan, that is rather like Scrabo tower only less elegant. Harris (1744) states that it was surrounded by 'a fosse which encompasses three-fourths of it and once probably surrounded the whole.'

From their pile at Castlereagh, known to the Scottish settlers as 'the Eagle's Nest', the southern branch of the Clannaboy O'Neills had authority over the entire parishes of Knockbreda, Dundonald, Holywood, Bangor, Donaghadee, Greyabbey, St. Andrews, and a large part of Drumbo, (O'Laverty), 224 townlands in all, a holding Harris (whose views were in line with those of the *County Down Handbook*) saw fit to describe as 'not contemptible'.

These lands were not exclusively peopled by O'Neills. Below the O'Neills were a dozen or so client families or septs, each of whom held a territory, and each of whom owed allegiance to them. In the latter 16th c. the lands of Dundonald were divided between three such families. The five south-eastern townlands were part of the Sliocht Aedh Breac (the section of Hugh the freckled). This comprised 14 townlands:

Ballenngcreve, Balleneganvie, Ballehenrie, Ballecaslanevery, Ballelissegowan, Ballerogan, Balle-M'Grenahan, Balleorane, Ballinrany (Ballyrainey), Balle-Lisewaden (Ballylisbredan), Ballewynnyearvell (Unicarvel), Ballyloghan, Balleregard, Ballecastlanbeg (Castlebeg)

and an island, Island Slesney (Rough Island). This sept would seem to have been a branch of the O'Neill family. Their establishment, no doubt by nefarious means, is an interesting example of the way branches of the top-heavy ruling family tended to push the middling landowners off their estates.

The central and northern parts of the parish were in the joint charge of the Sleught-Durnings (O'Dornans), and the Sleught Owen-M'Quin (the section of Owen, grandson of Quin). These were small septs, their combined territory, together with the district around Ballyhackamore, known as 'The Plaines of Belfast', consisted of the following 16 townlands:

Ballechackamore, Ballecarigogauntelen, two Balleneskeaghs, Carrowne-Calleduffe, Balle-Killemed, Balle-Kerowreagh (Carrowreagh), Balledamlady (Dunlady), Ballereagin, Ballyhugh, alias Ballylisnisca (Ballymiscaw), Balledundonnell (Church Quarter), Ballecloghan, Ballenechallen, Carrow-Kilneveveagh, Carrownecarne, and Carrownemullan.

Bordering them on the south east was the district of Castlereagh and Gallowgh, which may have been 'demesne' land. It included:

Ballehenoad (Ballyhanwood), Ballydengilnehir (Gilnahirk), [ ], Gortcrib, and Balletullecarnan (Tullycarnet).

Between Castlereagh and the territory of the Hubricks lay the wooded lands of the Sleught Kellies, which ran almost to Crossgar and included the familiar townlands of:

Ballybeine (Ballybeen), Balle M'Graffe (Ballymaglaff), Ballystoker (Ballystockart) and Ballerustell (Ballyrussell)

The lord of Castle Reagh, rather like the mayor today, would have been a fairly familiar sight in Dundonald, presiding at the investitures of local chiefs, and, an even more familiar activity, collecting dues and taxes, most notably an annual tribute, levied by the townland and renderable in animals, grain, cloth,

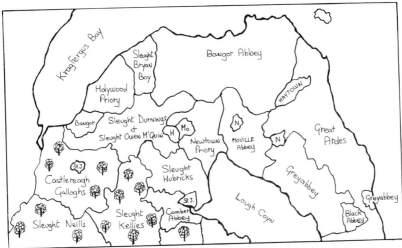

North Down at the end of the 16th century. (After J.R.H. Greeves)

butter, beer or honey – whatever the land produced. Our three chiefs also had to provide their lord (and his numerous hangers on) with 'cuddy' (food and entertainment) whenever he came a calling. All in all, the burden could be a heavy one, and our small septs would have had little independence.

Little is known about the local economy other than that it was probably mixed, with the cattle being booley'd in summer. The land produced enough to allow the rulers of southern Clannaboy to live in great comfort. Brian McFelim O'Neill, who became the 'captain of his nation' in 1555, was said to have possessed '30,000 beeves and other herds innumerable'. In the tradition of Aedh Buidhe, Brian became quite anglicised. In 1567 he was knighted, and confidential government papers describe him as 'a true subject'.

He was also an expendable one. In the late 1560s the crown was eager to extend its influence in Ireland, and Clannaboy was the weakest and the most accessible of Ulster's gaelic lordships. From 1567 on a sequence of English adventurers pressed the queen to let them into Clannaboy and the Ards. Sir Thomas Gerrard promised to take on Sir Brian if granted 500 soldiers. But they would have cost money, and spending horrified Elizabeth so Gerrard got nowhere.

Next came captains Browne and Borrowe, who may have had some success. In 1571, Elizabeth's principal secretary Sir Thomas Smith wrote:

Goodrich, Captein Barrow's Lieutenant, with fourteen men, kept and defended the castle called Castle Reau and went daily one quarter of a mile to fetch his water against five hundred that lay daily upon him.

While the above came to nothing, and may well have been pure fantasy (these were very macho times), it appears to have had the important effect of interesting Smith in the issue. Several months later he asked the queen for permission to plant Clannaboy and the Ards 'with a power of natural Englishmen.'[2]

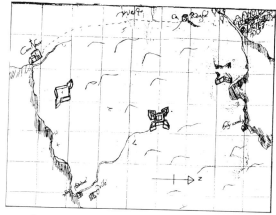

The tattered remains of Smith's map of c. 1572, showing the Ards peninsula sealed by three fortresses, one in or near Dundonald. Dundonald was claimed but never allocated and no fort was built here. Perhaps it was too close to Castle Reagh to be inviting. Comber had possibilities however, and Sir John Berckelay, a seasoned frontiersman, was granted 40 ploughlands to the north of the town, a district that included Dundonald's southern townlands. (P.R.O.N.I.)

Ignoring Sir Brian McFelim's rights and record, Smith drafted an erudite appeal to prejudice. Clannaboy, he declared, was 'inhabited with a wicked barbarous and uncivil people, some Scottish and some wild Irish', whom he mischievously identified with the people of Derry and Tyrone, lately risen in rebellion. As was the fashion, Smith couched his petition in the language of a civilising crusade. And more to the point (as far as Elizabeth was concerned), he promised to pay for everything himself.

His application was successful, and to the consternation of the Lord Deputy, who feared it would 'bring the Irish into a knot to rebel', Smith was granted what he could take in seven years, and so became the technical owner of 'Downedonoll' and its 'natives, male and female'.

Meanwhile what of Sir Brian? When the bad news arrived Sir Brian wrote to the queen, begging her to let him be. She replied 'comforting him'. When he defended himself by firing churches to deny Smith shelter (which may explain why Dundonald's church is shown as roofless in 1625), Sir Brian drew the snide observation (from the Lord Deputy) that he 'hath discovered his Irish nature'.

Smith's expedition was a fiasco and fizzled out when Smith jnr. was murdered (allegedly by being thrown alive to dogs) by one of his followers at Comber. By then a much more serious threat had emerged, for upon his death Elizabeth regranted Clannaboy to her favourite, the Earl of Essex. In 1573, amid mounting confusion, Essex landed at Carrick and posted garrisons at Holywood and Belfast. Two expeditionary forces now ran riot.

In October, after an abortive expedition to Comber, Essex defeated Sir Brian by the ford over the Lagan. 'All night', wrote Essex, the air rang with wailing 'after their country fashion, for the loss of them that were dead.'

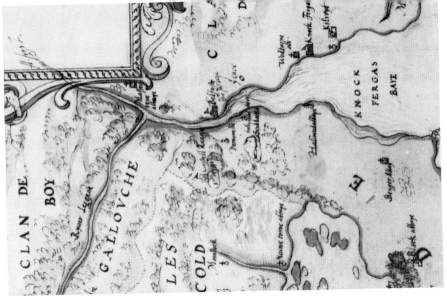

North Down c.1580. A visitor to the Ards at the turn of the 16th century described it as 'scarce and starving – a country without happiness and without religion'. (P.R.O., London)

A settlement was reached in 1574. Sir Brian's celebratory banquet was cut short, however, when his guest the Earl arrested him and had him executed on a charge of conspiracy. In the words of one annalist 'such was the end of their feast.' But Essex had no more success than Smith and Clannaboy remained in the hands of the O'Neills. After this, in spite of an abortive landing by another Smith in 1580 (the Smiths were nothing if not determined), north Down seems to have enjoyed a period of mending calm.

The O'Neills were finally deprived of most of their lands in 1605, when James I divided them up between Con O'Neill and two Scottish adventurers, Hugh Montgomery and James Hamilton. Hamilton, a former secret agent, then in his fifties, acquired the parishes of Bangor, Holywood, Ballywalter, Ballyhalbert, Craigavad and Dundonald, and licence to plant them with English and Scots settlers. (Now that there was a Scots monarch on the throne, it had suddenly become acceptable to be Scottish.) The Sleught Durnings, Sleught Owen M'Quin and the Sleught Hubricks were disposessed, but may have stayed on, (O'Laverty writes that there were O'Dornans in Holywood until the 19th c.)

Over the next ten or so years Con (whom the Montgomery Manuscripts describe as 'a drunken, sluggish man') frittered away the remainder of his estates. In 1609 'the ould King', as he was known, lived at Downaregan (probably Ballyregan). In 1613, their author continues:

we find him at Ballyhennocke, probably the present Ballyhanwood, where "a chestnut coloured mare" was taken from him, one Tirlagh Oge McByrne being tried for the theft, and acquitted. In the year 1615 Con resided at Tullycarnan (Tullycarnet?).

Con is said to have died at Holywood around 1618, and to have been buried in Ballymagan churchyard. By then he was a man out of time. The second, successful generation of adventurers had begun recasting north Down in the image of the Scottish lowlands. A new era was about to begin.

10 From plantation to rebellion

Eight important years

In 1606 Hamilton began to settle his six parishes with Scottish families. It was a huge gamble, for though he was followed over by a posse of relations with their tenants in tow, there was no guarantee that he would attract enough people to make the plantation work, or that the Irish might not rise and evict them. However, in the words of one commentator, 'Scotland (like the painfull Bees) did every yeere send forth swarmes', and by 1613 the health of the colony was such that it could afford to export some 41 families to another Hamilton property in Cavan.

What sort of people were Dundonald's new residents? The Rev. Andrew Stewart, who watched a generation of settlers arrive at Donaghadee, somewhat sourly described them as 'generally the scum of both nations, who, for debt, or breaking and fleeing from justice, or seeking shelter, came hither.' But along with the many labourers and would-be small farmers, who paid 8d each to cross from Portpatrick, came gentry of 'gud fashion', merchants (who would pay their rent in marmalade and pepper), weavers, carpenters, butchers, shoemakers, tailors, ditchers, coopers and smiths. A whole society transplanted itself, and brought to Dundonald the speech and manners of the Scottish lowlands.

The 'Towne' of Dondonell

The maps of the Hamilton estate drawn by Thomas Raven in 1625/6 show us a strange, embryonic version of the modern landscape. They also give us our first detailed glimpse of 'Dondonell', then a giddy metropolis of eight 'mudd' cottages and a roofless church, arranged on either side of the impressively named 'Towne Green', situated between the then road to Comber and the motte; with a suburb of two single room cabins over the river, on the rise that now lies between the traffic lights and the Spar. Opposite them, on the site of Wellworths, was a four acre common, suggesting that the energetic Hamilton had plans to develop Dondonell, though if these existed they fell by the wayside.

Cute old James Hamilton, laird of Dondonell. (National Trust)

On either side of the common were 'Lands howlden in Severall small parcels by the Townsmen'. These may have been villager's allotments. Interestingly enough no fences divide them. To the east, the land between what are now Cumberland and Moatview was reedy marsh, as was the land in front of the hospital. Beyond it, in Ballycloghan (which as the name implies could only be crossed using stepping stones) lay a large tract of 'wood and Bogge' dotted with islands. Dundonald House stands on Flat Island, Rosepark on Yellow Island, and the most distinctive of them, Island Ravera, sits in the grounds of Stormont, planted with conifers. (Look out for it near the gates.)

By far the largest island, a broad-backed drumlin of 64 acres, lay between Yellow Island and the village. It was in two holdings: the Quarter, (now Cumberland and Reaville); and Sander Dickson's farm, (now the cemetery). Short causeways linked the smaller islands, so it would seem that they did not go to waste.

The rector, John Lowthian (or Leatham) had nine acres in Ballyregan, some of which the church still holds. He had been ordained here by Echlin in 1619, and, at a time when many ministers were charged with the welfare of 3–7 parishes, Dundonald was lucky to have had a clergyman at all. Aside from the fact that he had a healthy £20 p.a.[1] from the tithes, little is known about him, other than that he would seem to have had strong presbyterian sympathies. This was enough to mark him out as a potential subversive and he was removed from office during the Laudian years.

One curiosity worth recording is that Lowthian may never have held a service in a church with a roof, not in Dundonald anyway, for when the church was refitted in 1634[2] he had been replaced by the conformist John Kynier, who by comparison was something of an establishment poodle. By then the tithes from the parish had fallen below the critical level and Dundonald was joined with Knockcolumbkill-Breda, Kynier ministering to both.

For scholarly company the minister would have had the teacher. (There had been a school here since 1614, probably held in the village's only two roomed cabin.) The teacher, as ever, was less handsomely provided for, receiving 'fyve pounds a year . . . besydes such monies as (he) shall have from the scholers'.

The lands beyond the village present a puzzling picture. The maps show a countryside striking in its emptiness. The valley was almost entirely unforested, the upland was moor, and apart from a farmstead near what is now Quarry Corner, and two dismal looking clachans near Rockfield and Cooper's Corner, the landscape is shown as being completely devoid of houses. (It has been suggested that for safety the settlers lived in hamlets and villages, however an equally likely explanation is that Raven was not asked to draw them.) The parish has been divided into 60 farms of between 6 and 213 acres. The four southern townlands, for example, the former territory of the Sleught Hubricks, are in fourteen farms, ranging from Edward Slowan's 8¼ acre lea, to George Mathey's 165 acres in Castlebeg and Unicarval, which included the gravelly 'Iland Castell Begg', a mile from Comber.

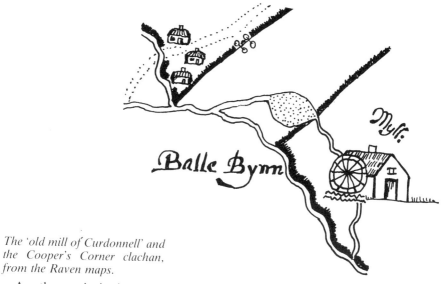

The 'old mill of Curdonnell' and the Cooper's Corner clachan, from the Raven maps.

Another curiosity is that most farms seem to consist of one large field. For example the 'widdow Cloyd' had a field of 30 acres in Ballyrainey, and Thomas Keevett apparently farmed a field of 87 acres. Though obliged to fence their lands, the planters may have gone on using the Irish field system. Alternatively, as well as farmsteads, Raven may have ignored internal boundaries, offering only a skeletal version of the 17th century boundary network. Remarkably, many of his boundarys (mostly hedged banks) can still be seen today.

Roads, cart-tracks, or as Raven neutrally describes them 'ways', are also shown, the main junctions being at the entrance to Rockfield, where there was a six road ends – Dundonald's spaghetti junction. The road to Newtown, which follows a delicate course between bog and ravine, fords streams rather than bridges them. However there were footsticks by the Moat Park playground (where the bridge is today), at Inchmarnock Drive and between Cumberland

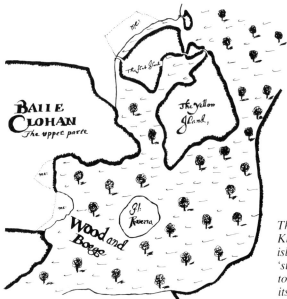

This archipelago lay between Knock and the village. The islands are probably the clay 'stepping stones' from which the townland of Ballycloghan takes its name.

and what is now the Old Dundonald Road. There was no Grahamsbridge. As its only passable building was the parish church, Dondonell became known as Kirkdonell, or Curdonell in the local idiom, (described by a visitor as 'broad Scotch hardly to be understood by strangers'), and during the early 18th c. it seemed as if this name would supplant the name Dondonell entirely.

Almost nothing is known about the lives of the first planters. Mary Dickie, who came over with her parents in the first flush of the settlement is (only just) an exception. Her headstone, formerly in the parish churchyard but now lost, suggests that for her at least, the adventure had a happy outcome:

> Here Mary Dickie lies beneath this stone
> Aged full 40 years excepting one
> September ye 16th she did leave time
> In 16 hund. years 30 and 9
> 22 years 8 months and 13 days
> Was married to James KIRKHOLME of Green Graves
> Beauty and vertue did in her agree
> And now her soul is blessed in Eternitie

The Unfought Battle of Dondonell

The 1641 rebellion shook the protestant settlement to its foundations, and revealed in north Down just how strong these were. In Dundonald there was apparently none of the gore that marked the first weeks of the would-be revolution elsewhere. However, one does not need to go far to find it. 73 Irish 'men, women, and children', were massacred at Ballydavey, near Craigavad, and another, Thomas O'Gilmore, was murdered on 'ye mountaine betwixt . . . Kirkdonnell and Holywood'.

Montgomery and Hamilton (Lord Clanaboy), now in his eighties, were each authorised to raise a regiment of 1,000 foot and a troop of horse from their tenants.[3] A fortnight later, while north Down was still relatively defenceless, Sir Con Magennis and a ramshackle army of almost 4,000 men attacked Lisburn. They were bloodily repulsed.

There was another scare in February 1642. This time north Down was slightly better prepared. Hamilton mobilised his makeshift regiment, and the Montgomery Manuscripts tell us that 'they made forts (by the vulgar called trenches) at Dundonald and other passes'. For all this, they were taken by surprise. The Irish advanced up the Ards peninsula, overcoming Montgomery's men near Mountstewart and ransacking Newtownards. Another group marched north from the Killinchy direction, however they were somehow put to flight at Battletown, a mile south of Comber. Fortunately for Dundonald this reverse discouraged the Ardsmen from pressing their attack, and the danger passed.

The balance of power tilted decisively two months later when a force of 2,500 Scots under Munro landed at Carrickfergus. Hamilton's motley tenant militia (which in spite of its recent showing, was probably as much a danger to itself as the enemy) joined them at Lisburn. Thereafter the conflict was carried on far from Dundonald, only coming close in 1649 when County Down's royalists, including Hamilton's son James, and no doubt a loyal band of tenants from Dundonald, were effortlessly scattered by a small parliamentary army near Lisburn. Though rumoured to have died 'or sunk in a bog, being corpulent', James survived to surrender to Cromwell and have a fine of £9,000 levied on his estates; a sum they were ill equipped to pay.

The Kirk

One important consequence of the Scots intervention was the setting up of presbyterian congregations. However, since many of Dundonald's people were presbyterian in all but name, this involved less of a shift in allegiance than a declaration of one. The catalysts in this process were the Scots army chaplains.

Thomas Peebles was chaplain to the Earl of Eglinton's regiment, stationed in

Artist's impression of the first meeting house at Dundonald, c.1670.

and around Newtownards, (or Ballybo as it was then coloquially known.)
Peebles, one of the architects of presbyterianism in Ireland, was a man of
enormous energy. Adair writes that he preached, enthused and persuaded 'not
only at the head-quarters of the regiment, but in all the neighbouring towns'.[4]
With his encouragement a congregation was begun in Dundonald in 1644, and
it is a measure of its poverty that when Peebles was ordained in the following
year, it was as minister of the united congregations of Dundonald and Holywood, since neither on its own could support him.[5]

'That confused and reeling time' (Adair)

One man who can not have relished the Kirk's arrival was the rector, James
Hamilton.[6] Not only did he at a stroke lose the bulk of his flock and much of his
influence, he was soon to find his own position imperilled. For the presbyterians in authority were no more tolerant than churchmen. Adair writes:

The presbytery (acted) against . . . scandalous conformist ministers . . . summoning
them before the presbytery, and, according as they found ground, either censuring or
relaxing them. They had greatest trouble with Mr.Brice and Mr.Hamilton of Dundonald, who obstinately adhered to their former courses, and denied the covenant and the
authority of the presbytery. Upon which these two hirelings were suspended,

He was still out some twelve years later. The report of the 1657 Commission of
Enquiry declared, 'Mr James Hamilton present Incumbent, but how outed we
know not.' It added, 'Cure at present served by Mr. Thomas Peebles, a
preacher in sallary.' The salary was an annual allowance of £100 (a huge sum)
paid by the Commonwealth to approved ministers.

    This follows a dramatic turnabout in Peebles' fortunes. Six years earlier
presbyterian ministers had been banished, and he had been forced into hiding.
By the summer of 1651 the tenacious Peebles was one of only six or seven
ministers remaining in Ireland. According to Reid:

changing their apparel to the habit of countrymen, (they) travelled in their own parishes
. . . to preach in the fields or in barns and glens . . . where the people willingly met
them.

    Intolerance of the Scots-Irish went considerably further. In 1653, in an
attempt to sever the link with Scotland it was proposed that the Scots of Down
and Antrim be moved to Munster. (For the Irish it was 'Hell or Connacht', for
the Scots it was Munster or the sword.) A list of 260 'obnoxious' landowners
was published. It included James Ross jnr., one of Dundonald's major
landlords, and Ninian Tate of Ballybeen, who donated the land on which the
presbyterian church now stands. However, though some of the victims were
taken to view their new estates, the climate liberalised, and this extraordinary
scheme was quietly shelved.

    With the accession of Charles II in 1660 there was another round in this long
game of musical pulpits. After seven quiet years (1654–61) Peebles was
stripped of his ministry and fled to Scotland, where his former commander, the
Earl of Eglinton wrote to the Bishop of Down and Connor on his behalf,
eventually securing his return. In the meantime, the resilient Hamilton once

again preached in Dundonald.

But what of the people these alternating clergymen served? The 1659 'Census', possibly a count of adults liable for poll tax, suggests a community of perhaps 200–300 people,[7] scattered fairly evenly through eleven townlands. Little has apparently changed since 1625. The village is much the same size, and the fertile lands of Ballyrainey and Ballylisbredan are still thick with small-holdings, amongst which may have stood the residence of Dundonald's only gentleman;[9] probably a member of the wealthy Ross family of Portavo near Donaghadee.

The 'Census' of c.1659: Dindonnall

Townelands[8]	No. of People	Tituladoes Names	Eng & Scotts	Irish
Castlebegg	06		06	00
Ballyrennie	12		04	08
B:Lishbredan	14	John Ross gent	07	07
Ballycren	05		02	03
Carri Reagh	11		09	02
Dunlady	06		04	02
Ballyregane	09		07	02
B:McSca	15		09	06
Church qr	09		06	03
B:Bine	07		05	02
B:Russell	08		06	02
Total:	102		65	37

This strangely shaped building is Ballyhanwood House, said to have been a 17th century Montgomery dower house. It was recently demolished.

On inspection, however, the superficial picture of a stable, harmonious community rapidly dissolves. The parish contained three communities, one episcopalian, one presbyterian, and one Irish catholic.[10] And the biggest surprise in the 'Census', particularly for anyone used to thinking of 17th century Dundonald as a Scots-Irish bastion, is that the 'native Irish' comprise almost 40% of the population.

What place had the Irish in the new order? A fairly menial one, it would seem. Of fourteen farms in the south-eastern townlands (1625), only one is held by the bearer of a possibly Irish surname. (The relative concentration of Irish here may be the result of a demand for farm labour.) The Irish were not allowed to hold land. In 1627, for example, Patrick Montgomerie held Bally-hanwood on condition that he did not let 'any part thereof unto . . . the meere Irish'. Anticipably, the 1681 Rent Roll shows that Dundonald had no Irish leaseholders. It would seem that the Irish stayed on as 'the sarvants', living as cottiers, and we read elsewhere that the settlers found them 'quick and clever at their work'. Dundonald's Irish population was scattered, poor, aggrieved and without formal organisation. It left no records.

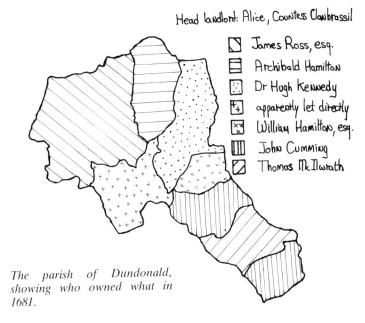

Head landlord: Alice, Countess Clanbrassil

◩ James Ross, esq.
▤ Archibald Hamilton
⊡ Dr Hugh Kennedy
⊞ apparently let directly
⊠ William Hamilton, esq.
▥ John Cumming
▧ Thomas McIlwrath

The parish of Dundonald, showing who owned what in 1681.

The activities of the smallest grouping, the episcopalians, are also largely unknown to us. The only people we have any knowledge of are the presby-terians, and this is entirely due to the chance survival of the Dundonald Session Book (part marriage register, baptismal record, ledger and Session Book), a tatty, leather-bound pocket book, parts of which are missing and parts of which have been eaten into by damp, which records aspects of congregational life between 1678–1713.

Love and Marriage

> In the middel of the (night) I Dreamid an
> I Dreamid my love another mans Bride
> So I became a ghossed and stumbled from
> Day unto Day By the reason my love
> was taken away I was sore Surprisd
> I soon did awake if this Comes to pass
> my poor hart it will Break

(Extract from poem found in Session Book)

Thirty-eight marriages are entered in the Book between 1678–93, 34 within the first five years, when the records were properly kept. Dundonald women married men from Bangor, Newtown, Belfast, Antrim, Magheralin, Donegore, and of course Holywood. Holywood men are not registered as outsiders so the strength of the connection can only be guessed at, but one entry (August 9, 1693) announcing the marriage of a couple from Holywood suggests close ties.

The form of marriage was then rather different to that of today. As the fateful day approached the marriage was proclaimed three times from the pulpit, usually on successive sundays. The last proclamation seems to have had more weight than the marriage, for example:

Thomas mc le Roy in ye paroch of Bangor & Agnes Newlands in
this paroch were proclaimed for the last time the First Sabbath of Der 1678

The first casual mention of the marriage ceremony comes two years later:

Hew Morfie and Jean Dempster in this paroch were proclaimed according
to the accustomed manner and married about a fourteen dayes thereafter

probably in response to a change in custom. By 1686 entries are brief and to the point:

Nor 8.86 Will:Deall and Janet patersone were married.

The need to make sure that the marriage produced children, particularly sons to work the land, meant that while premarital relations were not condoned, a sizable percentage of brides went pregnant to the altar. Engagements tended to be short and marriage followed pregnancy. If a couple courted for several years without the woman conceiving the courtship was often abandoned.

Children followed quickly. The baptismal records show that of the 18 grooms recorded as fathers, 5–7 had become fathers within a year, and 7–10 within two years. Large families were common, and as the tombstone 'ERECTED By James Mc__oyd in memory of Eight of his Childien who died young' reminds us, child mortality was high. Of the 163 children registered here, almost half will probably have died within the first month of life, and no more than 30 could have expected to see the age of ten.

The course of true love did not always run smooth. The baptism list hints at two difficult crises. The barely legible entry for March 8 1682 notes that,

'Henrie Neal had a daughter baptized born in fornication'. Eleven years later it is entered that;

James Rankin made public satisfaction for his scandal of fornication
with _____ and had his child begotten in fornication baptised named _____.

These entries offer an interesting insight into the way the community coped with problems such as unwanted pregnancy, for, disabled and excluded from the state, presbyterians developed their own self-regulating social system. It included a sophisticated problem-solving apparatus.

When the pregnancy was discovered the putative father would have been tried by the Kirk session, a sort of community court made up of congregational elders, and a body whose decisions were not lightly flouted. In this instance Rankin was found to be the father. He would then have been publicly shamed by being made to sit on the penitent's stool, under the pulpit, avoiding the eyes of friends and neighbours until, on the third or fourth sunday he would have received absolution and had his child baptised. The father's family were considered responsible for the infant's welfare; so Rankin's parents, or an aunt, may have offered to raise the child.

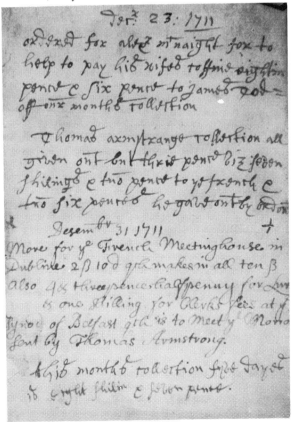

Early 18th century hieroglyphics from the Session Book.

All this highlights the immense power of the Kirk.[11] Another important source of its influence was the certificate of good character which the minister issued like a passport to anyone leaving the parish.[12] Without one it was difficult to get work and almost impossible to be admitted to another congregation. Ministers who withheld them from anyone whose character was less than saintly provided great ammunition for their episcopalian rivals. The curate of Dundonald, Joseph Finiston, was not above putting an unecumenical boot in. In 1711 he contributed the following to William Tizdall's indictment of presbyterianism, *The Conduct of Dissenters*:

Sir,
Kirkdonnel December 28. 1711

I had Occasion to be at Castlereagh . . . at a time when one James Moor, had a new Born Infant in the Agonies of Death, who being desired by some that were present, to send for me to Baptize the Child . . . was observ'd to be taken aside by one of the Elders, who was then in the House, after which he would not suffer any one to call me. In two or three hours after, the Child Died Unbaptiz'd.
Next Morning, I had Occasion to Travel by the Man's House. I called him out and . . . pressed him to tell me why he would suffer his Child to Die unbaptized, whilst I, whom he own'd to be a Minister of Christ, was so near him . . . why then says he, I will confess to you, I durst not do it, for if I did, I should neither be admitted to the Ordinances, nor have the benefit of a Certificate

A Population on the Move

If this seems like a trivial sanction it was not. The lack of continuity in the lists of landowners, and to a lesser extent in family names suggests that Dundonald's farming population was highly mobile. Though renewable, leases were short, and people hopped from farm to farm and district to district. Some fell out of society altogether and joined the endlessly circulating population of beggars.

The Sunday collection at Dundonald, known as the 'poores money' went largely towards supporting this itinerant mass. These collections were miserably small. The congregation was acutely poor, and as the wooden collection box was passed along, inside the mud and thatch meeting house, very few hands went forward. In 1679 the collection averaged 1s.8d and on some weeks it did not rise to 1/-(5p). Only heads of households were expected to give, and of these some put in no more than a farthing, others gave nothing at all.

The beneficiaries were 'our own poore', local pensioners like James Geddes, 'ye blind lass' Jean Egilshame, and Margaret Maxwell, 'a poor woeman'; and a sad procession of strangers, the stricken and the grotesque, who arrived with affidavits and letters of recommendation from (amongst others) the mayors of 'Darrie' and Carrickfergus: 'a Criple 4d', 'a distressed old gentleman', 'to a poor boy deformed in his foot twopenie', '1–4 given hereof to a poor distressed man yt had suffered shipwreck of all he had', 'a Grecian Priest so cald', 'two distressed men, William and Hew Montgomeries, who were robbed by ye torries, and one of ym sore wounded, lying sick of wounds 0–8', 'a poor cripple man carried on a barrow', 'one Elizabeth Thompson who had her husband taken by ye Turks and is yet in that miserable slavery 0–9', 'a hollywood boy', 'ye Scots man that was brocken by a law suit', 'ye French schoolmaster', 'to a lame soldier', 'To David Crawford, a broken man, taken by ye French, and long in prison, Eightpence', 'one Robert Anderson, Ballyrussel, who has suffered the loss of his goods for the truth – 6 pence', 'a blind woman', 'a Distressed French Protestant 1–0', 'one . . . who had his house burned by ye carelessness of servants -4 pence', 'to ane Irish man who had part of his tongue cut out by the torries 0–3', 'to one Patrick Savedge Living in Morne who had his house burnt and some of his children & all his goods in the fire 1–6'.

Where the state did not provide, the congregation provided for itself. Widows were frequent beneficiaries. Local boys were helped through college: 'Given to John Thompson for his incouradgement in his learning – two shillings', 'to a poore scholar going for glasgow on shilin'. Others were helped with the cost of burial: 'for making the grave of a poor woman who died beside us named Marion Wondrom 7(d)'; and there are regular, pathetic references to interring small children: 'For burying ye funline (foundling) . . . on shilin', 'given to John Fox... one shilling to help the burying of his little daughter'.

In spite of its penury the congregation responded well to appeals. In July 1680, 4s 7d was collected for M____ Stevens, 'who had her husband murdered by ye robbers in his own house'; and in September 1679, 24s 2d was raised for the relief of prisoners held by the Turks. Dues went to the Presbytery and the Synod; and while repairs to the meeting house consumed a small fortune, most of the money raised went on relief.

1690 and all that

Though the Book ends abruptly at the close of the year 1688, when Cobham left the parish,[13] and does not recommence until 'Anno 1693. After my return from our Calamities and troubles in Ireland', life in Dundonald was seriously disrupted only during 1689.

In January of that year, in common with their counterparts elsewhere, County Down's protestant landowners formed military associations and enlisted their tenantry in the county's defence. The decisive encounter came in March, when the Jacobites scattered their half-trained levies at Dromore. Resistance folded, and once again the roads through Dundonald became choked with terrified refugees, many seeking to flee to Scotland.

As the government's best troops were required for the campaign in the north-west, north Down was charged to the tender care of Magennis of Iveagh:

whose companies, composed of rude and half-civilised natives from the mountains of Mourne were stationed in the several towns. Their unauthorised and oppressive exactions were, for a time borne in silence; the people having few arms, and being destitute of a leader

However, a leader emerged. Among the thousands who crowded Donaghadee was one Captain Henry Hunter, an experienced soldier, who joined with leading townsmen to form an ad hoc militia. This boldly struck out for Newtown, which Reid tells us was on the eve of being plundered. Hunter engaged the garrison at Cunningburn, by Strangford Lough, and put them to flight.

Schomberg's army crossing the Holywood hills, on a road that has since largely melted back into the landscape. Part of it survives as the Ballymiscaw Road, identified as 'King William's Road' on Williamson's map of 1810. It is said that his army can be seen tramping the hills on the night of July 11th.

On the same day he dispersed a second party of this obnoxious regiment, stationed at Comber, and rescued that town also from their exactions.

Magennis withdrew to Downpatrick, but 'Hunter and his rabble' pursued and somehow managed to evict them. It was an astonishing turnabout. Reid records that:

By these unexpected successes the people of Down experienced a seasonable relief from the exactions of the soldiery; . . . the garrison in Derry were encouraged by the intelligence of these proceedings; and the greater leniency and moderation were henceforth observed by the Romanist authorities in other places, lest a similar spirit of revolt should be excited.

Not until James II arrived in Newry en route to Derry, were determined steps taken against the insurgents. On the last day of April the protestants were routed at the Break of Killyleagh, and driving groups of frightened militiamen before them, the Jacobites reoccupied the region, garrisoning it this time with a large contingent of regular troops.

This second occupation was also short lived. In August Schomberg's army landed at Groomsport, and Dundonald again changed hands. Following the inconclusive manoeuvrings of the autumn Schomberg wintered at Lisburn, Lord Hewett's cavalry being quartered among the farms of Kirkdonnel, Knock and Breda. Dundonald had no further involvement in the conflict.[14]

Nothing of the war's impact on the parish is known, however Reid's slightly apocalyptic review of the condition of eastern Ulster at the end of 1689 is perhaps worth recounting:

Houses had been every where plundered or burned; horses, cattle, and stock of every kind had been carried away or destroyed. The labours of the field had been suddenly interrupted in the spring; they were tardily prosecuted amid the alarms and discouragements of a campaign, and the scanty harvest had been only partially reaped through want of labourers.

The damage seems to have been quickly made good. In 1696 and 1699 the sunday collections yielded an average of c.2s 8d, tiny amounts which speak volumes about the poverty of the parish, but sums that are well up on pre-war levels.

To be or not to be?

As Cobham got older he became less equal to his nomadic lifestyle, and around 1700 he gave up the Dundonald wing of his ministry. While it is unlikely that he simply abandoned Dundonald, his departure left it badly in the lurch, and there were doubts as to whether the congregation could survive.

In 1702 the parish formally applied to the Synod to become an independent congregation, vouching to provide a living of 'twenty Pounds in Money, and twenty Bolls of Oats Yearly' to a minister. Their spokesman John McKitrick promised that they would also try to provide a farm, 'against Allsaints next'. As the Synod, which also had to weigh the minister's interests, considered this rather measly they in turn ruled that the congregation should also pay the first £3 p.a. of the farm's rent.

Putting on the poor mouth, the congregation made a determined attempt to have this small levy waived, but they were unable to wriggle out of it. At first no farm could be found, however, by May 1708 a twenty acre farm had been taken at £2.10 p.a., and in the autumn we read of Andrew Gibson being paid 3d 'for forking a stacke of ye parish corn'.

In spite of these inducements or maybe because of them, it was several years before the congregation could attract a minister. Over a dozen ministers (including Cobham and his son) are recorded as supplying the deficiency, some of them receiving beer for their trouble, the Rev. William Hunter of Belfast being notable in receiving five quarts, and hopefully some help with the journey home. The interregnum ended with the installation of James Stewart, a Scotsman and happily, a batchelor, on May 23, 1709.

Pewter and collecting pans from Dundonald   Presbyterian Church.

In the meantime the congregation made efforts to strengthen its position. In June 1707 it petitioned the Presbytery of Down asking that the townlands of Ballymaglaff and Ballyhanwood from the parish of Comber, and Craigantlet, Greengraves and Killarn from Newtownards be transferred to Dundonald. The Dundonalders pointed out that they had only eleven townlands while Newtownards and Comber each had over thirty, and gave eight reasons why the townlands should change hands. However, they didn't exactly make a stunning case for themselves. (Scraping the barrel, they resorted to the claim that the neighbouring preaching houses were so big that the people at the back could not hear.)

The campaign backfired. Comber sent a withering reply saying that they could all hear perfectly well, thank you. It answered Dundonald's reasons, and gave another seven why the lands should stay put.[15] Newtownards too (which the year before had promised its minister £40, 22 bolls of oats, and 300 loads of turf yearly), clung tenaciously to its townlands, answering that even if it wanted to hand them over (which it did not), it had no power to; 'the landlord will not allow of this annexation, but will make the inhabitants smart if they disjoyn from Newtown'.

It also accused Dundonald of trying to stir up trouble, and made the accurate but not entirely helpful point that had Dundonald saved the promised stipend during its years without a minister, it would now have enough to give one a decent living.

The lobbying was not entirely without effect. In 1711 the Presbyterys of Down and Belfast secured £4 annually from the Synod towards the minister's salary. This was paid for 17 years. Stewart's income received another fillip when the king restored 'Regium Donum', a small allowance paid to ministers. But these measures did not address the underlying problem.

The idea of enlarging Dundonald was revived in 1713, this time with the support of the Synod's Committee of Funds. It was so keen to minimise its outgoings that it advanced Dundonald's claim, but got nowhere, with the result that the congregation's existence remained precarious throughout Stewart's tenure, and on his death in 1748 the ministry lay vacant for another six years.

The presbyterians were not alone in having troubles. In the early 1730s a

Five well-worn lead communion tokens. These would have been coined by a local smith, and used to admit people to presbyterian communion. (P.H.S.I.)

dispute of the sort beloved by the novelist Anthony Trollope was brewing within the united parishes of Knock-Columbkille, Breda and Dundonald.

Owing to the ruinous condition of Breda church, parish business was generally conducted at Knock (or Dundonald), and this led to considerable discontent within the Breda wing of the parish. When the Rt. Hon. Anne, Lady Viscountess Dowager Midleton offered to build a new church in Breda at her own expense, however, it seemed that the problem might be amicably and advantageously solved.

But not everyone was happy at the thought of the focus of the parish shifting west. In particular, Lady Ikkerin of Castle Hill (whose estate lay between Stormont and Campbell College) was not happy at the thought of the parish's focus shifting west, and Lady Ikkerin was a most determined woman. In 1733 she made her opposition known to the bishop, with the result that when the showdown took place on the 21st May, at an extraordinary parishoners' meeting in Knock vestry, the aged bishop Francis Hutchinson was present. He witnessed the complete rout of Lady Ikkerin's party. As Hutchinson recorded:

the parishes by a majority of 279 against 7 voted for a petition for the removal of Knock Church into the townland of Breday. I viewed both places and thought the place more convenient and therefore approved

Quite undeterred by her neighbours' almost unanimous support, Lady Ikkerin promptly appealed to the Primate to veto the scheme. The hierarchy stood firm. In a long and mumbling reply the Primate ventured his 'humble advice . . . that a new Church . . . be built upon the Townland of Bredagh (and) be declared . . . to be the Parish Church of Knock, alias Bredagh'. The new church was completed in 1737, and was subsequently described as 'the neatest and most complete of its kind in the kingdom.'

The affair had important consequences for Dundonald. In his *History of the Parish of Knock*, Carmody implies that after this rebuff Lady Ikkerin in some measure turned her back on Knockbreda, and took steps towards making Dundonald an independent parish, the logic being that if she could not have a church at Knock, then she would have one at Dundonald. Whatever the reason, in 1758 Dundonald acquired its own minister, Edmund Leslie. However it seems unlikely that this was made possible by Lady Ikkerin's largesse. The Visitation of 1760 names the church's patron as Arthur Trevor, Wellington's grandfather, (described by Mrs Delaney as 'a sort of an old beau . . . a very honest, hospitable, friendly, good man with a little pepper in his composition') and a relative not of Lady Ikkerin but of Viscountess Midleton! The way in which the Church of Ireland was lifted to independence contrasts sharply with the struggles of the 'farmer's church', and says much about their respective characters at the time.

'A village in the middle of nowhere en route to somewhere else'
This discouraging quotation, drawn from Shirley Farrar's paper on Dundonald, sums up Dundonald's standing in relation to the 18th century road network fairly well. Indeed, if anything it is too generous, for as a glance at Sloane's map shows, the road system of 1739 seems to have evolved expressly

in order to avoid it. It was not on the routes between Belfast and Newtown, or Lisburn (then of a size comparable with Belfast) and Comber. The only traffic which passed through the village was that moving between Belfast and Comber.

A look at its geography reveals why. The old village lay up a cul de sac, virtually surrounded by marsh. Its site was useful militarily, but otherwise uninviting.[16] The problem, however, was that no good alternative suggests itself. To the west lay a district called 'the bogs', which ran to Ballycloghan. To the north and south lay hills and slobland. Had it been possible by some magic

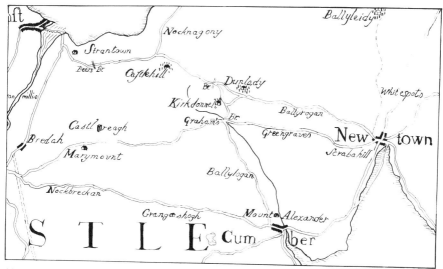

Sloane's map of 1739, showing Dundonald's relationship, or rather lack of it, with the early 18th century road network. (Linenhall Library)

to draw its scattered road junctions together, then something with potential might have been created, but it would have run against the nature of the place.

Further evidence of its obscurity is to be found in Harris's *Survey of the County of Down* (1740), and his *Antient and present State of County Down* (1744), both of which ignore Dundonald completely. Mid-18th century Dundonald's sole attraction was probably the 'Kirk Donnell Well', a chalybeate spring the waters of which were said to have the power to cure. (Its site is now in the grounds of the golf club.) But even in this it was blighted, for the waters had a thick scum and tasted 'very unpleasant'.[17]

Things got worse. The next important development, the laying of a road of the direct alignment type between Knock and Grahamsbridge, sometime between 1739–55, threatened to maroon the village completely by diverting the Belfast-Comber traffic along what is now the Old Dundonald Road.

This road and others like it were built mainly for travel by foot and horseback. As the volume of wheeled traffic increased, roads that would take a more level, and therefore more meandering course were mooted. These could arouse deep suspicion. When plans for a new road between Belfast and Newtown were published in 1757 and the farmers on the projected route found, to their horror, that contrary to assurances the overseers did 'not intend carrying said road straight' there was uproar. A strong protest was immediately lodged, but this proved ineffectual. The surveyors came out, but were unceremoniously sent packing, and on August 22, 1758 a second objection appeared in the *News Letter*. The proposed 'Great Road', claimed its opponents:

would not only be full of crooks and sweeps but laid over a greater number of steeper hills than if it were carried straight, as it ought and easily might, were partiality laid aside; these things being considered and to prevent the public money from being misapplied... we are resolved never to let it pass through our lands in any crooked partial way

This was followed by a warning:

if . . . any person whatsoever shall think . . . to enter into any of our farms by force to cut dig or abuse the same . . . under any pretence whatsoever . . . we are determined to repel force by force and exert our utmost abilities in defence of our just rights

In the face of this the authorities quietly demurred, and the Great Road was built on the direct alignment. Thus one of the earliest successful objections to highway construction in the county and perhaps the country was concluded, and work began on one of Ireland's last old-style, direct alignment roads.[18]

Murder Bridge on the Dunlady Road. No-one is now clear as to how the bridge got its name, however it is said that a man carrying a pig in a sack once rested on the bridge, but the pig started jigging and he fell over, breaking his neck.

The Great Road put Dundonald on the map. Between 1766–71 a coaching inn was built on a corner of the glebe in 'what is allowed to be the best Situation on the great Road . . . for the Public and Merchant business'; its landlord being none other than the rector. A daily long-car bumped between Belfast and Donaghadee, apparently strewing its passenger's posessions everywhere. Notices seeking articles 'Dropt between Belfast & Dundonald' regularly appear in the *News Letter*. Silver watches, and items such as a black silk cloak, 'a small Pocket-Book containing a great Variety of papers', 'one quarter of a hide of Ben Leather... and two Veal Skins', 'six pieces of Brown Linen', and 'a new Cotton Gown . . . with a great many other articles too tedious to mention', all went astray, as did much else besides.

The Protestant Parish

In 1766, alarmed by the 'Increase of Popery' the Irish House of Lords wrote to rectors asking for information on the number of protestant and catholic families in their parish. In Hazlett's absence, the curate Matthew Garnet replied:

Kirdonnell.- families, 149. There are only three Papists in the parish, one of whom is head of a family, but his wife and children are Protestants; neither Popish Priest nor Friar.

If the 'Irish' of 1659 are synonymous with the 'Papists' of 1766, then the century from 1659 saw the virtual disappearance of Dundonald's catholic/Irish population. There are several ways of accounting for this. Both the Session Book and Garnet's note suggest a slow and steady incorporation of catholics

Moat Park graffiti

into the protestant whole. (By the mid 18th century, for example, Irish families like the McGimpseys of Newtownards had become almost exclusively protestant.)

However, we should beware of overestimating this phenomenon, the list of 144 dissenters from Dundonald who petitioned parliament in 1775 includes only 4–9 people with Irish surnames, leaving the bulk of Irish unaccounted for. Another possibility is that the influx of protestant labour in the second half of the 17th century made possible the wholesale replacement of catholics on local farms; or again, it could be that catholics shared something of the protestant mobility.

That Dundonald's protestantisation was not an isolated event can be seen from the Religious Returns for 1764:

Parish	Episcopal	Dissenter	Catholic
Bangor	400	3025	12
N'ards	60	4750	50
D'dee	100	1848	—
Comber	315	1220	165

In spite of periodic food shortages, the population grew steadily until, by the 1760s, it was the turn of many protestants to become superfluous to the needs of the local economy. The answer for some was emigration, and Dundonald's exodus of catholics was followed after 1718 by one of protestants, mainly presbyterians, most of whom went to North America. Amongst the estimated

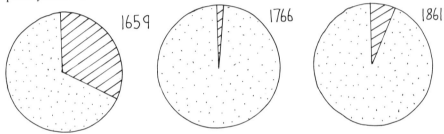

Catholics as a percentage of the parish population.

200,000 who emigrated were John M'Dowell of Ballyhanwood, who got caught up in the Hearts of Steel and fled the country charged with incendiarism; and the Rev. William Ray, who sailed on the New Hope in May 1765, inviting 'whatever of his Friends that chuse' to come with him (and given the customs of the time, it would have been odd if none had followed.) People left in droves. Indeed at one point it seemed as if the Ulster plantation might turn out to be no more than a stepping-stone for the settlement of North America.

In spite of this haemorrhage the local protestant communities seem to have gone from strength to strength. Jacob Hazlett, who became rector in 1766, inherited a parish that was independent in name only and turned it into a going concern. He sold Milch Asses and 'exceeding good old Oats' from the rectory. He had the church repaired in 1771, and a tower added three years later. In 1773 he set up a school; having the teacher double as parish clerk. Nor was he above a little social engineering. Noting the country was 'ill supplied' with smiths, he had a blacksmith take the cottage by the high road, promising 'a good workman . . . great Encouragement'. (Likewise when his inn needed a landlord, he sought a 'Person of some Property whose Character . . . will bear the nicest Scrutiny.')

The church repairs would have been carried out to the sound of much wailing and gnashing of teeth. For as well as having to pay tithes, presbyterians were obliged to help maintain episcopal buildings, so it is likely that the church will have owed its continued existence (in part) to non-conformist money. Decisions to undertake matters like this were made at Vestry meetings, so when in

1775 an Act was passed taking away the Vestry voting rights of dissenters, it is hardly surprising that reaction was sharp, and that in Dundonald the petition which led to the repeal of the offending clause was 'most Heartily & sincerely' subscribed to.

The presbyterians were also making progress. Firstly, the continued existance of the congregation was no longer in doubt, indeed in 1769 the meeting house had been extended. Secondly, after three short ministries, the arrival of James Caldwell in 1772 began four decades of relative stability.[19] Whereas Stewart had been 'an extreme subscriber', Caldwell did not hold with the Westminister Confession, and when the Presbytery of Bangor split in 1774, Dundonald stuck with Bangor, well known for its liberal, New Light views. The Presbytery regularly gathered here, and their influential 1771 denounciation of the Hearts of Steel was issued from Dundonald. Not all their assemblies were of such moment, however, and at another meeting in 1787 it is recorded that the entire attendance consisted of Caldwell and his dutiful elder, Mr Blow.[20]

The gentry

At the time of the split the parish's leading families were the Lamberts or Lambert-Tates of Dunlady, and the Cummings of Unicarval, who were almost all Dundonald posessed in the way of polite society. (It is worth noting that in spite of the proximity of the Ikkerins and the Earls of Mount Alexander, no-one within the parish rose above the rank of esquire.)

The Lamberts were a prominent county family, and they appear to have had

Dunlady House, seat of the Lamberts, now better known now for its ghosts. These include a woman in white, the image of a blood-red hand which mysteriously appears on a wall, and a room which cannot hold glass.

considerable wealth and influence. They can be associated with Dunlady House from around 1720,[21] for in that year a George Lambert of Dunlady served as High Sheriff of County Down. (In his will of 1723 he left his brother Robert 'my coconut tip'd with silver, my ring I wear, and a broad piece of gold'.) George was succeeded by his brother Robert, who also became High Sheriff. He died in 1752, whereon he was succeeded by his son Robert, who held sway for the next thirty years.

The family's wealth had several sources. They ran a large farm and stud farm. They owned the townlands of Ballyoran and Dunlady, and holdings near Comber, Greyabbey and Downpatrick. (A handful of illustrated Dunlady leases survive. They show that as well as pounds, shillings and pence, the tenants were obliged to furnish trimmings such as 'two fat Hens at Christmas', and appropriately, as Lambert was a keen huntsman and a governor of the County Down Corporation of Horse Breeders, 'a Hund whelp' for the master every year.)

They also had mining interests. Harris mentions a 'good slate quarry' at Dunlady, and Lambert had had another in Tullycavy, which he claimed produced slates 'as good as ever were made'. However, though affluent, Robert was occasionally stumped for cash, and appears to have been twice reduced to auctioning the furniture, possibly to meet gambling debts. (These

This cryptic mark appears on one of Dunlady's gatepiers.

embarrassments were temporary, and his fortunes recovered sufficiently to allow him to settle £800 p.a. on his daughter when she married.)

A good example of their influence would be the building of the Dunlady Road in 1762, when Robert used his position as High Sheriff to have a road laid between Dundonald and Bangor. To minimise any possible inconvenience, he had it run past his demesne. He had an eventful year as Sheriff and the *News Letter* of 1762 is full of his injunctions and decrees.

Robert Lambert died in 1783, and was buried in the parish churchyard. While Mrs McTier suggests that he may have been a bit of a rogue, almost everything else points to his having been an archetypal gentleman of his time: a lover of hunting, racing, and society, and a deeply conservative individual, who, while he backed reform, would not let land to 'Papists', or to any of 'those

Richard, Earl of Annesley, who married Ann Lambert in 1771. Prior to his elevation Richard was a Customs official in Dublin.

wicked and deluded People called Hearts of Steel'. With his death the name became extinct here.

His daughter Ann married Richard Annesley in 1771, and when Richard unexpectedly became Earl of Annesley in 1802 the couple moved to a smart address in Dublin. Dunlady became a dower house occupied in 1814 by Lady Annesley; and in 1823 Atkinson describes it as 'the seat of Mrs Macilroth, mother of the Countess of Annesley.' On her death the house was let. Thereafter, epitomising fallen grandeur, it took a middling place amongst the parish's half dozen or so country seats.

The Cummings were to the south of the parish what the Lamberts were to the north, on a slightly less grand scale. Their connection with the parish can be traced back to the Subsidy Roll of 1663, when a John Cominge is associated with 'Ballylishbredan'. The family established themselves ten years later when John bought the townlands of 'Ballylisbredin, Castlebegg also Bailycastlebegg and Unicarvell'; snatched from the disintegrating Clanbrassil estate for £552 'and a Boale of Oats yearly', stealing a march on James Ross, who was also interested in acquiring them.

John's heir, also John (a Dublin attorney), seems to have been childless, and on his death the estate was divided between his brothers: with John getting Ballylisbredan (and the family seat), and Thomas and William jointly taking Unicarval/Castlebeg.

This split proved to be the family's undoing. Around 1740, the Lisbredan branch vanishes, apparently broken by a 'Controversie and lawsuit' entered

Unicarval House, home of the Cumming family, and the scene of a grisly murder on the eve of the 1798 rebellion. The bottom right window is blind.

into by their Unicarval cousins, who seem to have disputed the inheritance. Thereafter the focus shifts to Unicarval, home of Elizabeth and William Cumming. He had been baptised by Cobham in the mudwalled meeting house in 1699, and was described on his death in 1776 as 'a most sincere friend and benevolent neighbour'. (A sentiment his cousins would hardly have echoed!)

What happened in between is largely a mystery. All that survives about him are a couple of newspaper advertisements, which record a spot of servant trouble. In 1753, for example, one of his men ran off with part of the family silver; and a few years later another, described as 'a Highland man (who) spoke a broken language (and) wore scurvy old brown Cloathes' (William evidently picked his men carefully), ran off with his nephew's boots and spurs.

The house at Ballylisbredan has not survived, however William's delightful home at Unicarval is still standing. Its age is uncertain. The architectural evidence is contradictory, and while tradition dates it to the 1740s, there was clearly a good house here as early as 1696. The rent of this house and three acres was then £3.12.2 plus:

2 boules of well cleaned barley
18 good fat hens
9 days work of a man and horse
or in Lieu for each hen 4d and for each day's work 12d

The Cummings lived in the parish for over 150 years, leaving Unicarval around

1830. According to tradition they morgaged the estate in the 1820s to meet the bail money of a friend, who rather ungraciously absconded, with the result that it had to be sold.

The soil

This sort of continuity was unusual. The land seems to have circulated at a dizzy rate. For example in 1732 Capt. James Ross of Portavo held twelve farms here under eight tenants. Seventeen years later, when the estate was sold to meet debts, only three of these remained. Advertisements in the *News Letter* show that between 1745–70 well over half the leasehold land in Dundonald came onto the market, sometimes at vastly increased rents; for example a 47 acre farm in Church Quarter, 'having plenty of moss and marle', and let for £17 in 1739, was split in two and offered at £60 apiece twenty years later. This rise may not have been as outrageous as it seems. Tenants were encouraged to improve their holdings and the new rent may reflect added value.

Some had no choice but to add value, as land was often hived off and let raw. In 1767, for instance, Henry Ranken of Dunlady let 20 acres in Ballymiscaw which, he enthused, had been 'newly marled; with 158 Barrels of Lime', with another '202 Barrels to be given to the purchacer free of Expenses.' And the catch? Only that the would-be farm had neither fields nor farmhouse. However if he couldn't offer a farmhouse Henry offered the next best thing, free timber and glazing, and 'ten pence per perch.... for ditching until it is made into Six Parks'. No wonder the population was emigrating en masse.

Alternatively, some farms went lock, stock and barrel. In 1772 William Blair let 21 acres in Ballyrussell with:

All his Household Furniture, with all Farming Utensils, both very good, a Mare with a Foal of this year; Cows and Heifers; several Stacks of Corn, a Stack of Hay, and some Turf (with Moss and Meadow, some of it very lately limed)

The ripening grain was often thrown in too. When McCully the miller died in 1770, as well as his 'Cows Horses . . . Arks, Field Gates, Horse Racks (and) Cow Stakes', his executors offered, 'about twelve Acres of excellent Wheat, a few acres of Barley, about twenty acres of Oats, and a few acres of Meadow.'

The instability was endemic. Though renewable, leases ran for three named lives or 31 years, whichever was longer. The named lives were usually relatives of one or other party, and in the case of the Annesley leases, this led to some curious disparities. For instance Robert Cinnamon's 18 acre farm on the slopes of Dunlady was held on the lives of Robert Viscount Joycelyn, and Richard Viscount Powerscourt, two of the wealthiest minors in the kingdom. A blunt reminder that three lives and 31 years could be of comparable duration comes in a 1768 lease of lands in Ballyoran to James McCully. McCully's two year old son, cited on the original lease, had died within six months of the signing. Fortunately lease lives were renewable, and on payment of 'one British sixpence', the life was replaced by that of McCully's brother, a youth of 'about seventeen'.

More striking still, however, is the extent to which life existed courtesy of the land. Farms were incarnations of the land they stood on. Fields were houses in

'Shucktown', off the Gransha Road. Look carefully and in the middle of the ruined cottage you will see an 18th century, one roomed, mud and sod walled cabin. It went with a 7 acre farm. The blocked remains of its original door and windows can still be seen.

Johnny Morrow lived at Shucktown around the turn of the century. He had led a riotous life until one evening, drunk, he staggered into a mission tent and was converted to God. He set up a small 'meeting house' in a byre at Shucktown. This proved popular, and his lane became known as 'Church Road'. He is pictured outside his newly whitewashed cottage, with his wife by his side (she had left him, but returned after his reformation), and an open bible in his hand.

kit form. Dundonald's cottages were made with mud from the nearest marl hole (or locally quarried stone), roofed with thatch from the fields around them, heated with turf from a nearby bog,[22] and supplied with water from an adjacent well. Fields were fertilised with dung or marl. Nothing went to waste. In 1772, for example, Andrew Jackson let his 100 acre farm in Ballyregan 'with a Portion of Turf; Ash for Car and Harrow and Scollops for Thatching'. 'Straw fit for Thatch', could be bought from the mill.

Though to a high degree self-sufficient, the parish was also plugged into a circuit of country fairs and markets. The most convenient were at Comber, Newtownards and Belfast, however farmers sometimes travelled further afield to get what they wanted. In 1766, for example, Andrew Allen of Ballyrainey went to Mullacrew to buy 'a Parcel of Cows', and drove them home across three counties. (We know this because at Jonesboro' on the Armagh/Louth border he was joined by a small pig, which followed him home. When he got back he advertised for its owner.)

Dundonald was also a district of stud farms. Some half dozen are known, by far the largest being Lambert's, where, 'for as little as two guineas', favoured

Mather's place, behind the Ulster Hospital. It is also built around an 18th century mudwalled cabin. Like Shucktown it was lived in until quite recently. Sandmartins nest in its crumbling gable.

mares could be covered by Old Tickle Me Quickly, Frosty Face, Lightening, and Sir Thomas, whom he insisted was still up to the job, in spite of 'villanous reports' to the contrary.

Thomas Kennedy operated in a much smaller way from his farm near the meeting house. Then there was Dalzell of Ballylisbredan, who catered for the shady end of the market. His stallion Rainbow, the sire of Hero Black, could be availed of for 'Half a Guinea and a Shilling to the Boy'. Business was good, until Hero Black's owner took space in the *News Letter* to deny that the horses were related, and to call Dalzell a fraud. Dalzell made a great fuss about 'so base and False an Imputation', but quietly dropped the pedigree claim.

The advertisements also throw up some mysteries. Where, for instance, was 'the Mansion-house of Ballyrainey', sold as 'fit for a Gentleman' in 1765? Or the Ballymiscaw flax mill 'new built' in 1763? And what on earth was 'The

Dundonald Club', which met at Hamilton Thompson's on Thursday September 3 1767, 'Dinner to be on the Table at Three of the Clock.'?

They record some fascinating social snippets, such as Dundonald's first known divorce, or rather separation, a very civilised affair which took place in 1762, when James and Margaret Green auctioned their goods, split the profits, and vowed to live 'separate for ever hereafter'. (Its first known elopement follows two years later, when Margaret McCully escaped from her husband Alexander, who seems to have been less wounded by her departure than the fact she left with 'several valuable things'.)

Both advertisements and leases contain interesting topographical details and long disused place names such as Archy's brae, and Long Stone Park Farm. In 1763 the Lambert estate leased 'that Parcel of Ground in Dunlady commonly called Archy's bray containing by Estimation Thirty five acres' to one John Hamilton, stipulating that if he builds a stone dwelling on it he can have £6 'and as many Brown Slates as will . . . cover the Rooff'. Towards the bottom of the scale, in 1768 Lambert let five acres 'lately taken off the Grove field... with the House and Garden thereunto belonging' to William Gowdy, aged 'about twenty one', for a stiff £10.4.9. p.a., payable, as ever, on May and November 1st, and due within 21 days on pain of eviction. Gowdy could marl his land from the Bog of Allybrook.[23] For fuel he had 'two Days Baking of Turf in the Mosses in Dunlady'; and he undertook to grind his grain at 'the old Mill of Cordonald'.

Many farmers such as these had a sideline or a trade. Gowdy, for instance, did a bit of horse breeding. John and Gawn McRoberts of Ballyoran were farmer-blacksmiths; and Gawn, 'a friendly, jolly fellow and nobodys enemy but his own', acted as auctioneer, adviser and willmaker to the neighbourhood. He was also a great bullet player, and was for some time the popular champion of County Down. One of his greatest duels was fought against the champion of Co. Antrim, in a game played on the road between Mountstewart gate and Conway Square, Newtownards, the players being accompanied on the way by crowds of excited supporters. Gawn's grand-niece Mary wrote that as:

the Co Down champion had been "on the spree" for some time previously the result was for some time doubtful but in the end he won what his supporters thought a glorious victory

Gawn drowned in a horse-pond around the year 1800, after losing his way in thick snow.

By this time the flourishing town of Belfast had begun to make its presence felt. However its influence was then almost entirely benign. It became the main market for local produce, and to an extent Dundonald shared in its prosperity. Even so, we should be wary of taking too rosy a view of the local economy. The poor harvests of 1726–8, and the failure of the potato crop in 1740–1 brought distress to even the most sheltered parts of County Down. Large scale emigration continued. Indeed, so many left that in 1777, a year after Adam Smith in *The Wealth of Nations* had explained the role of towns in nourishing the surrounding countryside, an unknown contemporary source quoted by Stevenson described the Dundonald district as 'black and barren'. While this

'The old mill of Cordonald' (l) and its adjacent scutch mill. This photograph is thought to have been taken in the 1930s. Both mills have since been levelled. (John Lennon)

probably misrepresents the material condition of the parish, it may well have summed up the mood.

Wind and water

Though Dundonald had little to offer in the way of water power, the industrial revolution did not entirely pass it by.

Industrial Dundonald was built along the inconspicuous 'Sally river', which rises in Carrowreagh, runs down the Glen Hill, and threads its way through the drumlins of Ballyoran to meet the Inler at Millmount. This tiny, fleet stream once powered a staggering ten (and possibly twelve) grain, bleach and flax mills. Their heyday was the late 18th/early 19th century, when for most of its length the river was a complex of dams, sluices, and guttered mill races. There was nothing quite like it for miles. By 1880, however, the good days had gone, and by 1914 all but two mills had fallen out of use. Five have been demolished within the last thirty years.

The granddaddy of them all, and the last to close, was the 'old Mill of Cordonald', which stood near the Co-farm on the Millmount Road. It was probably the corn mill mentioned in the 1680 Book of Survey and Distribution (as one of only seven in the entire barony), and may even have been the structure drawn by Raven in 1625, but this is probably wishful thinking. This old, thatched mill was added to or replaced around 1800. After about 1818 the mill, old or otherwise, was owned by the Galways, and in 1833 it is recorded as being powered by a 12ft wheel. Though the mill has now gone, part of its fine sandstone mill race and an impressive section of sluice gate can still be seen, as can the outline of its kidney shaped dam.

It's heir, and the district's finest surviving mill is the bleach mill built by Hugh Barnett in Killarn in 1752, now the Old Mill Kennels. However Hugh (one of the Barnetts of Barnett's Park) did not long enjoy his investment. In 1755 the mill was in the hands of his heir James, who did not share Hugh's enthusiasm for the bleaching trade and let the mill at the end of the year. Barnett was eager for profit, too eager, and if an arrangement was made it fell through. Eighteen months later he tried again. This time his terms were more generous and the letting was successful. His advertisement makes clear that the mill lacked nothing, having:

a good spring to supply the wash mill, led from the fountain in pipes round the boiling-house, with a large drying-loft, wash-mill, beetling-engine, two large furnaces with keeves and racks and all other bleaching utensils, with a good dwelling house, all new and slated

The mill 'with Ease' bleached 1200 pieces yearly, the loft dried 20 pieces of cloth at a time and by 1773 'two new Slate-Cabins' had been built for the mill workers.

One item the Barnetts did not invest in was a watch house. This proved a false economy, for linen kept getting pilfered from the green. The last straw evidently came in 1773, when the loft window was broken and five pieces were stolen. The forces of property reacted swiftly. Local notables led by Lambert, pledged a mighty £110 towards the conviction of the thieves, and a quarantine

Barnett's mill today. Its 11 metre wheel is said to be the largest in Ireland.

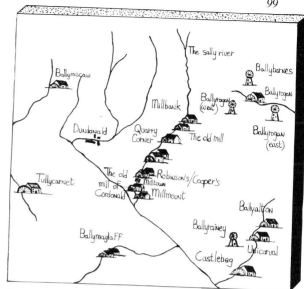

Map showing the location of the district's water and windmills.

zone was established around the green.

The complex grew under the ownership of Stitt of Comber, and in 1837 it processed 5,000 pieces (some 60 miles) of cloth per year. The mills then had the luxury of being fed by two ponds, one above Millbank, the other by Cooper Hill (now marsh.) They were powered by 18ft and 14ft wheels, sizeable engines, but mere sprockets compared with what was to come. Around 1850 the business was taken over by Munce, a Newtownards baker, whereon the mills were amalgamated and converted to handle corn. The mill and miller's house (complete with sealed room) survive, as do parts of the machinery, and the mill's glorious, rotting waterwheel, said to be the largest in Ireland.

The histories of the stream's other eight or so mills are obscure. Few can be dated with certainty, and only one (the little flax mill formerly situated at the foot of Carrowreagh Gardens) can confidently be ascribed to the 18th century. Most of what is known about them comes from the 1833 Valuation, which paints an intriguing picture of life on the river at the height of its prosperity.

Andrew McIlwaine's flax mill stood near the head of the stream at Millbank, jammed into the hillside between three small dams. This was a busy centre with flax coming in from farms roundabout, and being carted off in uncombed bales to Belfast. McIlwaine's office, with its encrusted, undulating slate roof, survives, as does the soundly built mill. Its dark recesses contain the rusty axle, and the knot of machinery that once drove the scutching blades.

The pair of mills which stood near Carrowreagh Gardens are the most obscure of all. Both may date to the 18th century. Their original use is unknown, however in 1833 there was a beetling mill, with loft and drying house here. By 1861 the older mill had fallen out of use. The buildings have not fared well, and their small remains are presently being sized up for a Scrabo stone fireplace. The field opposite was known as the Sour Brae; perhaps the flax was soured here.

The Quarry Corner scutch mill is another of the departed brethern. It was notable for having the old Belfast High Tide Mark built into one of its walls, and as the only mill in the district to convert to steam. To their shame Dundonald's latterday mill owners have not been protective of their wheels. This mill's wheel was spirited off around 1940 by 'a man from Ballymena.'

Below them, on Cooper's farm, were the Ballyoran Mills, a corn and scutch mill run by the Robinsons (father and son) until the early 1890s. Both the two storey corn mill and the 'T' shaped scutch mill were driven by 15ft wheels (13ft according to the 1833 Valuation). The mills survive, however the canny gentleman from Ballymena struck here also.

Further downstream, near Millmount, stood another nest of mills, amongst them the venerable old Mill of Cordonell. Almost nothing now survives, however in 1770 this was the site of:

a valuable Corn Mill, a Bleach-green on which fifteen hundred Pieces of Linen may be done in the driest Season, having two Bleach mills, containing two Beetling-engines, three Pair of Rub-boards, and Wash-mill, a Buck-house with Furnace, Kieves, Rack, and all the utensils necessary for the Bleaching business... all strong and in good Order

It is possible that the profits from this lively business built Millmount.

Off river, there were mills in Ballymiscaw, Castlebeg, Unicarval, Ballymaglaff, Ballyrainey, Ballyalton and Tullycarnet. Of these, only the Ballymiscaw

Enter the dark hole in the centre of the picture and you will find yourself in the remains of Ballyalton's little flax mill. Nature is inexorably taking its course.

and Ballyalton flax mills, and Castlebeg's small beetling mill (built for the Andrews family between 1741–62), are unquestionably 18th century. Ballyalton alone survives.

The wind was another eagerly exploited source of power, and small windmills were built in the townlands of Ballyrainey, Criagantlet, Ballyrogan (two), Ballybarnes and Ballyskeagh. All seem to have been flax mills.[24] These led a brief precarious existence and we can chart their drift into dereliction. In 1834 two were working, two were stumps and two lay empty but still had their sails. Twenty-five years later Craigantlet and Ballyrainey were still going strong; however while Ballyrogan west was back in action, Ballyskeagh was in ruins, and Ballyrogan east and Ballybarnes have disappeared from the map.

There was widespread, small-scale quarrying. However if Ireland's Surveyor General Francis Dobbs had had his way Dundonald might have become a pit village. In 1725 Dobb's quest for coal brought him into County Down, where after several borings he arrived at the following cautious opinion:

I imagine in that sandy country from newtown to Belfast, which I take only to be the Rotten top of that Freestone, there may be a probability of some... for in those beds in the Freestone the Coall generally lys

The search began in earnest in the early 1780s, when the Bangor and Newtown Mining Company sank a number of shafts into the valley's New Red Sandstone, some of them to a depth of 80m. The bores seem to have several times penetrated the sandstone, fishing out dark shales, which in their enthusiasm the miners proclaimed to be 'the cap of coal'. To settle the matter (and reassure their more restless backers) the company called in Joseph Jackson, a high powered Dublin geologist, who spoilt everything in 1786 by reporting that:

freestone is incumbent on the primitive at... Killarn Glen, at Kirkdonnie Glen, and in James Chambers' land, as proved by boring . . . sufficient proofs, in my opinion, that there are no seams or bands of coal contained within the district perscribed.

By 1834 expectations had become more realistic and the Parish Memoir records Dundonald as a useful source of greywacke and freestone, the latter being 'of a very fine quality much used in the construction of the New Dock at Belfast.' Quarries had been opened in Church Quarter, Ballyhanwood, Ballybeen, Ballymiscaw (two), Ballymaglaff, Carrowreagh (four), Ballyrussell and Ballyrainey, where shale and sandstone were extracted. None were very big. Gravel was dug in Carrowreagh, Dunlady, Ballybeen (two pits), Ballymaglaff and Castlebeg; and there were subsequently sandpits in Ballymaglaff and Church Quarter (off Church Road), where a leather purse containing thirty two 16th and 17th century coins and a curious early 18th century ring inscribed 'I die or I shaing (change)' were turned up in 1928.

'We the Volunteers of Dundonald'

It is impossible to imagine the explosive effect the news of the American Revolution had in Ireland, particularly in the presbyterian parts of Ulster, which over the previous half century had become closely bound to the American colony by ties of kin. Many found the colonists example utterly intoxicating: here were their brothers, sisters and cousins seeking by their own exertions to make themselves free.

The contrast with their own circumstances was vivid and and depressing. The Irish election of 1776 had been unusually corrupt, with a swill of pensions, titles and bribes securing 'the Castle' what it hoped would be a parliament sufficiently beholden to resist the strong desire in the country for reform. The government's designs worked well, however it met with an unexpected reverse in the potwalloper borough of Antrim, where the freeholders rejected the landlord nominee in favour of an independent, Captain Wilson.

This small success was keenly welcomed in Dundonald. Every year on June 18th, the anniversary of Wilson's victory, 'a very respectable number of freeholders' gathered at the village inn to celebrate the day when 'by the spirited exertions of the people the chains of lordly aristocracy were broken'. These were hearty occasions; 45 or 46 toasts were regularly drunk. Proceedings began soberly enough with glasses being raised to 'The King and Constitution', 'The revolution of eighty-eight', and 'a hearty drubbing to the French'; however the company then went on to toast electoral reform (frequently), 'peace with America', 'The 20th of June 1215' (the Magna Carta), 'Strafford's fate to all corrupt ministers', 'Freedom and Prosperity to Ireland', 'Mr Grattan', 'The Protestant Interest', 'The memory of Alfred the Great','May the King know his friends from his enemies','The Memory of Andrew Marvell', 'May the lovers of liberty always have cause to rejoice', ending rousingly with 'Liberty to all mankind'.

'The Commodore' was one of the leading members of this group of liberal *bon viveurs*. He invited 'lovers of liberty and freedom' to dine with him on the second anniversary of Wilson's election, and his epitaph in Dundonald churchyard seems to capture something of the spirit of the time:

> Here lies beneath this stone
> The Commodore who oft-times shone
> In cracking jokes with merry guests,
> And charming songs with merry taste;
> Punctual and just in all his dealings,
> Yet Said himself he had his Failings,
> Bad Qualities, if he had any,
> Were very few, his good ones many,
> His heart and hand were always ready
> To serve the Poor & help the Needy-
> Had gratitude in high Perfection,
> And died in hope of Ressurrection,
> 20th May, 1779, aged 48 years.

The organisation that gave this radicalism expression was the Volunteers. Dundonald had its own company by 1779. They wore blue (Irish made) uniforms and were armed with flintlocks, which they used 'with the greatest exactness'. The Dundonald Volunteers eagerly endorsed the reforms advocated by Grattan and the Patriot party in the Dublin parliament. On the 4th November 1779, for example, in company with Volunteers all over Ireland, they met to demand the removal of English restrictions on Irish trade. In the following year, they met to demand parliamentary independence, and to take part in mock engagements near Belfast; and in 1782 a delegation from Dundonald attended the influential Dungannon convention.

With the winning of 'the constitution of 1782', the need for extra-parliamentary activity waned, and the Volunteers went into a sort of suspended animation. And there they might have stayed had it not been for the French revolution. This, and a feeling that it was perhaps time to finish the work of '82, refired the Volunteer spirit.

In the winter of 1792–3 the parishes of north Down again met to air their views. The Newtownards Volunteers rejoiced at the 'Emancipation of the French nation from the Chains of Despotism'. Donaghadee called for a parliament to represent 'ALL THE PEOPLE'. Comber denounced the 'depraved and morbid' state of Irish democracy. Castlereagh, chaired by Hugh Montgomery of Tullycarnet, railed against 'enormous Taxes ruinous to Trade, (and) Pensions of the most scandalous nature', and insisted on 'an immediate Reform of Parliament'.

The 'Inhabitants of the Parish of Dundonald' met on January 1st 1793 to denounce 'gross corruption' in government and demand 'an equal Representation of all the People', declaring that 'no Man, nor body of Men, dare say that the tenth Man of Ireland is represented in Parliament'. In case anyone doubted their resolve, they made it known that:

We, the Volunteers of Dundonald, will rub the dust off our Arms, and join our Brother Soldiers in every legal means to obtain our just rights.

Who were these dangerous radicals? Few of their names are now known, however the meeting was chaired by Col. Robert McLeroth of Dunlady and Daniel Blow of Primrose Park (Rosepark), who was shortly after charged with printing seditious libels. Its secretary was Robert Stewart, who had led the company during the heady year of 1782. The rank and file, no less committed and no less militant, would have been the ordinary presbyterian people of Dundonald.

The government's response was to arm itself by forming a militia. The people of Down were well aware that this might one day be used against them, so the Militia Act was most unpopular. When the Governer and Deputy Governors of County Down met at 'the hamlet of Castlereagh' to carry its provisions into effect M'Skimmin writes that a 'vast body of people' gathered outside; and when the Governor's escort, a troop of the 17th dragoons, went off to water their horses:

A furious discharge of stones was made by the people on the house where the governors were met, its windows staved, the sentinel wounded, and his horse knocked down. Shots were now fired from the house.

The dragoons returned in haste and a melee followed, during which six or seven died. Word was sent to Belfast and units of the 38th regiment with two cannon were sent up, however by the time of their arrival the crowd had fled.

The Volunteers disbanded in 1793, and thereafter the Society of United Irishmen carried forward the cause of reform. However, though the United Irishmen flourished, their moment had essentially passed by the summer of 1798, when the remains of the movement careered to disaster.

The '98

Dundonald was not involved in the fighting in 1798. It was too near the purged and garrisoned town of Belfast to become a rendezvous for dissent. However given its Volunteer history, and that it was a presbyterian community with a New Light minister in the heart of the planted regions, it would be strange if its sympathies were not strongly republican, and membership of the United Irishmen high.

Not everyone, however, was prepared to take up arms. The majority probably sought peaceful change. The population also included an embattled and unsung minority of loyalists, some of whom, like John McRoberts, were yeomen. This gave the crisis here the character of a civil war. Families divided. For example, while John McRoberts kept the King's peace, his brother Gawn (encountered earlier) seems to have been busy making pike heads.

Let us take up the story from early 1797, when the anti-government party held the field and were actively arming. Passions ran high, and occasionally there was violence. Towards the end of February, for example, a party of men arrived at Unicarval seeking weapons. Cumming refused them, barred the house and shot at the crowd. If he had intended to scare them, the plan backfired, for they 'immediately broke open the windows and door, rushed into the house and murdered him, mangling the body in a most inhuman manner.'[25] There were outrages on both sides. A few weeks after the murder, 'By way of showing his attachment to the laws', a drunken yeoman fired into the village inn (Hamilton Thompson's, now a well known rebel den), 'the ball . . . cutting through the servant girl's clothes.'[26]

When General Lake arrived in Belfast later that month, the government recovered the initiative. It now sought out arms. Gawn McRoberts' apprentice, 'one called Grainger', was almost caught red-handed. He was 'busy at the pikeheads' when to his horror the militia appeared:

when he saw the soldiers coming he hit on a rather ingenious plan of tying the heads together, and strapping them over his foot and going out for a stroll, with the intention of leaving them behind a ditch, however good a plan that might have proved at another time it did not do for the soldiers discovered his secret and arrested Gawn . . . he being the owner of the forge.

Gawn would not say who the pikeheads were for, and would have been shot at noon the next day, had his brother (who had influence with Castlereagh) not obtained his pardon.

The rising, when it came, took place within a framework of enabling myth. Fantastical apparitions were seen, and angels appeared in churchyards at midnight, predicting England's ruin. There was a revival of religion. Bizarre ideas circulated. Prominent amongst these were the alleged prophecies of Columbkille, said to exist in a manuscript called *The Irish Chronicle*. These predicted revolution; and for some reason Dundonald was particularly noted as the place where the prophesies would be fufilled':

Here a young maiden with two thumbs on her right hand, was to sit upon a large stone (the Longstone?), and to hold the horses of three kings during a great battle in which Ireland was to be, as it were, three times lost, but at length won. During this conflict the wheel of an adjoining mill (the old Mill?) was to be three times turned round with the blood of the slain.

Before this could happen however, the maiden, perhaps some spirit of the American Revolution, had to cross the Atlantic three times; and two briars 'growing in the same neighbourhood at a considerable distance from each other', had to intertwine. Both had done so, and a glorious revolution was believed to be at hand. 'Though no-one even pretended to have seen . . . *The Irish Chronicle*', writes M'Skimmin, 'all appeared to believe in its marvellous predictions' and they contributed greatly to morale.

On the eve of rebellion the only sizeable government force in north Down was a contingent of 270 York Fencibles under Colonel Stapylton, stationed in

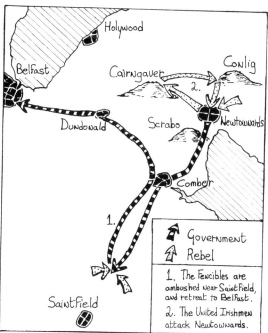

The manoeuvrings in north and mid Down on June 8th-10th 1798, immediately prior to the battle of Ballynahinch. It is tempting to see the rebellion in north Down as an attempted resolution of conflicts inherent in the original plantation.

Newtownards. North Down planned to rise on the night of June 7th, but the government moved first, arresting most of its principal officers.[27] When mid-Down rose on Friday June 8th the Fencibles and yeomanry marched south, leaving a token garrison in the town. They walked straight into an ambush at Saintfield, but managed to pull back in good order to Comber.

North Down rose on the evening of the 9th. Nervous about being cut off or ambushed a second time, Stapylton retreated through Dundonald to Belfast, abandoning the Newtownards garrison to its fate. Early on the morning of Sunday June 10th, 'Pike Sunday' the United Irishmen closed on the isolated garrison.

The attack was a fiasco. Secure in the market house and well supplied with ammunition, the garrison greeted the rebels with fusillades of musketry, whereon they fled in confusion, running 'above a Mile before . . . Prayers, Entreaties or Reproaches or Threats could induce them to halt.' They regrouped on the Cairn Hill (the United Irish had a great fondness for mountains), where desertions and reinforcements wholly changed the compo-

sition of the force. When discipline had been restored, the new army marched
to Conlig, where they made ready to attack again.

In the meantime, however, the garrison fled, allowing the rebels 'quiet
possession' of the town in the late afternoon. They had little time to enjoy their
success, for shortly afterwards a messenger arrived instructing them to join the
general muster at Saintfield. The response was almost mutinous, and only after
'much flattering' did they make the night march south.

For two sweltering June days the north-east of County Down belonged to the
United Irishmen. The green cockade was worn, military camps were set up and
makeshift garrisons posted. A Committee of Public Safety on the French
revolutionary model was set up in Newtownards. Dundonald lay on the fringe
of this fledgling statelet, and when Lake's successor Nugent dispatched a force
to re-take Comber and so cut off the United Irishmen's retreat, it no doubt
promptly fell into line.

The insurrection lasted less than a week, and the end of organised
resistance[28] was followed by an undisciplined campign of reprisal. Again there
is no dependable evidence as to how this affected Dundonald, however the
parish may have fallen within the ambit of Colonel Atherton, who made
punitive forays into the country around Newtownards. As he wrote to Nugent
on June 20th:

I have had tolerable success today... we have burned Johnston's house at Crawford's-
Bourn-Mills – at Bangor, destroyed the furniture of Pat. Agnew . . . at Ballymaconnell
Mills, burned the house of McConnell, Miller and James Martin . . . We hope you will
think we have done *tolerably* well. Tomorrow we go to Portaferry . . .

In *Betsy Gray*, W.G. Lyttle writes of a squadron of dragoons stopping near
Dundonald, where they met a farmer digging potatoes;

'How far is Belfast?' shouted one of the troopers.
The man was deaf, and, not hearing the question, did not look up. He's a rebel, I'm sure,
said the trooper, and raising his carbine he shot the poor man dead.

Near to the same place the same party seized an inoffensive man and strung him to a
beam which projected from a farm house, where he was strangled to death. That beam
was only recently cut down.

Unfortunately, it is hard to imagine a less reliable source than *Betsy Gray*, and
these anecdotes are probably best seen as rebellion folklore.

The avenging was not entirely one-sided. The staunchly republican congregation of Gilnahirk (an offshoot of Dundonald) were so out of sympathy with
the monarchical views of their minister Francis Pringle (who is said to have
spent the rebellion in a hayshed in Ballyhanwood, eating only a raw egg laid by
a brooding hen) that they compelled him to resign in the following year. He
emigrated to America.

With the arrival of Cornwallis as Lord Deputy the 'pacification' became
more orderly. The leaders of the rebellion, including 'Lambert Brice of
Dundonald' (about whom nothing more is known) were court-martialled, and
hung in Cornmarket.

11 The long nineteenth century

Pew and preare Book

In June 1808 Hamilton Thompson, the 'Actin Church warden' presented the parish with a handsome new Vestry Minute Book costing 11/4½d. (We know its price because Thompson was persuaded, no doubt reluctantly, to reimburse himself several weeks later.) Thanks to Hamilton's generosity (and the whiskey that made it possible!), we can begin to follow the work of the Vestry and the workings of the church in some detail.

In Dundonald the Select Vestry fell some way short of being an unofficial parish parliament. It had limited powers and few of the gentry had much to do with it. In their absence it was made up of middling farmers, men like Alexander Rabb and John McRoberts, and occasional tradesmen like the carpenter Thetford Young. They met every Easter Monday to fix the rate of a levy known as 'the Cess' (usually 1d per acre) which was used to meet church running costs.

About half of this went on the wages of the church's two part-time employees, the clerk and the sexton. The sexton, Jane McMukan or McMeeian was engaged to 'open the Door likewise the gate and to keep the Church in good Cleanliness', for which she got £2 per year. However, the job was no plumb and the appointment of John McNall 'to continue in office during his good behaviour & no longer' (1833), suggests that suitable candidates were not always plentiful. The clerk, James McClure, had £5 p.a. due quarterly but not always paid so, and on June 27 1808 the following doleful entry occurs:

Receved from Hamilton thompson Acten Church warden for the perish of dondonald £1.11.9 the Remender of my Salery for the year 1807

Most of the rest went on the church. In 1808 the folio bible was rebound at a cost of 13/-, and 6/8d was 'pead for a preare Book'. The seating was spruced up in 1809, when £1.13s was spent on locks for the boxed pews in which the grandees sat (the wealthy rented boxes in church as they might in the theatre), ensuring that if the hoi polloi strayed from the free seats at the back they would soon perforce find their way back there. Hugh Cuddy (a member of the latter group) fitted these for 6/6d.

There was always something needing fixed. In March 1809 Cuddy mended the east window for 2/2d, several years later 8/6d was spent on 'slates & draning', and in 1830 £1.10s went on repairing the windows of the 'Spire'. In 1831–2 the church was roughcast and whitewashed, and 5/11½d was spent on 'notice boards for Church yard'. The period saw other, grander improvements. A new bell was bought in 1814, and in 1819 the Rev. Dillon laid the foundation stone of a splendid new rectory. However, in spite of a generous grant, the building work left Dillon out of pocket, and the entry covering it has a slightly martyred air:

cost £830 – received only £800 from the Board of First Fruits: erecting offices and all other improvements amounting to nearly £400 sterling, at the sol expense of the Incumbent.

The Vestry also supervised the burial of the destitute. The accounts for 1814–15 included:

To burying a strange woman 0:17:11
To burying Sara Todd 0:14:4

and after 1842 a halfpenny an acre (£5.10.9) was levied for 'Coffins for the poor.' The minutes for 1842–4 show how it was spent:

To Thetford Young for three Coffins – 1:10:0
To Mrs Moody for Calico tape + & – 0:7:9
To gravedigger for making three graves – O:3:0
To two Stools for resting Coffins 0:5:0

The bell of St. Elizabeth's, 'erected in the spire' in 1814, at a cost of £56.6.3d, all but £14 raised by subscription.

The Vestry saw to the welfare of 'deserted children', and there was usually at least one 'orphant' to support. In 1809 £3.0.6 was 'pead to john Sinclair for sending (a) Child to Dublin and Baying frocks for it'. In 1830 £5 was levied to support 'a deserted Infant lately found in this Parish', and seven years later £4.5s was raised towards its education.

The church looked after its poor. In October 1808 there were seven women on the parish, four of them widows. Six months later 12/2d was divided amongst them, Widow James receiving 4/8d as her boy had 'goat his leg Brok'. Though it buried 'a strange woman' in 1814–5, and lodged 'a poor Woman' in 1845–6, by and large the church supported its own, using its 'poors money' as a form of patronage, to be spent in shoring up the communion's crumbling fringes. The wandering beggars that fill the pages of the presbyterian Session Book are conspicuously absent.

The earlier minutes also include much that is interesting and obscure, some of it wilfully so. For example in March 1810 the Vestry prepared 'Sevirl Charges against the Incumbent', but the secretary is too discreet to say what these are. (This is characteristic, to trace the entrant's true feelings one needs to multiply each hint of emotion by ten.) The parish was also obliged to raise men to serve in the North Downshire Militia. The militia were still unpopular, and in order to reach its quota in 1810 our peace-loving parish had to bribe 'three Healthy young men' with £20 apiece.

The Baptism, Marriage, and Burial records have also survived, and each is of interest. All highlight the minuteness of the congregation. (For example, there are years in which no-one dies.) The Baptismal register[1] is also interesting for the light it casts on the problem of illegitimacy.

Between 1820–33, not notably an interval of loose morals, 22 out of the 106 infants baptised here are registered as bastards. Thereafter matters begin to be handled with more delicacy, 'His wife' being added to the woman's name to denote a married couple. Through the register's pages flit irresponsible and apparently irresistible beau's such as Thomas Williamson:

May 27 1820 Thomas Son of Thomas Williamson & Anne Breen Donlady – Bastard
July 25 1820 Anne daughter of Thomas Williamson of Donlady & Jane Smiley Ballybeen – a Bastard

and unlucky or imprudent women like Mary Mc_____ of Ballybeen, whose family had enough influence to have their name blanked. Foundlings such as Esther (1830), John (1850) and Hugh (1853) were almost always illegitimate and not infrequently the product of incestuous liasons. And this was not an Anglican foible. It is unlikely that the presbyterian records would tell a very different story; and given that this was an age without contraception, we can only wonder that the figure is not higher.

The Toll War

As will be clear to anyone who has had the stamina to come through this book chronologically, Dundonald, like most apparently sleepy country parishes, could readily be brought to the boil. An issue on which passions ran particularly high was the question of the Long Bridge tolls. Traffic coming into Belfast from

County Down had to pay a toll of dubious legality in order to enter the city.[2] This 'much incensed' local farmers and there are said to have been many angry disputes at the bridgehead.

Finding the situation intolerable, the farming community east of the river resolved to end to the tolls. In October 1814 farmers representing Dundonald, Knockbreda, Holywood and Moneyrea met in a Castlereagh 'retiring house' to plan their campaign, Dundonald being represented by two of its most substantial farmers. As an opening salvo they published extracts from McNally's weighty *Justice of the Peace* in the *News Letter*. Then they hired a council, a Mr Warren. For most of them this was a step into the unknown, and with a prudent wariness of the law and those who practice it, the minutes include the proviso that 'should Mr Warren appear dilatory another lawyer is to be chosen'.

The delegates fears turned out to be groundless. The issue was soon settled in the courts, and in the words of one campaigner they 'succeeded so well in the accomplishment of their object that scarcely any imposition . . . has been attempted since.'

Squire John

The year 1809 seems to have been notable for the arrival in the parish of none other than Black John Cleland, scourge of the United Irishmen and one of the most hated men in County Down. In 1805 he married Esther Jackson of Mount Pleasant, and when he gave up the rectorship of Newtownards (the only one of his four clerical jobs which involved any work), the couple are thought to have settled on her estate, changing its name (c.1830) to the rather more familiar 'Stormount'.

Uncomplimentary stories about Cleland abound. As Castlereagh's agent he is said to have accepted only gold coin from the tenants, which he supplied to them at a mark-up of up to 5/- per £. There is considerable evidence that as a

This drawing, thought to be a caricature of John Cleland, appeared in a scurrilous pamphlet lampooning Castlereagh on the occasion of the 1805 County Down election. It also includes an intriguing reference to 'the Dundonald elephant', whoever or whatever that may be.

magistrate he was grossly partial, and during the mid 1790s he seems to have locked up political opponents virtually at will. As rector, 'the *pious* Father in God John Cleland', as he was described with heavy sarcasm, is reported to have delegated his duties to the extent that he was rarely seen in church. The family are said to have been cursed, and on settling in Dundonald they are believed to

The story of Stormont, showing (l-r) the Widow Neill's farm (1732), the prosperous late 18th century farmhouse, the Georgian country house (c.1830), the Scots Baronial castle (1859), and the 1932 Parliament Buildings.

have been ostracised by their neighbours.

Not much is known about Cleland's life in Dundonald, however Cathal O'Byrne, who disliked him intensely[3], relates that Cleland closed the old 'King John' road by putting gates at the borders of his demesne and allowing fewer and fewer travellers passage, until the gates were closed entirely. (An anecdote which probably says more about the old road's decline than Cleland's villany.) What O'Byrne also fails to mention is that this was part of a Napoleonic-style grand design, for Cleland sought to replace both the existing roads with a third road of his own devising. However his plan met with stiff opposition and only the section between Quarry Corner (then Mill Corner) and Newtownards was built, Lord Castlereagh's tenants apparently proving more amenable than those of Dundonald.[4]

Cleland apparently lived without great show or desire for honour. (He is said to have refused a peerage at the time of the Act of Union.) However, with a touch of *nouveau riche* vulgarity, John's eldest son Samuel had a grand new house built when he came of age. Aesthetically this seeems to have been a disaster, contemporaries describe it as 'plain', and 'very gloomy in appearance', and dissatisfaction with the castle, as it was known (though it was not castellated), may have been one of the reasons behind the celebrated rebuilding of the 1850s.

John Cleland died in June 1834 aged 80. That November Samuel married Elizabeth Joyce of Thornhill, Knock (the girl next door), who had also recently lost her father. He was 26 and she 17. Little is known of Samuel's life. Thomas Stott of Belmont implies that when young Samuel was something of a rake; spoilt and wealthily loutish, adding that he proposed to Eliza following 'copious libations to "Bacchus"' after his horse had won at the Maze. More reliably, he also mentions that the accidental death of Elizabeth's father, a close friend, shocked Samuel and 'greatly changed' his behaviour. It would seem that he inherited his father's unpopularity. Stott writes that around 1840 'there was no intercourse in the neighbourhood in the way of visiting with the Clelands', and recalls that his father pitied Samuel's 'isolated life'.

Samuel died in bizarre circumstances. The train of events that led to his death began when he discovered that his head groom (one of the few people he trusted) had been systematically defrauding him. According to Stott, (who had the account from his father, who had it from the single witness), Samuel then became:

> so incensed that he *then* and *there* dismissed him, paid all the wages due, and had the house cleared, "vowing he would not rest until he had it down." . . . so keen was he that he collected all his men and led them off to pull it down, and had all but one gable levelled when the dinner hour arrived. He went up to the house and had his lunch, and so intent was he that he that he came back again before the men. When the first of them came he said . . . "come let us see if you and I cannot have it down before them," or words to that effect. Taking a pick he attacked the wall . . . when all of a sudden it fell, crushing him under its extreme weight

The incident caused a great sensation, not least because of the family's notoriety. It was widely rumoured that the death was not an accident; and there will doubtless have been much talk of poetic justice and the family curse.[5]

Elizabeth, completely shattered, had a pharonic mausoleum (one of the largest in Ulster) erected to his memory. It takes the form of of a (now cracked) blue granite box cornered with mock columns on top of which sits an elegant six columned cupola. It is a monument to rival the Kempe Stone. Samuel, the remains of his parents, his brother (who died under age), and several of their progenitors were dug up and reinterred in lead coffins in the vault.

The mausoleum, the spiked church tower and the motte combine to create what the historian J.S. Curl called an 'unforgettably dramatic composition', and in his painting 'Dundonald graveyard' Neil Shawcross has captured something of its power. Stott writes critically of this 'display of wealth', but it is surely cynical to see the mausoleum as other than a simple, powerful, and in its way touching expression of grief. Widowed at 25, Elizabeth would have many

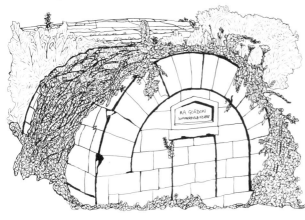

The Gordon Mausoleum, fastened with ivy, in Dundonald churchyard.

'That aul thing should be blew t'hell er that. Those Clelands were the biggest rogues in the country.' The Cleland mausoleum, in a corner of Dundonald churchyard, said to have been built high to be visible from Stormont.

opportunities to remarry, but remained spouseless for the rest of her life.

. . . and Squire Robert

Robert Gordon, a Belfast wine merchant, and his wife Catherine moved into Summerfield (now Knock Golf Club) around the end of 1809, buying the estate off Robert's older and wealthier brother David (who had lived there since 1801) for £5,500 plus a morgage debt of £1,000, which Robert (the poor relation) did not apparently clear until the 1820s. David and his family went to live in great style in Florida Manor, near Killinchy, however he continued to buy property here and retained an active interest in the affairs of the parish until his death in 1836. The Gordons were one of Belfast's leading commercial families.[6]

Summerfield was then a large, unassuming late 18th c. house, pleasantly situated amongst trees, neat boxwood hedges, and walled fruit, herb and flower gardens. To the east it marched with Bessmount (now the Nurses homes), to the west Primrose Park (now Dundonald House), and to the north west Stormount. To the north lay the old Belfast Road and several small farms, three of which had a right of way through the demesne. Before the estate's gentrification this had not been a problem, but the Gordons found it a nuisance and not withstanding a vogue for all things pastoral, took exception to their neighbours driving cattle through the grounds.

Old Daniel Blow was a particular offender. Blow owned two of the farms, and according to the Gordons he was 'constantly passing from one road to the other'. His son-in-law Joseph Russel was apparently worse again.

After putting up for as long as he could bear it Robert followed his neighbour's example and put up gates at either end of the track, giving a key to Blow. 'After much trouble', the gates were accepted. When Blow died in 1810 Primrose Park was let to Russel, who, much to Gordon's chagrin, continued to use the track freely until 1827, when David Gordon intervened to buy the house and two of the rights of way for £2,400; an expensive price for a lowly cart track.

But this was not the end of it. The third right of way belonged to the delightful Rev. Cleland, whose estate had swallowed up the third farm. With the anullment of the other two rights, this became an important bargining counter and Cleland used it to maximum advantage.

The inevitable deal was struck in 1829. In return for the final right of way David Gordon gave Cleland Primrose Park at the price he had paid for it, and Robert threw in enough land to allow Cleland to lay an avenue down to the road. This seemed to settle the matter.

However things were just hotting up. Joseph Russel, now consigned to one of the farms that had belonged to Blow, claimed that one of Primrose Park's two rights of way correctly belonged to his farm and made clear that he intended to use it. Ignoring him, Gordon had his men build a wall across its entrance. But Russel was not to be easily deflected. One Saturday afternoon he came 'with three men duly prepared with Clubs etc and . . . Demolished the Wall.' (This will have set the tongues wagging in Gape Row!) Gordon's reply was to remake it, and in case Russel doubted *his* determination, to cut a 'fosse' across the track to make it useless. For good measure he threatened to take Russel to court, whereon Russel wisely let the matter lie.

'An improved and improving country'

Meanwhile, what had been happening elsewhere in the parish? For once it is possible to say, for in the 1830s, after thousands of years of grubbing after scraps, the local historian encounters an almost embarrassing wealth of information: the Census of 1831, the Valuation and the Ordnance Survey of 1833; and best of all, the Poor Inquiry of 1836, in which the Reverends Dillon and Finlay comment, guardedly, on the condition of the parish poor.

Let us start with the village. Since 1625 it had 'jumped' from the moat to the Newtownards Road, and quadrupled in size. (Not that that is saying much!) In 1831 it had 34 houses, most of them 'neat' single storey, one or two roomed cottages. Ten years later it had 41 houses and 190 people, suggesting that much of the expansion was recent. This was as big as it got.

It had two bars, one in what is now the Moat Inn, the other perhaps on the site of the Cherryhill Inn (Thompson's may by now have gone). Between these stood the semi-legendary terrace of cottages known as the White Row or 'Gape

Row', so called because all that passed before it was microscopically scrutinised from behind its half doors.[7] In the 1830s it housed the families of respectable tradesmen, but the Row went downhill. Agnes Romilly White (1934) gives the impression that it was lived in by a swarm of obese old tea swilling spinsters, who spent their days yacking and out-staring curious travellers. Passers by included Franz Lizst, his grand piano, and John Keats, who passed on a walking tour in 1818.

Life focused on the 'very badly' kept high road. Like the village it had its routines. The mail car to Donaghadee swept through at 9.30am, and coaches from Portaferry and Comber passed in the other direction, returning in the evening. The locals raced them, and bets were often laid. Clog-wheeled carts were still in use. The heaviest traffic was on market days, when farmers packed the Moat Inn at 4.00 and 5.00 in the morning, breakfasting on eggs and potatoes; returning in the afternoon with a cartload of sweet smelling dung. Not everyone confined themselves to buying manure, and the local lore is full of tales of tipsy farmers being driven home by their horses.

The parish had five bars[8], against 9 in Knockbreda, 28 in Comber and 'about 50' in hedonistic Newtownards, though in the hopeful words of one resident, their hold would soon 'be diminished by the influence of the temperance society there'. Legal alchohol was only part of the problem. In the 1820s the country is said to have been 'in great danger of being demoralised by illicit distillation', however the shebeens disappeared after the reduction of a tax on malt, and in 1836 Finlay could report that in good livin' Dundonald, 'This pernicious practice is unknown.'

Though the parish could boast a smith, a carpenter, a painter, two shoe-makers, a grocery and a string of mills, the local economy was overwhelmingly

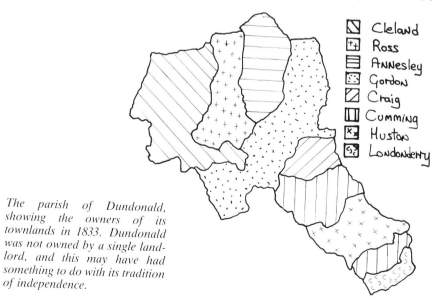

Cleland
Ross
Annesley
Gordon
Craig
Cumming
Huston
Londonderry

The parish of Dundonald, showing the owners of its townlands in 1833. Dundonald was not owned by a single landlord, and this may have had something to do with its tradition of independence.

agricultural. Of its 285 families, 37 were involved in manufacture, 38 in trade and 210 worked on the land.

The landscape had changed greatly since 1625. The smaller marshes had been drained, the turf had been worked out and the hedgeless, bankless farms had been divided into hundreds of small irregular 'Parks' or fields. In 1833, as a result of reclamation it at last became possible to run a road through the 'wet & rushy' meadows between the Elk Inn and Grahamsbridge, and so the Comber Road (originally 'the Meadow Cut') was born.

The land was divided into some 160 farms and the men who farmed them were the backbone of the parish. Bordes calls Dundonald's farmers 'respectable yeomen'; and Lewis (1837) observes that 'Every improvement in the mode of tillage and the construction of farming implements has eagerly been adopted' here.

Holdings ranged from 3–110 acres but were generally between 10–40 acres, held at £1.10-£2.10s per acre. Finlay estimates the average size at about thirty acres, which would compare well with the county as a whole. He writes that 90% of the land was tilled, with potatoes, wheat, oats, and barley being grown in rotation. Yields were high. According to Bordes the land produced 15–18cwt of wheat, 12–15cwt of oats, 15–18cwt of barley or 150–300 bushels of potatoes per acre. New crops were tried out, and it is recorded that when turnips were first sown in Ballyhanwood 'Hundreds' came to see the wondrous new vegetable.

With the possible exception of the Clelands and the Gordons, the resident gentry were middling families ('rich savages', according to O'Donovan), and apart from Dr Herron of Camperdown, and the dissolute Captain McDonald of Dunlady, all were plain 'Mr's'. The big houses were now Stormount and Summerfield, followed by Rosepark, seat of the Crawfords, Bessmount, seat of the Corrys, and Rockfield, home of a merchant family, the McCleans, who were (amongst other things) importers of 'Fleecy Hosiery' and 'Cotton Pantaloons'. Most of these sat on the sunny lower slopes of the Holywood Hills, enclosed by plantations and maintained by new money from Belfast. None of the 18th century gentry remained.[9]

Dundonald was relatively prosperous. According to the OS Memoir:

The lower parts of the parish have a tolerably rich and fertile appearance and even those which are _____ present a cultivated aspect. . . . the whole district has the appearance of an improved and improving country.

However its bounty was not evenly divided, and though the parish lacked the extremes of wealth and poverty found elsewhere, the condition of its poorest groups was unenviable. At the bottom of the heap were the families of the 100–140 farm hands. However, though poor they were not impoverished. Men worked for upwards of 1/- a day and Finlay writes that there was 'no want of employment'. Dillon estimates that 'A healthy stout labourer' could earn £15.13s a year. (Finlay says £19, well above the county average.)

Unmarried, live-in female servants made up 'the principal part' of the workforce. Women reaped for 1/- a day (with meals), made hay for 10d and weeded for 6d. Hand spinning and weaving were 'the usual occupations in the

Spinning at Ballyoran, c.1910. (Molly Greeves). The Ordnance Survey Memoir of 1833 noted that spinning and weaving were 'the usual occupations in the cottages'.

cottages'. Women embroidered for Scottish finishing companies, working long hours for fiddling wages. Children were put to work early. Describing the lot of a labouring family with four children Finlay wrote that 'the two eldest are generally hired out to the farmer and the two youngest are one half time at school and the other half employed in labour.'

Over half the man's wages went on food. Potatoes and milk, oatcakes, herrings and occasionally a piece of bacon and a cup of tea, were the rule here, according to Dillon. It was a fairly nutritious diet and many would have envied its variety. The spuds were generally baked or boiled and flavoured with herbs; and Andrews of Comber mentions that 'the fare is always best when the females dispense with tea and the men with whiskey.'

Dillon describes the worker's dress as comfortable, and on Sundays 'decent and respectable'; and Blake of Comber notes that 'shoes are generally worn now'. Confirming this picture of relative plenty Finlay adds that 'In the premises of a day labourer there is frequently to be found a cow, almost always a pig, and other appearances of comfort.' In the premises means exactly that, animals often shared a cottage with their owners.

The district's cottages were whitewashed to striking effect. As Mrs Riddell wrote 'the whole place looked green and white by reason of the green fields and the whitewashed houses.' Whereas the newer cottages were built of stone, roofed with slates and fitted with sash windows, many of the older ones were made of mud and thatch, and 'badly lighted (with) no ventilation but through door & chimney'. Some 10 or 12 of the poorest of them were shared by two families.

Possessions were few. Furnishings were basic. Blakely of Comber writes that many cottages were 'without furniture of any kind', and in a damning reply the parish priest of Newtownards described some as 'hardly equal to repel the wind and rain', and noted that people 'often lie on straw on the floor'. An indignant Maxwell of Newtownards writes that only when the letting of such hovels is forbidden 'shall Ireland cease to be *accursed*'.

The replies from Dundonald are extremely bland. Looking down his nose somewhat Dillon calls the furniture 'as good as could be expected in that class of houses', and the bedding 'comfortable . . . for that class of people'. Finlay the improver is barely more informative. He writes that as far as he knows bedding is generally satisfactory, except, of course, 'where the occupants are slothful'.

As a rule the labourer worked for his landlord, often a smallish farmer who found it hard to make ends meet. (Finlay describes labourers as 'better off than farmers.') Andrews, who succeeded Cleland as the Marquis of Londonderry's agent, describes these men as 'the most grinding landlords on the earth', but this was often because they were under pressure from the like of Andrews, the head landlord's agent. Neither Dillon nor Finlay remark on this sensitive subject, merely noting that the rent of a cottage and garden was somewhat high at £2–3 p.a., for, though prices and wages had fallen after 1815, rents had stayed at their inflated wartime levels.

Evictions seem to have been rare. Much more worrying was the practice of 'throwing', the amalgamation of farms, which according to Andrews threatened to 'unhinge the whole frame of our agricultural society'. In Killinchy, where ⅓ of farms were of 1–10 acres throwing was prevalent, and the Rev. Green records that in most cases the former tenant was left in a 'most indigent and helpless state,' fit only to 'resort to Belfast'. In Dundonald the picture is apparently happier. Dillon writes that though landlords were anxious to throw, 'I do not recollect a single instance of a man of character and punctuality in paying his rent being disposed.' But then it would be very odd if they were.

Asked whether the lot of the poor has improved or worsened since the war, the correspondents from north Down are divided. Only Dundonald sends in an unambiguous reply. Dillon and Finlay are cautiously upbeat.

The emigration figures tend to confirm this picture. While Newtownards had a 'very extensive' emigration, and Comber lost 'not less than 100 persons every year', Dillon estimates that fewer than six per year left Dundonald. Finlay, ever more optimistic, puts it at four. (McIlwain of Newtownards adds that the emigres were often 'the ornaments of society in the sphere in which they

The Rev. William Graham. (British Museum)

moved', and notes glumly that the outflow was offset by 'an influx from the south of the worst of mankind', by which he may mean catholics.)

Is this rosy picture a true one? How in touch were Dillon and Finlay with what was happening here? These are hard questions to answer. The most obvious explanation of Dundonald's good health is Belfast. However the differences between it and neighbouring parishes are sometimes so marked that they are difficult to explain entirely in terms of local variation, Belfast not withstanding. It is tempting to see the origins of these discrepancies as lying, in part, in the personalities of our authors, neither of whom seem to have been very strong on social concern. Both their allegiances clearly lie with the local establishment, and it is difficult to get rid of the feeling that much has been glossed over.

God's river

Finlay did not live to see the enquiry published. He died in 1834, aged just 47, and was succeeded by a young man named William Graham. Graham's was a passionate, proselytising christianity. In the words of an admirer, 'His fire was the means of quickening dead consciences to life', and while Finlay was no slouch, Graham may well have taken Dundonald by storm. (At the very least he will have refilled the pews. Sandy Hanna writes that many in the congregation took exception to Finlay's Unitarian views, with the result that there was a regular Sunday pilgrimage to Strand Street, Holywood, where the message was more orthodox; one long gallery being 'almost entirely filled' with people from Dundonald.)

Graham left in 1842 to become the General Assembly's first Missionary to the Jews, a position perhaps better suited to his talents. Graham served in Damascus, Hamburg and Bonn. He worked hard. In 1859, for example, he reported that he visited 1752 Jewish families in 258 towns and villages, sold 62 bibles, held four weekly services (two in German), and sent out 300–500 tracts in the post; the only thing he does not mention is making converts, perhaps they were not to be measured statistically. Graham also possessed a fine critical mind and his commentary to Paul's Epistle to the Ephesians became a standard text in the U.S.A.

Thomas Toye was another hellfire preacher who made a deep impression here. He first visited Dundonald in 1830 on the invitation of William Galway, and Galway's daughter Jane has left us an account of one of his descents on the unsuspecting populace. The following exchange took place near Millmount, probably in Milltown, at the death-bed of an old and apparently well adjusted woman:

she told him that she did not feel she was a sinner; that she was not afraid to die; that God was merciful. He told her that she was guilty and condemned before God and that she must be born again . . . "Leave me," she exclaimed, "and let me die in peace. I cannot bear your words."

He redoubled his efforts:

"You are asleep; you are ignorant of your danger; hell fire is waiting to devour you. I will pray to God for you." "No," she said, "I want none of your prayers; begone!" He left and never saw her in life again.

This was Victorian evangelism at its worst. However, though some recoiled, many were won over; not least Jane Galway, whom Toye eventually married. He retained a strong connection with the parish, working closely with Graham's successor, the Rev. E.T. Martin, and his presence was to be critical to the success of the Revival here. (Finlay's was something of a transitional ministry. He was proceeded by a liberal and followed by arch tories, for while Finlay was whiggish, Graham and Martin were political conservatives and during their ministries no important church occasion was complete without the presence of the redoubtable Dr. Henry Cooke.)

Enter the constabulary

Not everyone in Dundonald, however, was engaged in practicing christianity. In 1842 we read that Benjamin McBride 'a notorious Thief', was arrested for stealing fowl from Ballybeen, and 'was for that and his former evil deeds sentanced to be transported.'

His prosecution was a conspicuous success for law and order when one was desperately needed. Fowl stealing went on at an 'alarming' rate in Dundonald and Castlereagh, and the arrest made people feel less powerless in the face of it. The most interesting aspect of the case, however, is that McBride was caught and frog-marched to Belfast by the ordinary citizens of Ballybeen. Dundonald had no police force.

The arrest prompted the revival of the Toll Fund. In high spirits after McBride's conviction the survivors of the original committee, or their heirs, decided to use it to fight crime. They began by giving £5 to those who had helped put away McBride, however, as this had apparently taken twelve people the money came to be spread a little thinly. The committee acted again in 1845, after a spate of thefts of 'Fowl, Butter and Cheese'. A reward was offered. Bills were posted throughout the countryside. The thief or thieves were not caught, however the publicity seems to have had a sobering effect, and while we read of no more prosecutions, we hear of no more kidnapped fowl.

This interesting experiment in policing ended in 1851 when it was agreed to divide up the Fund and dissolve the revamped, anti-crime organisation. This was an event of some significance. In the ten years between McBride's arrest and this decision, the responsibility for law and order passed from the citizenry to an organised police force. Dundonald's first station was set up in 1849, when it was presided over by a constable Hicks.

The County Down burnings
The arrival of the constabulary followed a drastic change in what might be called the psychological climate. By 1848 the relative, and for some extremely relative, well-being of the 1830s had given way to uncertainty. The cause was not the famine, which affected Dundonald only indirectly, but the disease and recession that followed in its wake.

It is most unlikely that anyone here died of hunger. Holdings tended to be highish, the economy was mixed, and in as far as it is clear, oats and cabbage as well as potatoes were grown on the garden plots. However, the parish did not escape hardship. Though no details have come down to us, many families must have found it hard to avoid falling behind with the rent and evictions may have followed. Nor did it escape disease. Refugees from the west brought typhus to Belfast and it spread from there into eastern Down, taking several hundred lives.

The effects of the recession were worse still. The following account of the health of the Belfast markets appeared in early 1849:

The past year has pressed heavily on all classes. We commenced the year with the reasonable prospect that we were to work out the difficulties of '46 . . . but political events on the Continent and at home . . . deprived us not only of the usual markets for our productions, but dried up our energies and resources. Our farmers are everywhere . . . oppressed.

Many found their positions imperilled. Even landlords, whose incomes shrank and became less regular as tenants defaulted, often found it hard to cope, and the depression hastened many into bankruptcy.

Landlords, of course, had a well established way of dealing with defaulting tenants: they evicted them. Usually with reluctance if for no other reason than eviction meant writing off the back rent, and it is a measure of the depth of the depression that for a time the number of evictions dropped. What is exciting about the 1840s is that tenants here, and throughout Ireland, evolved a form of reply.

They organised. The Ulster Tenant Right Association was formed in 1847, and campaigned to have rents reduced and the Ulster custom legalised. However there were other forces organising, and not all were so constitutionally inclined. On the evening of the last Saturday in 1848 stacks of oats, hay and corn, were set alight in Dundonald and Castlereagh. Mrs Dinnen of Castlehill lost a stack of hay and Samuel Carson of Ballymiscaw lost part of a stack of oats. Several days later haystacks were burned in Killarn and Ballyrogan, and an attempt was made to fire a stackyard in Craigantlet.

The attacks made a deep impression. Under the headline DIABOLICAL OUTRAGES, the *Banner of Ulster* declared that these 'daring' affronts:

which are unfortunately too common in the southern and western districts of this unfortunate country, but which, happily, are rarely perpetuated in Ulster, have caused the most intense excitement and alarm throughout the county Down.

Dundonald vented its feelings at a vexed and angry meeting in the schoolhouse, chaired by John Andrews. It was decided to set up a night watch of at least two men per townland, to ask for a police station and to offer £50 (subscribed there and then) to anyone who could catch the incendiaries. The watch was soon in place. The *Banner of Ulster* reported that 'a number of farmers, well armed, sit up nightly in almost every district'. The result was a certain amount of chaos. People got very jittery and several policemen in 'coloured clothes' (plain-clothes) were very nearly pitchforked.

There were further outrages. John Roddy of Carrowreagh discovered two men in his haggard, but they escaped after a furious pursuit. Later that night James Bowden of Ballymiscaw fired at a man he saw prowling round the farm: 'The ruffian . . . cried out, "Oh, God, you have killed me;" but on being searched for he was nowhere to be found.' The burnings spread to Newtownards and the Lagan valley.

Robert Gordon of Summerfield, who led the campaign against the incendiaries. (St. Elizabeth's)

The parish met again. At an 'influential and numerous' gathering chaired by Robert Gordon (and attended by, amongst others, the young John Cleland), the local magistrates Gordon and Saunders deputed 125 'Special Constables' to aid the police. Saunders and Gordon (who must have made a most unlikely chief constable!) were widely praised as giving a lead to the whole county. The parish fell under arms.

But the burnings continued, under the cover of the long winter nights. Ferguson of Dunlady had a haystack fired but managed to dampen the blaze. Another was set alight on John Young's farm in Ballymiscaw. A newly hired hand was arrested in suspicious circumstances but nothing was learned.

Hopes rose again several days later when a man carrying 'lucifer matches' was picked up off the Falls Road (then a region of stoutly protestant farmers). The man was apparently villany personified. One newspaper, clearly anxious not to prejudice his trial, described him as 'a low-set, miserable looking creature . . . with a long Jewish beard . . . whose mendicant habits . . . and idiotic expression of countenance, added to a knavish tact, have rendered him an accomplished agent to the conspirators.' Although charged with two Dundonald burnings he was not convicted of either. The hoped for breakthrough did not occur.

The turning point came when, in terror, a young Newtownbreda woman apparently discharged a fowling piece primed with grit and pebbles into the head of a would-be arsonist, and her sister, not to be outdone, stabbed another with a bayonet. The incident became celebrated; partly because no bodies were found, the only evidence of the imbroglio being a trail of blood and a shot-riddled, blood stained cap.

The northern press lionised the 'virgin heroes', the proprietor of the *Northern Whig* declaring that had he been nineteen he would not have left the spot until he had made Grace McVeagh his wife; however the catholic press were cool, and an exchange on the ethics of their action followed. Characteristically, genuine debate proved impossible and the discussion degenerated into farce when the papers who had been hostile took up the story that the shooting had been staged.

Grace McVeagh's opponents claimed that she had bought a quart of bull's blood in Hercules Street, Belfast, that afternoon. In reply her supporters produced an expert to swear that at least *four* quarts had been spilt, and lambasted 'the hollow hearted calumniators of a heroic young female'. Two inquiries exhonorated the sisters, however they shaped up poorly as heroes, being 'rustic in their manners', and subsequently showing 'little of that firmness . . . which they so remarkably displayed'. With hindsight it looks as though the Misses McVeagh were pawns in a ruse to frighten off the incendiaries. If so it was successful for shortly afterwards the burnings ceased.

The whole affair remained deeply mysterious and in the absence of any explanation there was a riot of speculation. Cynics suggested that the burnings had been 'got up by loyally-disposed men in order to obtain employment . . . as rural policemen.' Others blamed Chartists. Many suspected the navvies working on the district's new railway. Some, who had firm ideas on good and evil, deemed it a 'Romish plot'.

Rather more astutely, the Chief Secretary to the Holywood Sessions Court thought it might be an attempt to split the Tenant Right Movement by sowing suspicion between farmers and labourers, for in Dundonald at least, all the victims were middling farmers. All agreed that the perpetrators could not be local men. (Dundonald passed a resolution 'acquitting' locals, and blaming *agent provocateurs*: 'instruments of those desperate characters who have been disturbing the peace of other unhappy districts of Ireland.') No-one dared face the awful possibility that it might be some of the 'humbler or destitute' of the neighbourhood; however the *Freeman's Journal* noted that the district's militrisation coincided with the fact that:

a large number of ejectment degrees were issued at the quarter Sessions lately held at Newtownards and Hillsborough . . . the people of the district speak very mysteriously regarding the landlords and the police.

One implication being that the burnings were aimed at filling the area with police, in order to forestall a genuine campaign of disobedience.

If the burnings were engineered by the landlords, then they failed in their object, for within a year the farmers and landlords had fallen out, and only months after chairing the first crisis meeting John Andrews had become a pariah. In March 1850 a government spy reported from Comber that, in north Down:

all the farmers are combined to reduce the rents, & in order to do so they have appointed a secretary & a committee in each Parish or District composed of two respectable farmers from each townland. These associations are most secretly formed, for I am as yet unable to learn anything definite about the Committees of this district. . .

Nor did he, and as a result little is now known about the movement, other than that it was active and well supported.

Attempts were made to organise a rent strike, enforced by coercive letters from parish committees. *In extremis* anyone who moved into an evicted man's farm had his animals and crops spoiled or his outhouses fired, with lighted turf being set into the thatch. The case was debated as well as fought, the reformers arguing that rent reductions were as much in the interest of the landlord as the tenant. (As John Moore of Milecross put it: 'Sir, if rack rents are to be kept up until our poor fellow-countrymen are brought to the workhouse or grave, what will my Lord Vane do with his impoverished and desolate Newtownards and Comber?')

Newsrooms were set up in barns and outhouses where papers were read out, particularly the *Banner of Ulster*, which was to the Tenant Right Association what the *Northern Star* had been to the United Irishmen. As in the 1790s the presbyterian clergy were well to the fore. The rhetoric was similar too. The poster advertising a 'Great Baronial Tenant Right Meeting' in Newtownards in October 1851 ran:

Let the Sychophant and the Slave who prefer poverty & degradation to comfort and the chain of Tyranny, & oppression to the liberty of freemen, "at home by their fireside stay," but let the HONEST MEN OF DOWN, who love their Wives their Children & their Brethren COME ONE AND ALL.

The meeting, called to demand an end to 'Rack Renting', became a test of the movement's strength. It took place in spite of intense landlord opposition, with the Marquis of Londonderry threatening to confiscate the tenant right of anyone who attended. Trouble was anticipated and 20 extra constables were drafted into the town, however the magnificent assembly (as it was described by its supporters), passed off peaceably, in spite of attempts by several drunken 'bailiff looking persons' to stir up trouble.

The gathering, which included Sam Carson, William Trotter and William McIlwaine of Millbank (some of Dundonald's most prominent farmers), was treated to a number of eloquent addresses. David Gordon, the parish's biggest landlord, was mercilessly lampooned, as was the Marquis of Londonderry, 'the great captain of the Peninsula', whose cause, according to the *Banner of Ulster*, even the landlord press had given up as indefensible.

The campaigners left in good spirits, however the Association did not achieve its aims. Coercion, sectarianism and a rise in agricultural prices took the energy out of the movement, and after the defeat of Sharman Crawford of Crawfordsburn in the 1852 general election, it ceased to be a force in County Down. However the story has a happy ending, for ultimately the struggle was successful beyond the wildest dreams of the early campaigners, and many would have lived to see their goals achieved.

The age of the train

"The cows will all cast their calves, Brother," said Mrs Waule, in a tone of deep melancholy, "if the railway comes across the Near Close; and I shouldn't wonder at the mare too, if she was in foal."

"Let'em go cutting in another parish." . . . said Solomon. "But some say this country's seen its best days, and the sign is, as its been overrun with these fellows trampling right and left, and wanting to cut it up into railways; and all for the big traffic to swallow up the little, so there shan't be a team left on the land, nor a whip to crack."

George Eliot *Middlemarch*

The Comber train at Dundonald station (c.1930). The station is fondly remembered for its flower beds, which regularly won the B&CDR's best kept station award, and for the waiting room's welcoming fire.

The Belfast and County Down Railway Company was formed in the spring of 1845, at the height of railway mania. At first the company intended to build lines to Holywood, and to Newtownards, via Dundonald and Comber, but this cautious plan was soon revised in favour of sending them on to Bangor, Downpatrick and Donaghadee, and after beating off challenges from rival consortiums, (one of which planned a vacuum-propelled system that made the B&CDR's plans look antique), the company received its licence in 1846.

The line to Holywood was opened two years later. Receipts were high and little time was lost in driving the main line east towards Dundonald. Two things made this easy, the co-operation of local landlords, some of whom were shareholders, and the absence of east Belfast, which did not begin to be built until the 1870s. Taking advantage of the depressed state of the iron trade, the directors struck a 'very good deal with a respectable company' for rails, and another with a second for sleepers. Nonetheless money, or the lack of it, proved a constant impediment and the work progressed in fits and starts.

Technically, the route presented few problems. The track follows the glacial overflow channel fairly faithfully, and apart from a deep cut around North Road, a couple of smaller cuts in Tullycarnet and some fairly heavy banking in parts of Ballybeen, the laying of the line to Dundonald was straightforward, and it was carried over the Comber Road on a bridge adorned with a wrought iron trellis. The only obstacles between here and Comber were occasional patches of marsh, but these were easily overcome, and, advancing like a giant worm's cast, the line reached Comber in late 1849.[10]

Its opening on May 6th 1850 was a gala occasion. Festooned with brightly coloured banners and flags, and crammed with waving people, the train puffed back and forth between Belfast and Newtownards frightening cattle and carrying 'about a thousand' passengers in the course of the day. To the delight of the stationmaster, Hans Magee, it made short stops at Dundonald's unfinished station, which with its 300m platform, was to become the second longest on the line.

At first the line did well, in spite of fierce competition from the coaching companies. By the 1860s, however things had gone badly astray. In a letter to the *Northern Whig*, 'A DAILY TRAVELLER' compared the B&CDR's second class carriages to turf carts, complaining that they 'admit water almost as freely as if they had been made for a showerbath'. In a damning report the Royal Commission on Irish Public Works found that the company was badly run, the track, stock and engines were worn out, and that trains were 'continually' breaking down. In the 1870s, however, a new management restored the company's fortunes. It tempted back passengers with an unrivalled range of discounts and blandishments, and began to compete keenly for freight traffic.

Flax, tow, yarns and whiskey slid between Belfast and Comber at 2/6 and 3/- a ton, well below the authorised rate, a dubious practice which bankrupted most of the region's road haulage companies. The B&CDR won commuter traffic by building stations at Bloomfield (1879) and Neill's Hill (1890); by which time the suburbs had engulfed Ballyhackamore and begun to infiltrate Knock. A long car service was introduced between the city and Dundonald in

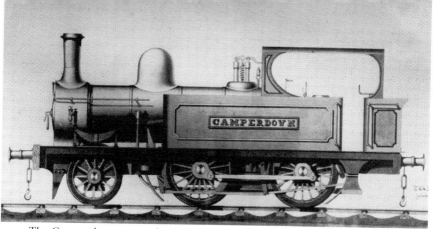

The Camperdown, named after the halt at Camperdown farm. (The Fishers)

1890, and a second line was laid in 1891–3.

The extention of the tram system to Knock in 1905 led to a cut-throat struggle for passengers. The B&CDR fought back by deploying one carriage trains, and in spite of intense competition from trams, charabancs and omnibus companies, the company retained a fairly healthy market share on this route until the 1930s. However, beyond the north Down pale traffic slumped, and in 1953 just after its centenary, (a doubly ironic piece of timing, as Dundonald was just then beginning its massive expansion), the line was closed.

The railway to a certain extent re-oriented the parish. In the late 19th century the station attracted some small scale settlement of a genteel kind, followed more rudely by 'Tintown' and 'Timbertown' after World War One. However, its position (out of the way at Grahamsbridge, with halts at Henryville and Camperdown), meant that the line mainly benefitted the southern reaches of the parish, to which it became essential.

School and hedge school

In the 1830s Dundonald had two small 'hedge' schools. One had about 50 pupils and was maintained 'by the scholars'. The other had 25 pupils and managed on fees and £20 yearly from the rector. The smaller one was run by the Church of Ireland, the larger by the presbyterians, and it will by now surely surprise no-one to learn that there was a certain amount of rivalry between the two.

The parish school's difficulty was that it needed to attract presbyterians to survive. It did so, but this created something of a dilemma. If it pushed the Church of Ireland line too hard, the parents of its presbyterian pupils would have complained of indoctrination and withdrawn their children – and it certainly wasn't going to espouse presbyterianism. Its solution, rather daring for the time, was to set aside the Church of Ireland catechism and refrain from offering 'particular religious instruction' of any kind.

Around 1835, however, its problems disappeared. In or about that year David Gordon built and endowed 'A large and handsome school-house' on the Comber Road (now the bottom storey of the Orange Hall). The grant transformed the parochial classroom into a modern, well-equipped school. This fact was not lost on people, and in 1837 the Church Quarter School, as it became known, enrolled more pupils than its presbyterian equivalent.

Needless to say the Kirk did not take this lying down. Resources were pooled and under the minister's direction a fine two storey school was opened in October 1844. The effect on the parish school was catastrophic. According to one source '*when this school came into operation* . . . (it) closed, there being no *children to attend it.*'

Once the school had been set up the Rev. Martin wrote to the Board of National Education, asking it to meet the running costs. The school was duly inspected and the Board's inspector had high praise for all he saw. However local opinion was sharply divided. The Church of Ireland curate, Arthur Farrell, gave the new school a decidedly icy reception, writing that he considered one school (i.e. his) quite sufficient. However when the inspector talked to 'a respectable yeoman of the village' he got a very different story. No-one could afford the Church Quarter School, he was told. The fees were 4/6 and parents were regularly 'prosecuted in *Courts of Law* for this payment', spluttered the outraged yeoman.

Writing of the need for '*a school to meet the wants & wishes of the people*', he approved the new school in 1845 and it received books for 100 and the salaries of its staff. In return it was usual for the words National School to be inscribed on the building. The Rev. Martin agreed to do this, but on his terms, which were that 'the word Congregational' should be prefixed.

Like many National Schools, the school was essentially an extention of the church, and its management committee, an educational version of the Kirk Session, ran the school accordingly. The school day ran from 10.00am to 5.00am in summer, 3.00pm in winter. It began with 1½ hours of religious

Dundonald Congregational National School, built on the Green in 1844. Note the scratches at waist height by the door, made by children sharpening their slate pencils. In the 1840s there was also a small library here. The presbyterian church is alongside.

instruction given by the minister using the presbyterian catechism, (rather naughty, for this book had not been sanctioned by the Board). The rest of the time was mainly taken up with reading, writing and sums.[11]

The Church Quarter School struggled on until the 1870s, when poor attendance forced it to close. (In 1871 it had 27 pupils against 169 attending the presbyterian school.) And it is noteworthy that no Anglican attended the presbyterian school until the Church Quarter School shut down. Anglican numbers picked up shortly afterwards, but by then of course it was too late.

These schools did not serve the whole parish. During the latter 19th century there were also schools at Ballystockart, Greengraves, Ballyrogan, Creighton's Green. Craigantlet, Tullycarnet (Gilnahirk), and Ballymiscaw. Let us take a brief look at the workings of one of these, Ballymiscaw, the school 'on top of the mountain'.

Ballymiscaw school is perched nearly 200m above sea level midway between Dundonald and Holywood. Like most of the outlying schools, it was built and run by local farmers. Some of these, such as Ballystockart, remained fairly independent of the churches, however Ballymiscaw willingly fell under presbyterian influence and its committee gave the church a free hand.

It opened in 1855 with 48 pupils. Though their ages ranged from 3¼ to 15¾, they were taught in one class and not surprisingly many made slow progress. Absenteeism was common, particularly at harvest time, and young children with no older brothers or sisters sometimes stayed at home during the winter. Pupils usually left when they were old enough to work on the farm; however the records show that Belfast was becoming an ever larger employer. In the 1860s for example David M'Gill and James Carnduff, both farmers's sons from Killeen, went off to work in the big smoke; David as an apprentice, James as a writer to an attorney.

Like Dundonald, it kept a six day week, all of Saturday being taken up with religious instruction. It was furnished with 'an abundance of desks and forms', a book cubboard and a fire, which kept at least one end of the room warm. Its teacher was William Bowden, 'an excellent young man' who to his credit admitted children who were too poor to pay. Like many of the district's old National Schools, Ballymiscaw has only recently closed and many of its former pupils can still be found here.

The picture-postcard parish

We begin this glance at the second half of the century with a look at Dundonald through the eyes of an admirer, the Carrickfergus born novelist Mrs J.H. Riddell. Mrs Riddell, the Barbara Cartland of her day, wrote over fifty novels including a string of highly successful big house romances. Prominent amongst these was *Berna Boyle – A Love Story of the County Down*, which appeared in installments in 1883, and was first published in one volume in 1885.

Set in Dundonald in 1850 it tells the story of a frought romance between Gorman Muir of Ardilaw (Dunlady) and 'sweet lipped' Berna Boyle, the daughter of a wealthy widow who rents Clear Stream Cottage nearby. Mrs Riddell, who came here herself in the same year, seems to have regarded her new neighbours with a sort of fond contempt. Her at times acid, at times saccharine novel is filled with work-shy peasants, God-fearing, upwardly mobile farmers and amoral, mildly decadent gentry (probably the Clelands).[12]

What makes *Berna Boyle* fascinating (and maddening!) from a historical point of view is that local scenes and lore are often incorporated wholesale. (This gives the book its substance, and while it does not make her flimsy leading characters credible, it at least convinces the reader that they move in a real world.) We read of the County Down burnings, and the fate of the Misses McVeagh, who apparently rigged the whole thing and 'were glad enough' to get to America.

There is a graphic account of the death of Eliza Cleland's father and even a glancing reference to her dowry. Mrs Riddell tackles the land war head on, when her rugged but sensitive hero takes on an evicted man's farm, knowing that it has been embargo'd and that two blacklegging tenants have been burnt out. Its landlord, Lyle Garnsey had also given up working the farm when his spuds were uprooted and his corn was cut while green. However, Gorman sends the ruffians packing, after shooting them in the calves with bay salt. (Mrs Riddell is firmly on the side of property.)

She writes affectionately of the Rev. Dillon (Mr Crommles), who 'loved his ease . . . and would exchange cordial good mornings with the rankest Dissenter'; and of his congregation, which even on gala days never amounted to fifty souls and often dwindled to half a dozen:

There was always the Rector, a good easy-going old clergyman, whom it certainly could not . . . do anyone any harm to go and listen to; the clerk, who struck the note with the pitch-key always too high, who always sang wrong, and thought he knew a great deal more than Mr Crommles; the sexton, who stoked a huge stove set in the middle of the church; the Rector's churchwarden, who wanted to see fair play about the few halfpence collected every Sunday, which halfpence were divided, after service, between two old women representing the poor of the parish; and a certain magistrate who always attended divine worship "hail or shine".

The church was one of the snuggest spots in the parish:

The pews around the stove were usually as scorchingly hot as pews can ever be without flaring into flame. It was a deliciously warm church. Even Dissenters, driven to the top of the hill either by choice or necessity, felt that there was a good deal of comfort about THE ESTABLISHMENT . . . and were certainly of the opinion, as they walked demurely home, that if they got no rousing doctrine, they had received the benefit of a capital fire.

In contrast to the sparsely peopled parish church, the meeting house 'swept in the bone and sinew of the countryside'. It had life, vigour and a welcoming atmosphere. However, though she pined for the 'delights attaching to Dissent' old Mrs Boyle attended the parish church. To do so tried her sorely ('such a church! Never a new bonnet to be seen in it') but it was the price of gentility and had to be paid.

Dunlady House (Ardilaw) appears as a 'tumbledown old barrack', which has fallen from its high estate to the point where it simply 'went with the land':

It had sunk surely, if slowly. First it was let to a Newtownards man, who, having gone to

India without a penny, came back, to quote the country-side gossip, possessed of "millions and millions."

Then a sporting character (McDonald), . . . who, it was creditably asserted, fought mains of cocks in the dining-room and had boxing matches in the great barn, remained in Ardilaw for the space of two years, at the expiration of which term he drank himself to death, greatly to the satisfaction of many worthy people. After that the place was let for the summer to persons able to drive across to Holywood "for the bathing". Then it went down another step, and was rented by a Belfast shopkeeper, who wanted country air for his children, and grass where those children could tumble about and grow up wild.

How much of this is fact, how much fiction? Such accounts are impossible to assess, and this is what makes *Berna Boyle* such an infuriating source. But some assessment must be made, and the strongest clues are in the book itself. Mrs Riddell was not big on invention. Her strength lay in providing a poisonous commentary on the world around her, and while the book should be approached with caution, it would seem that the central romance has been tacked onto a fictionally enhanced version of Dundonald life.

Her account of the village, however, is straight reporting and worth recounting in full:

But the merest hamlet! Spite of the railway station less than a mile distant; the post-office and public-house combined, situated where the Comber Road branches off from the Newtonards; the smithy hard by; the church, perched aloft on one of those quaint low hills that have won for the county a not inapt comparison to a basket of eggs; the police barracks, the remarkable-looking Rectory, the mail-car running along highway twice a day, the Presbyterian meeting-house – surely the smallest and most unpretending of picturesque villages!

Only one side to it, and that extremely imperfect! First a row of one-storied-cottages, where dwelt the local cobbler and tailor, both deadly jealous of town ways and town notions. Then fields advanced boldly to the front, succeeded, after a short space by the police barracks, a couple of its occupants, privates in the Irish constabulary, being generally encountered lounging on the footpath opposite. A little further, a few more cottages were scattered beside the road; at the extreme end of the village, beyond the lane which still winds up to the gate of the graveyard, stood proudly forth a shop, where nothing could have been bought, it might have been supposed, that any human creature would desire to purchase. Close to the turn leading to the Rectory was a second smithy, for the neighbourhood was (and is) one much given to farming, and found constant need of a farrier's services; a few detached houses, farm and otherwise, lay back from the left hand side of the road – the right being skirted, as stated, by humble cottages; the whole place looked green and white by reason of the green fields and the white-washed houses. Up on the hillsides lay great masses of trees and belts of plantation, and higher still you could see roads winding over the heights whence lovely views were to be obtained of Belfast Lough, and the Antrim mountains, of Scrabo close at hand, and, on a clear day, a glimpse of Scotland.

By the middle of the century Dundonald enjoyed the sort of Belfast-derived prosperity that in 1813 had led a traveller to describe the Lagan valley as 'one continued garden'. It was far enough from poverty, and wealth, to be considered picturesque, and close enough to town to have an audience. (It would then have been as convenient to Belfast as, say, Donaghadee is today.) And while it lacked the more modish attractions of Holywood, the fact that it attracted relatively few visitors was in itself an attraction. Mrs Riddell writes of it as a place of retreat:

Dear, simple primitive village: could there ever on earth have been a more delightful place for one, world-tired and weary, to pause for a moment and take breath?

Though Dundonald had escaped from its early 18th century anonymity, it had not apparently come so very far: Bassett's *County Down Guide* deems it 'a railway station', and Smith's *Belfast and its Environs* (1853) omits it entirely. Universal appreciation was clearly some way off.

Upstairs, downstairs

For fifteen years after Samuel's death Eliza Cleland was the parish's first lady. Attitudes to the Clelands seem to have softened during this period, and the image of ' the widow Cleland', lofty, bereft and grieving, like a prototype Queen Victoria, undoubtedly struck a sympathetic chord. Even Mrs Riddell did not dare to write about her scaldingly, and Eliza appears in *Berna Boyle* as 'the Marchioness', a shadowy, background figure. The facts of her life are scarcely clearer. Stott remembers that in her youth she was 'undoubtedly a very fine looking woman . . . tall with golden hair and a fine figure', but otherwise little is known about her.

After Samuel's death Elizabeth apparently took little to do with the management of the estate. The diminutive Miss Murdough managed the household, hiring and firing as the occasion required. Her office at the end of the hall was the Castle's power centre. It had a deck of pigeon holes for letters, and a battery of speaking tubes and whistles through which she could get in touch with almost any room in the Castle. Miss Murdough (who, we are told, was a Scot and had a great affection for the old country), had her mistresses complete confidence. She paid the wages, supervised the buying, and had the carriage and pair at her disposal for shopping trips to town.

She managed a large and international staff. As well as maids of all descriptions, there was the chef, a coachman, a butler, a valet, a gamekeeper, grooms and stable boys ('that rough swearing stable clan'), gardeners, a French butler's assistant, a smith and a carpenter, Mr Telford, whose young son Barney was hired as the post boy in 1853. Many years later Barney wrote a long vivid letter describing his experiences at the Castle, and what is known about life at Stormont is known from him.

On his first morning Barney turned up at 6 o'clock, heart thumping. There was no-one about. So, at something of a loss and anxious for him to make the right impression, his father thought it would be a good idea for Barney to collect the post. On his return he met none other than Miss Murdough. She was appalled at the sight of him sweating and straining with the massive post bag and gave him a good dressing down, telling him there was a pony and cart for that sort of thing. Then she dried him off and took him down to the kitchen:

There were a big crowd there, what with housemaids, chambermaids, and ladies maids, butler and valets, the noise and clatter of dishes and spoons and girls talking, but it all stopped as soon as we entered. She introduced me something like this – "Ladies and

The grieving widow: Eliza Cleland in middle age. (Robert Cleland)

Gentlemen, this is our new post boy. He bids me to say that any letter you have to mail must be in my office by 8 o'clock morning and 5 o'clock afternoon and any letter directed to any person in the Castle will be found in my office after 9 o'clock a.m. and 6 p.m. barring accidents." Of course I said nothing of the kind but it gave me a good introduction.

Barney, who owned what he stood up in and a spare shirt, was provided with a wardrobe of tailored suits from J&J Magee of High Street, Belfast, young Samuel Cleland's seconds. His main duty was to carry the post to and from the village, bringing back little extras like an occasional pouch of tobacco for Mr Arnoldi, master John's valet. However, his most enjoyable (and most exhausting) job was to act as Margaret Cleland's chaperon and companion, duties previously undertaken by Mr Beattie the coachman, who had become 'tired of her continous escapades on the Newtownards road', and was only too willing to hand them over.

Margaret, then about fourteen, was lively, headstrong, affectionate, and something of a tomboy. As a result of a throat complaint she talked as if she had a hare lip, though her features were perfect. This difficulty required Margaret to sleep sitting up. The family had sought treatment from specialists in England, France and Germany, but in vain. Only violent exercise gave her any relief.

One of the two snarling griffins which can be found at Stormont's main entrance. It holds a shield inscribed with the initials J C.

She wrestled with her brother Sam and her French maid Marie, and when they were not about she wrestled with Barney. They dressed in body tights made of 'material like fine moleskin, close and tight, not a wrinkle that you would catch hold of and no seams to rip open.' As Joyce Wilson has remarked, it is hard to imagine a young Victorian miss engaged in such unladylike activities.

Margaret loved to explore the countryside around the estate, and Barney went with her. One of her favourite circuits was along the Killeen Road towards Craigantlet then down Ballyregan to the village, calling at the rectory on the way. Another was along the Knock Road to Ballyhanwood, calling on Tom Morrow for 'a drink of cold spring water', then home along the Comber Road.

These were not entirely companionable journeys. Like a moslem wife Barney had to keep a respectful distance (generally 30 metres) behind Margaret and:

When she was going to stop for a walk she shot out her left arm like a semaphore as a signal for me to ride up . . . and walk the horses round until she was ready to go ahead again.

In spite of such strictures the two became friends, and Barney and 'Cis' shared many adventures. On one occasion the pair were chased by angry bees. On another Barney pulled Margaret from a swamp: and on a third his dog saved her from a fate worse than death when she was attacked in a corner of the demesne. Then there was her secret correspondence. Unknown to her mother Margaret was writing to a French youth, and Barney had to resort to all sorts of tricks to get the letters through.

Barney's letter casts little light on the lives of the rest of the family. We know that Margaret's four brothers went to Eton, and that the eldest, Master John, went on to Cambridge. The Londonderry connection remained important. John is thought to have met his wife through the Londonderrys, and on his marriage they presented the couple with a silver salver, recently sold to the

Margaret Cleland, in her late teens. She was bright and vivacious, and Barney mentions that she exposed the tip of her boot when on horseback, an act then considered very daring. (Robert Cleland)

Onassis family. However, we are much better informed about life below stairs.

'Being so far from the city', the family found it hard to keep servants, especially young ones, and partly to remedy this dances were held in the servant's hall under Mrs Murdough's supervision. At these the butler's assis-

Artist's impression of Stormont Castle (The Builder, 1858). The castle was largely built to this design.

tant played the latest continental waltzes, polkas, quadrilles, and the Sir Roger de Coverly, and Mrs Murdough, keeping her end up, played highland flings on an old harpsichord. These happenings were eagerly anticipated throughout the parish, for a number of young farmers known to Mrs Murdough through the church (and certain to be of the right stuff) were invited along. Some brought their sisters, some brought their wives, but happily most were single, and the maids had partners in plenty.

Everyone let their hair down. Barney writes that the fun went 'fast and furious' until midnight, when everyone made for the dining room where a big supper had been laid out. Then the dancing began afresh, and went on till near dawn.

Eliza's regime ended with the rebuilding of the Castle. In September 1856 Eliza, John and Margaret left for France, taking with them two maids and two drays full of boxes. After a farewell dance the house was closed and the staff were discharged, Mrs Murdough staying on three or four weeks to tie up the loose ends. With this Eliza and to a lesser extent Margaret went into a form of exile. We have few clues as to their feelings on the subject. Barney is factual:

One day Sis told me that this would be the last summer in the old house as the family would all be going away on September and it would be four or five years before they would be back or perhaps never, as Master John would be getting married and might want all the new Castle to himself as he was now of age and had full control. She would be going back to France and her lovely blue Alsatian mountains.

It was probably John who turned the big, plain house into a proper castle. Where Samuel had been slightly cheapskate in building in brick, John spared no expense. The old house was remodelled in the highly fashionable 'Scots baronial' style. It was cladded in Scrabo stone, and all manner of dizzy and extravagant embellishments – battlements, towers, turrets, and of course the snarling gryphons at the entrance steps. When built the Castle would have been a soft, sugar brown colour. Its present forbidding duns are entirely due to a Dorrian Grey-like accretion of dirt.

As well as the splendid ballroom, the new Castle contained fourteen family bedrooms, a variety of reception rooms, with mock Byzantine and neo-classical interiors, complete with fluted columns, Greek statues, gorgeous early 18th century Gobelin tapestries and much expensive and it must be said, fairly tacky furniture from London. It was to this flamboyant edifice that John brought his new wife Therese Maria, daughter and heir of Thomas Leyland of Haggerston Castle, in 1859.

Three years of Grace

The Year of Grace, or 'year of delusion', as it was tartly described by one presbyterian minister, was of course 1859, when a wave of ecstatic religious feeling swept Ulster and elsewhere. The Revival began in Connor, Co. Antrim in the spring, and by early summer conversions were being reported from Belfast.

The Revival hit Dundonald in June, when the village seems to have been visited by converts from Connor. Surprisingly, in the light of what followed, the occasion seems to have been a complete anti-climax; no-one got over-excited, and the converts moved on. The real action began several weeks later, when in the middle of the Sunday service two women suddenly 'uttered piercing screams', and had to be removed. Twelve more were 'stricken' on August 14th, at a service taken by Toye (for whom this was a dream come true). The Revival began to take root.

The critical meeting took place on the following Sunday, and we are lucky enough to have an account of the day's proceedings. In the morning a 'gentleman from Belfast' (Mr Toye?) reduced most of the bible class to tears 'so deep was the impression made'. Thus began an extraordinary day. At church that evening many people, (including one 'remarkable for sin') were overcome and had to be helped out. Astonishing scenes followed. *The Revival* reports that:

Others . . . were stricken with conviction by the roadside, and some after they had reached home. The pastor of the congregation and his friend were engaged till a late hour of the night, in visiting those who had been spiritually impressed. As they passed from place to place they found that groups of persons were collected here and there, for religious exercises. From various houses the sounds of praise and prayer were heard ascending, and from others, fervent aspirations for mercy. Never before, perhaps, in Dundonald . . . on a Sabbath evening was there such a spiritual harvest as on the last, when the Great Husbandman gathered many sheaves into his garner.

After this came the deluge, with prayer meetings being held at Rockfield, Millmount and in the Ballymiscaw, Tullycarnet and Craigantlet National Schools. Perhaps the most extraordinary of these took place in September at Millmount, in Galway's barn. Toye delivered a characteristically terrifying address and so many were seized that the barn took on the appearance of a hospital ward.

The Rev. Givan of Castlereagh has left several graphic descriptions of conversions, one of them involving a man who 'had been living for years in gross sin'. This man underwent an experience which Givan compared to exorcism: 'His tongue was protruded, he foamed at the mouth, he could not speak, occasionally he uttered a wild roar (and) laboured under a sort of unnatural panting'.[13]

Not everyone was comfortable in the face of such scenes, and doubts about their religious character were aired in the press, particularly in the *News Letter* which held a fairly free debate on the pro's and con's of the 'Great Awakening'. 'If the revival be God's work', asked one pertinent correspondent, 'how does it happen that it falls, principally, on females, who are peculiarly susceptible to nervous derangement?' Did conversion not leave people fit only for 'apartments in the asylum?', asked another. Reassuring letters like 'THE REVIVAL – A MEDICAL OPINION', were offered in reply. (The *Newsletter's* main rival the *Northern Whig,* confined itself to unsubtle attempts to discredit the movement, such as its gloating report on the case of a born-again twelve year old convicted of stealing corn.)

Conversions of catholics were reported with particular relish, as in Knockbreda, which sent a message to Gibson, the Revival's first historian, reporting

Dundonald Presbyterian Church, built in 1839. The back of the church faces the Green, so only presbyterians normally get this view!

the 'first case of awakening a Roman Catholic, very satisfactory'. Comber, Holywood and Newtownards were also forcibly smitten. 'In no part of the province so far as I can learn has there been a more genuine work of grace than in the town of Newtownards', declared one of its schoolmasters, citing as proof the conversion of the town's bellman, a notorious drunk, discreetly identified as 'J K'.

The Revival was not a spontaneous outpouring. Though the churches remained officially ambivalent, it was organised and made possible by ministers of religion. It should also be said that it was mostly a working class phenomenon, and mostly affected presbyterians not least because its catalysts were mostly presbyterian preachers.

Moreover, in Dundonald anyway, the Revival did not come out of nothing. The district had three covenanting societies, and in the winter of 1858, as if by divine foresight, the meeting house had been enlarged, even though the presbyterian population was then falling. Givan makes the point that in Castlereagh the number of communicants had steadily risen during the years prior to the Revival, so here at least, the background to the Revival was a rising interest in religion.

Nonetheless, its effects were impressive. In Dundonald the number of communicants increased by 50 to 102. In Castlereagh the number rose by 100, and in Ballymacarret, where there had been 'scarcely twenty', the number rose to 150. John Weir remarks that at 'Dundonald, Rathfriland and other places in the county of Down meetings were being constantly held, and with marked results.'

While there can be little doubt as to the Revival's impact, it is easy to overestimate its lasting effects. Many soon fell back into their old ways. However, the church here harnessed something of the energy of '59. The Bethesda Mission Hall, built on a hill on the Greengraves Road (formerly the Bethesda Road) is a creation of the Revival. Bethesda was a work of love. The money that paid for it was collected in pennies and ha'pennys from the cottages roundabout, and there are stories that the stones that built it were brought in barrows by local women. Bethesda was opened by Dr Henry Cooke in the summer of 1862 in a carnival atmosphere. A band led the worshippers to the hall, and the crowds were so large that the service had to be held in the nearby field, which, to this day, is known as 'Cooke Hill'.

Polite society I: Rockfield

Rockfield, a large Georgian house with classical trimmings, was built around 1800, probably by the McCleans, a family of Belfast merchants. They lived here for some fifty years.

The estate was gentrified by degrees during the first half of the 19th century. By 1833 it had been extensively planted, and lush formal gardens had been laid out to the rear. By 1859 the transformation was complete. The old farm had disappeared, and a lordly demesne with over 1½ miles of sheltered coach paths stood in its place.

As a finishing touch someone added several of the instant antiquities without which no estate was considered complete. Stones carved with spirals (said to have come from the bishop of Derry's palace) were introduced, and two horseshoe shaped benches each made of about half a dozen stones were sunken on the fringe of the estate. Trees and moss grew, hedgehogs settled in the beech

Rockfield House, Ballyoran. The chimney of the original farmhouse can be seen to the left.

Helen Greeves, at the time of her move to Rockfield. (Gordon Greeves)

leaf mould, and soon these bowers looked as old as time itself. They attracted stories long in the townland, and perhaps correctly attributable to its medieval chapel and holy well (mass was said to have been said here in penal times.) Erudite archaeologists have puzzled over the significance of these plausible stones.

When Adam McClean the younger died around 1847 the estate was briefly let to Farrell the curate, then taken on by James Shaw, a Belfast soap and candle manufacturer. The Shaws were followed in the 1870s by a military family, the Symingtons, who lived here until their batchelor son Robert, a linen merchant, sold up in 1906. The house was then taken by Leopold and Helen Greeves, he being one of the Greeves who owned the Cooper and Conway Street mills, she being a Marsh of Marsh's Biscuits.

Both were quakers and lived simply. Leopold tried his hand in linen warehousing, but he proved an innocent abroad: his first business failed, and he was swindled out of his second by his partner. He was much happier reading (he had a fine library of Irish books) or playing billiards (they had a full-sized table, made from a single sheet of slate). Both loved hunting, and Helen was considered the best horsewoman in County Down. She was also very popular, and when the girl's school were asked to write on the theme 'If you were someone else, who would you like to be?', one girl wrote 'Mrs Greeves, because she is always so kind.'

II The Galways of Millmount

Millmount is also Georgian, but where Rockfield is unmistakably a country seat, Millmount looks like a Merrion Square townhouse which has been transplanted in the country. Oddly enough, though built around 1810, the house does not appear in any of the contemporary lists of gentleman's seats. This may have been because its owner, William Galway, was a farmer. His hobby was smithwork (he is said to have invented Ireland's first horsedrawn potato-digger), and one imagines him having little time for gentlemanly airs and graces.

The Galways, who can claim descent from James I, (no mean feat given James' predilections), moved here from Malone around 1818, buying Millmount in preference to Belmont (now Campbell College), as its fields were better supplied with water. The farm then consisted of the house and outbuildings, a corn and flax mill, eight workers cottages, and 104 acres of top quality land.

If William was not considered a gentleman, his son and grandson were, and the estate faithfully reflects the family's rise in status. In 1833 Millmount seems to have had few pretensions. By 1900, however, it could boast magnificent mature gardens (amongst which strutted peacocks, until they broke the byre windows), a croquet lawn, tennis court, a leafy tree-lined avenue and a small ornamental lake.

Raspberries, damsons, pears and gooseberries grew plentifully. (This bounty occasionally proved too tempting; salmon were mercilessly poached from Galway's dam and an artful thief once locked the family in the house while he ran off with the apple crop.) The back lane, overhung with cherry trees and dripping with honeysuckle, bluebells, violets and wild roses, was a favourite haunt of artists in search of arcadia.

Millmount, home of the Galways; later the Co farm.

This natural abundance contrasts sharply with life indoors. William and his wife Margaret raised their family with a puritanical severity. Both were dedicated covenanters and books like *Erskine on the Assurance of Faith* and *Crumbs from the Master's Table* circulated in the home.

The rising generation were very much in the same mould. (This was before the days of youthful rebellion.) William's daughter married the Rev. Thomas Toye, an old family friend; and his heir William helped set up Bethesda. This William died prematurely in 1869, leaving his wife Jane to run the farm and raise the family, and she did both with a rod of iron. Jane, an imperious *grande dame*, who is reliably said to have gathered in her skirts every time she passed the Theatre Royal, sought to keep the farm in the family, but none of her sons was interested and for a time it looked as if it might have to be sold.

Eventually, she prevailed upon her youngest boy John Meneely to take on the farm. However Jane did not retire gracefully, and for several long, abrasive years the farm was somehow run jointly. It is said to have been a great relief all round when John got married and Jane finally retired to Donaghadee. In the meantime Millmount prospered, and it entered the new century as Dundonald's largest farm.

III The Robbs of Ballybeen

Then there were the Robbs of Ballybeen House, gentleman farmers, whose home is now a Housing Executive office, and whose farm now lies under the Boy's High School, Fisher Body and the Ballybeen estate; all formerly prime agricultural land.

Helen Robb driving cows along Robb's Road around 1920, with Ballybeen House in the background. Note the footpath, a dirt track marked off by a grass kerb. (Kathleen Robb)

Jane and Sandy Robb and their family outside Ballybeen House around 1897. Alec Robb in sitting on the pony. (Kathleen Robb)

The Robbs, or Rabbs as they then were, are said to be descended from seven Scottish brothers who came over during the plantation. Our branch came to Dundonald from Ballysallagh near Bangor around 1812. Socially, the Robbs would not then have been considered anything special, however by 1861 they had increased the size of their farm from 62 to 136 acres, and had risen to close to the head of the second rank of Dundonald families, amongst well-to-do farmers like the Galways, and the McRoberts of Ballyoran, and some way ahead of the Kirkwoods of the Beeches, the Chancellors of Solitude and the Killops of Dunlady, rising families, all of whom could be considered, or considered themselves gentry by the turn of the century.

Four generations of Robbs lived at Ballybeen, and the successive heads of the family, each called Alexander, were all long livers. The first lived until 1852, whereon the farm passed to his nephew, Alexander. He had eleven children, one of whom died near Gettysburg, fighting for the Union. His heir Sandy also emigrated. Believing that he had no chance of the farm Sandy went to Canada to seek his fortune, prospecting for gold at Cariboo (and with some success, the family jewellery includes a Cariboo nugget). When the gold rush subsided he trapped and farmed, writing long homesick letters ('Write soon . . . nothing will be uninteresting'), and sending back for a wife, preferably a good County Down girl. (For once, the family were unable to oblige.)

Sandy fully intended to live his life there and probably would have had tuberculosis not taken two of his brothers, giving him the option of the farm. When his father became unable Sandy returned, got married (at last!), and took charge. 'Fearless in his advocacy of what he believed to be right', and progressive in his ideas, Sandy entered public life as a land reform campaigner, however the first Home Rule crisis turned him into a 'liberal unionist'. He took the *News Letter* instead of the *Northern Whig*, and beat no less than Sir Daniel Dixon to obtain a seat on Down County Council. He also became the treasurer of the presbyterian church, and helped to steer it through a sticky patch in the 1880s, when the Rev. Martin, who had not received his stipend, took the deeds of the church and held onto them until he was paid.

The family grew, expanding to the point where it had some difficulty in housing itself. Pella Cottage on Church Road came in handy in this connection. Alexander senior lived here after releasing the farm. 'Esker' was another Robb clearing house. Sandy built it for his sisters Mary and Suzanna, who when young are said to have been known as 'the beautiful Miss Robbs of Dundonald'. Neither married. In her youth Suzanna had had a lover, however her father disapproved and threatened to shoot him if he ever found him in their yard. The two were forced to meet secretly, and courted in the strange riverless glen behind Morven Park, but in time the hopelessness of the affair bore in on them, particularly the young man, who spent a night in a forlorn and drunken stupor at the foot of Dunlady Hill, and shortly afterwards died of pneumonia.

This was her only love, and Suzanna was faithful to its memory. She claimed her lover's grave annually until her death, and it distressed her to recall the affair in old age. Both now lie in the parish church yard.

The McRoberts of Ballyoran (l-r) Frank, Kate, Johnny, and of course Mary, looking suitably regal and composed. (Barry Kirkwood)

IV The McRoberts of Ballyoran

Their neighbours the McRoberts (whose ancestors we met in Chapter 10) were also very definitely in the ascendant. William McRoberts was thrifty and hardworking, and under him the farm grew from 25 to 83 acres (1859). That these gains were preserved was in part thanks to the emigration of all but two of William's eight children, which more or less left the field clear for his fifth son Francis to inherit the farm intact.

Under Francis the farm annexed another two of its neighbours, growing to its maximum extent of 125 acres. It grew in more ways than one. Francis and his wife Agnes had seventeen children, at a rate of almost one a year over 18 years. This left Agnes in a state of permanent exhaustion and in such feeble health that her eldest daughter, the formidable Mary, effectively supplanted her taking charge of the house and the raising of the family. The eldest children went to school in Dundonald. However as the family's means increased, and the younger McRoberts went by janet and trap to the Model School in Newtownards, and then on to a select finishing school in Derry.

In 1878 the family built a new home, Ballyoran House, which the Rating Inspector deemed 'A very superior Ho. for a farm of such a size in fact too good.' The McRoberts were clearly getting above themselves. When Francis died in 1891 (after an injured big toe became septic) the children entered society unchaperoned, joining the county hunts and throwing stylish parties.

V Hanwood House

One of the finest of this new crop of mansions was Hanwood House (overlooking the Ice Bowl), built by Hugh McClements towards the end of the century. Hugh, known as 'The Dandy', because he always turned himself out in a frock coat and tall hat, was a fussy old batchelor who had to have everything just so. When he went into Belfast for the day, for example, he always left his long-suffering sidekick Hughie Nicholson a long list of things to do, leading the droll Hughie to ask him, 'Just how long is it you'll be away, sir?'

His disreputable neighbour Barr was a continual source of irritation. Barr grew no vegetables that anybody knew of, but he always took a load to the mart on Fridays, and the Dandy became convinced that Barr was selling his. Rather than confront him, however, he hid in his depleted vegetable garden intent on catching the thief in the act. The first night passed uneventfully. On the second he heard rustling in the cabbages. 'Stand Barr or I'll fire.' he called. Getting no response he loosed both barrels, killing one of his calves.

When McClements died the house was briefly taken by Hugh and Jane Dickson. Hugh, one of the rose growing Dicksons of Hallmark, arrived here from Knock, where against all advice he had set up his own nursery. The hills behind the house became fragrant with roses, amongst them some twenty strains of Hugh's own invention, pride of place going to 'the Hugh Dickson', a big fluffy crimson affair not entirely unlike its creator.

Though a talented breeder, Hugh proved an unmitigated disaster as a businessman, and the family had to bale him out several times. When Jane died of cancer, Hugh married one of his employees, a Miss Anna Service, who ran Hugh's domestic affairs as strictly as she had had to run his business, locking everything away on the children, whom she thought hopelessly spoilt, and to whom she became the archytypal wicked stepmother. Hugh's shortcomings as a provider made economies necessary, but Anna carried them to extremes and her meaness became notorious.

Hugh's heir Sandy revived the family's fortunes. He rejuvenated the business, employing forty in season and exhibiting successfully at Chelsea and Harrowgate. There was always chaos at showtimes, with everyone joining in to wrap the specimen roses in damp tissue paper, and pack them off in long wooden boxes. Sandy and his beautiful, high-spirited wife Tess brought life and joy back into the house. Both were dedicated socialites, and life became a pleasurable round of shows and house parties.

Then things began to go awry. Sandy lost control of his drinking, and as the business began to suffer he got worse. His behaviour became tyrannous and unpredictable. Tess left him, fearful for her safety, and he became estranged from his children. Eventually he reformed, but the damage was done and he ended his days alone in the big house, sober and remorseful.

While the above concerns rose, other estates were just as surely on the way down. Dunlady comes to mind here, but its decline halted with the arrival of Thomas Killops (c.1867), who took the house on his return from the Clondyke goldfields. Ballyhanwood House (not to be confused with Hanwood House, above), degentrified, became 'Barr's place'. Camperdown, formerly the home of Dr. Herron, a navy surgeon, and a certain 'William Douglas, gent', was taken on by a farming family, the Fishers. At first the estate retained many of its decorative features, but the land was now required to pay for itself, and by degrees the farm lost its frills.

The creme de la creme
Far and away the richest and most eminent Dundonald families were the Clelands and the Gordons. The Gordons are something of a mystery. Though Robert Gordon senior is recorded as being a firm presbyterian, his children Catherine and Robert were for most of their lives members of the Church of Ireland, and as we shall see shortly their conversion (if such it was) was to prove the church's salvation. Neither married. Robert died in 1894, and his more vigorous sister Catherine, an 'unfailing friend to the poor and needy' died six years later, aged 94, whereon the estate was let then sold.

The Gordons were a county family. The Cleland's horizons were much wider. They mixed in London society. John Cleland married Therese Marie Leyland of Haggerston Castle, Northumberland, and Hyde Park House, London; a wealthy heiress. Eliza and Margaret then moved to Paris. Little is known about their lives there, however they belonged to an international class, and would not have lacked friends or society. After Eton John's brothers James, Frederick and Robert joined the cavalry. Robert became a Lieutenant Colonel in the 9th Queens Royal Lancers, and died defending empire. James took a commission in the hussars, and Frederick, the 'delicate' brother, who when young had gone to Italy to paint, eventually joined the Scots Greys.

In spite of the stigma attaching to the family, there is no evidence that the later Clelands were bad landlords. Indeed John is remembered as an enthusias-

Robert Cleland, who died of wounds received while leading a cavalry charge during the Afgan campaign of 1878–80. The charge, like the celebrated charge of the Light Brigade, had been ordered against overwhelming numbers, and with little chance of success. (Robert Cleland)

tic improver.[14] His chief innovation is said to have been to put wooden floors in the cottages of his tenantry, however the tenants are said to have stayed fixed to their old habits and the floors are said to have rotted away.

In a way, this little story could almost be seen as a metaphor for John's life. His marriage to Therese went sour. (The Cleland version of events casts Therese as the villain. She is said to have become uncaring towards John, and to have felt more love for her pug dogs than her children; whom she is supposed to have consigned to top of the draughty main tower, so great was her desire to avoid them.) John became melancholic and began to drink heavily.

Outwardly, however, all seemed well. John became High Sheriff of County Down in 1866, and Deputy Lieutenant three years later. Therese became one of London's leading society hostesses. The family travelled frequently, dividing their time between London, Essex, Stormont, Haggerston and Paris, as the season demanded; Therese's only complaint about Stormont being that it had too few bedrooms (a mere 14) to allow her to entertain on the scale to which she was accustomed. (Haggerston had 100.)

As John got older his melancholy deepened. A story told by the Rev. Cotter in the 1940s offers what might be a characteristic insight into his psychological world. Cotter relates that Cleland had a horror of being buried alive, and insisted that a spare key be kept in the vault, just in case. The story may be exaggerated, it may be wholly untypical of him, but then again it may offer some clue as to his cast of mind in his later years.

Eliza Cleland died in 1892 and was effectively sanctified by proxy two years later, when at Margaret's behest the Vestry named the parish church 'St. Elizabeth's', in her honour. Margaret had an elaborate stained glass window (by Mager of Munich) installed to her memory. This depicts St. Elizabeth, a 13th century Hungarian noblewoman, who like Elizabeth was widowed when young. (She was a fashionable subject, Lizst had recently written an opera about her.) Margaret ('Cis') ended her days in Bordeaux, where she became dominated by her housekeeper, eventually leaving her money to the woman's son.

On John's death in 1893 the Clelands left Stormont, letting it to a shipping magnate, Charles Allen; Arthur, John's heir, having already married and set up home near Ascot. Therese moved to England where she remarried (a young guards officer), taking her fortune out of the family (a loss that was partly offset by an increase in ground rents from east Belfast). Arthur and his wife Mabel, (the only daughter of a Lt. Colonel D'Aguilar of the Grenadier Guards), considered moving back on Allen's death, but they liked Ascot, and found the Troubles off-putting, so they put the estate on the market and it was sold to the newly established government of Northern Ireland in 1920.

The have-nots
Not everyone lived in a fancy house, or even had a house to themselves. Overcrowding was worst in the village where according to the 1861 Census 47 families shared 26 cottages. Gape Row was all double-let: in No.3 Kanes shared with Thompsons, in No.8 McKibbins shared with Scotts, and so on, with families living downstairs and sleeping in the loft.

But this, in a sense, was the good news, for conditions round the corner were infinitely worse. The village's old quarter, the area between the Green and the crossroads known as 'Meetin' Street', was then a miserable slum. Most of its cottages had passed the end of their useful life and several were decrepit to the point of falling down. Two were pulled down in 1864. Three more were described as 'soon to be thrown down' in 1864 but were still standing a year later. Another was described as 'Ruins' in 1867.

Dundonald was late in getting rid of its sub-standard dwellings. (Comber, Newtownards and Bangor removed the last of theirs during the 1850s.) As most of the village belonged to the Clelands, it could be said that they were slow to get rid of the worst of their housing. However the charge would not be fair. John Cleland had direct control of only Gape Row. The rest of the village was sub-let to very small time landlords. Andrew Moody, who owned the grocery containing 'nothing that any human creature would desire to purchace', had five tiny cottages at the foot of Meetin' Street. John McCrea, who ran the nearby spirit grocery let another three, and Patrick Crawford had the five nearest the meeting house. Cleland seems to have cleared these when the leases ran out.

In some ways the rest of the place was no better off. The cemetery area is a case in point. In the 1860s it was one of the poorest and most densely settled parts of the parish. Here lived the old, the disabled, widows and the simple, in cramped cottages (including one 'Long thatched cottage') that barely qualified for rates.

In 1861 the parish had some 90 'third class' cottages, and eight dwellings so abysmal they were classified as fourth class. (Four of these disappeared with the renewal of Meetin' Street.) Third class housing was also very poor, and in case second class is beginning to sound luxurious, remember that the Clelands stabled their horses in second class accomodation. Gape Row was considered second class under this scheme. Standards were low with the result that almost any dwelling of over one storey or with more than three rooms was considered a 'mansion' or a 'castle'.

The texture of the countryside I

The countryside, as ever, was in a state of flux. The 19th century saw two housing revolutions. The first had begun in the late 1700s, when the district's mud and thatch cabins (many of which probably dated from around the Williamite wars) began to be replaced by long slated cottages made of stone. This was followed, about a century later, by the mass arrival of two storied houses.

There was a drift from tillage to husbandry. In 1851 just over half the parish was under crop and this percentage declined steadily until 1914. By 1900 two of the district's three cornmills had closed. Oats, potatoes, wheat, rye, beans, peas, parsnips, cabbages, turnips, carrots, vetches and mangels were grown. The most notable absentee being today's main crop, barley. Another surprise is that very little flax was grown (1851). The reasons were financial. Most farms grew cash crops, adapting production to demand. Dundonald's smallholders, more directly concerned with survival, mostly grew potatoes, cabbages and

The view from what is now Dundonald Primary School to the moat, c.1895. The gate piers (top right) mark what is now the school's entrance. (Agnes Johnston)

Gibson's farm, Ballyskeagh, c.1914. The farm covered 13 acres. In the 1860s most of the houses in the parish would have looked very much like this.

oats.

The lowlands had been drained and made less spongy. Fields got smaller. The landscape became intimate and tightly enclosed. For example Ballyoran, which was shown as three fields on the Raven Maps, had 50 fields in 1859. Over the same period Dunlady leaps from 9 fields to 178, and Carrowreagh from 7 to 186. Fields multiplied around key lines, and then slowly began to revert to them. (This relentless sub-division was largely a late 18th/early 19th century abberation. Ten years ago the above townlands had 24, 83, and 88 fields respectively; one field in Carrowreagh containing eight of its mid-Victorian equivalents. To put it another way, the modern landscape is in this way reverting to that of the early plantation.)

The parish acquired hundreds of miles of earth and hedge boundaries. Not surprisingly, these were constantly falling into disrepair, and not just on poor farms. According to Barney Telford, Stormont's boundary with Castlehill was 'rotten – just a big sand ditch full of rabbit holes . . . if cows got near it they just walked over'. Occasionally decaying boundarys were hastened on their way. In

Nightengale's farm, Carrowreagh. During the late 19th century many of the district's smaller farms disappeared; their farmsteads fell into dereliction. In 1860 this was the centre of a 20 acre farm.

1829 Charles Blackwood, gentleman, of Pella Cottage, paid the rector a fine of 2/6, after 'cutting thorns & injuring the fence round the Churchyard . . . for wh. offence Mr Blackwood was sincerely sorry'.

Big farms became larger. Many small farms vanished. Formerly independent farms became out-farms on larger holdings. (All the estates mentioned earlier were agglomerations of small holdings.) Expansion was usually benign, but occasionally leases were not renewed and small farmers were put out, to find a new farm or to labour.

The most far reaching changes, perhaps, were the Church and Land Acts of 1869–1903, which enabled farmers to buy their land, ending generations of renting; and it is interesting to speculate on how the prospect of possession of the soil affected attitudes to the Home Rule Bill which followed shortly after. During the interval, Gladstone, the dethroner of church and landlord, became a hero amongst Dundonald's farmers.[15]

With the introduction of Home Rule, however, Gladstone somewhat abruptly fell from favour. An Orange Lodge was set up and met in what is now the Elk Inn. Membership soared and in 1884 it leased the old school on the Comber Road, where it has been ever since. There was fierce anti-Home Rule sentiment, the fear being that the work of nearly 300 years was about to be undone.

This feeling is well summed up, perhaps, in the story that one morning during the passage of one of the Home Rule Bills, a strong north westerly wind carried the sound of the shipyard sirens over Ballyhanwood. Hearing the fanfare and interpreting it (how else) as signifying the worst, one old farmer crossed the yard to where the boys were reddin' out the byre: 'Y'needn't muck the byre, boys,' said he, 'the Home Rule Bill's bin passed.' Ruin would surely follow. The muck could lie.

The texture of the countryside II: A farming family

We could not leave this look at the land without taking at least a glance at the lives of one of the families that farmed it.

The Morrows of Ballyhanwood are one of Dundonald's oldest farming families. Today they run three highly successful farms in Ballyhanwood, and have provided the province with councillors, two presidents of the Ulster Farmer's Union and a deputy leader of the Alliance Party. However it was not always so. On the contrary, their story is a tale in the log cabin to Whitehouse mould.

Said to have arrived in the 17th century, after having been chased out of Scotland for sheep stealing, the Morrow family are initially thought to have been associated with the village, finding their way up to Ballyhanwood by about 1730. The family flourished and by the late 19th century held nine good farms in Dundonald and Gilnahirk. The district teemed with Morrows, who were tied by blood and marriage. At least six cousins wed and it is joked that only the arrival of the motor car saved the family from inbreeding.

At the centre of this complex web, or as close as anyone could confidently get, was old 'Mr Tom'. Tom and his wife Jeanie farmed the top of Ballyhanwood. Their courtship tells us much about Victorian romancing. They met at a fair; after which Tom visited Jeanie three times, once to introduce himself to her parents, once to propose and the third time to take her home as his wife. They were married for over 58 years and had nine children, the clean shaven Tom rearing five bearded sons.

Their home, the whitewashed 'mansion house', now more humbly Lough-view, was built around 1845 and when new was evidently considered very grand, or at least too grand for the likes of yon' Morrows. It faced a neat lawn, bordered with roses and dominated by a giant monkey puzzle, beyond which

Richard Morrow outside the smithy at Gilnahirk, c.1885. (Phyllis Morrow)

Richard Morrow in his favourite clawhammer coat outside 'the mansion house' c.1920. (Phyllis Morrow)

lay the fruit garden, usually in gooseberries and raspberries, and a sheltered orchard planted with Beauty of Bath and bramley apples. In the shimmering distance lay Strangford Lough, the Mournes, the Holywood Hills and of course the great grimy city. To the rear lay the yard, three-quarters enclosed with outhouses, amongst them the stable, the carthouse with its sprung trap and Surrey cart, and the family's ancestral home, an old and partly mudwalled cabin; all built on a hard shale terrace, which opened through stone gate piers to four fields.

The farmwork was divided into man's work and woman's work and there was plenty of both. Jeanie kept the house, raised the children, milked, dropt, and fed animals. She would also have picked potatoes, made hay, spread horse manure (spreading cow manure was man's work), made the butter and kept the fowl, taking the egg, fowl and butter money. The rest, with some overlap, was mainly Tom's work. This included the food shopping, for the farmer often took the grocery list with him to market.

Traditional customs were observed. Fairy thorns grew unhindered, and a charm in the form of a clutch of four calves feet, cut from the knee, hung in the byre, possibly to ward off blackleg. The blacksmith pulled teeth, and sick 'bastes' went to Mr Jemison who was 'as good as any vet'.

Tom was born in 1814 and lived to be 102. He was prodigiously strong, and his then batchelor sons William and Richard did not take over until he was well up in his seventies. Where William was a soft-centred, easy going sort, Richard was thrifty, shrewd and dour. (It is said 'He woulda skinned a louse for a ha'penny.') He died in 1945 ('the Lord forgot him') aged 95.

By then there were other Morrows in Ballyhanwood. For, as in the best blockbusting dynastic novels, the family divided into two distinct wings, holding largely incompatible philosophies. Whereas the 'mansion house' tended to be Orange, masonic and Tory, their kin down the road in Hill House were outspoken liberals. While the 'mansion house' Morrows circulated in the staid atmosphere of Dundonald, their relatives attended progressive Gilna-hirk. And while old Tom Morrow vowed to fight Home Rule 'even if the gun had to be held up for me', his relatives down the hill were cautious Home Rulers.

There have been Morrows in Hill House since the 1840s. Mr Tom's counterpart here was William Robert, known as 'Lame Willie' (to distinguish him from 'Tom's Willie', 'Willie a' the Mill' and 'Willie a' Heathery Hill'.) Though William was not an exceptionally tall man, a rogue gene surfaced and he and his wife Jeanie had three 6ft 4inch sons, collectively known as the 'nineteen feet of Morrow'.

When William died, his sons Adam and William tried to run the farm jointly, however this didn't work, and the farm had to be divided before the brothers came to blows, or worse. Farm splitting was often a recipe for disaster, but both the new farms survived. Adam stayed on at Hill House, where, stung by the loss of half the farm, he became compulsive about buying land, and ran up fearful debts which his tortured wife Minnie tried to help meet by selling snowdrops from their lane in Belfast. William inherited an old thatched cottage and 23 acres, which he turned into an efficient, modern dairy farm.

For a closer look at the workings of a typical Dundonald farm of the period, let us briefly examine the accounts at Henryville, where Willie a' Heathery Hill ran a good mixed farm.

Willie sold spuds, wheat, hay, grass and oats, and counted on the potato crop to see him through the winter. His cash book for the year 1877–8 shows that his monthly income was extremely erratic, falling from £132 in May when he sold heifers and the winter wheat, to only £7 in July, when he had 30/- from potatoes, £3 from grass and a few pounds from butter and milk, which brought in a small but vital regular income. In spring, the time of repair and renewal, he bought a plough, had the horses re-shod and had gates mended and wheels respoked, paying the carpenter 22/- and McKibbin the smith £4.7.6. June was the month the rents came in, but also the month he payed the 'Cess' and his share of the Rev. Martin's stipend (18/-). June outgoings included turnip seed, potale, manure, lime from Castle Espie, coals (the fire stayed in late that summer!) and medicine for an unknown ailment.

Willie had Henryville for £110 p.a., but it had not been a great year and he had to borrow £50 from a cousin to make ends meet. The next biggest expense was wages for his men, Hugh and Tommy. Each had about 14/- per week. But the cash book only tells us part of the story. Behind the figures lay an invisible economy of exchange and barter, most notably between farmer and man. Besides his wage each labourer had a rent-free cottage, plus wood, potatoes, buttermilk and vegetables: perks which would probably have equalled the cash value of the wage.

Society I: dwindling Dundonald

The most important consequence of the changes on the land was a collapse in

Adam Morrow reaping. (Judith Morrow)

the rural population. In 1837 almost 1,700 people lived in Dundonald. In 1900 it had a population of about 1,000 . In this it followed the national trend fairly faithfully, with the exception that its decline had little to do with the famine, indeed during the famine decade the population rose.

There was a drift off the hills. Some townlands were decimated. Between 1851–1901 the population of Carrowreagh fell from 190 to 81, and that of Ballymiscaw fell from 311 (1841) to 145. It was not just the uplands which failed to maintain their population, between 1841–1901 the population of the village more than halved. However, whereas its numbers began to pick up around the turn of the century, hill numbers did not. Most of the newcomers had little to do with farming, and had no desire to colonise the increasingly bloodless uplands.[16]

The religious balance also changed. Catholic numbers rose slightly. The Anglican population rose (fairly) steadily. The presbyterians fared least well. Their numbers almost halved, falling from 1442 in 1834 to 729 in 1901; even so the parish remained overwhelmingly presbyterian.

Society II: 'The bone and sinew''

Labour was cheap and servants were common. Most worked in the larger houses, but many of the bigger farmers had a servant or two about the place. Whole families could be in service. In 1861, the last year for which figures are available, there were some 174 servants in the parish, and it is unlikely that numbers would have fallen greatly until the sale of Stormont and the social changes of the 20th century. Most were local, but the more highly qualified people tended to come from further afield. As we have seen the Clelands drew the upper echelon of their staff from all over western Europe.

Visitors who were not servants were usually farmhands. Men from Fermanagh, Armagh, Cavan, Tyrone, Londonderry and Donegal found their way to Dundonald. Some spent most of their lives here. A few married local girls, others became part of the family they worked for. However when they died they usually went home, and in the 1930s the body of one old trouper, Peter Quinn, was reportedly carried back to Cavan on his next-of-kin's roofrack.[17]

While the men delved the women sewed. In 1841, 142 women are recorded

The famous Cariboo Road at Great Bluff, British Columbia, c. 1869, in a photograph taken by Sandy Robb, who helped to build it. (John Robb) A great number of Dundonald people emigrated during the middle and latter part of the century, and Sandy seems to have emigrated together with other Dundonalders, as part of a sort of local expeditionary force. His letters describe his adventures, the marvels to be found in his strange new country, its biting winters, and every so often his homesickness: 'You asked me, my Dear father, whether I ever think of home. If you had been as many years as I have away from home you would not have thought... to ask the question. Since the day I left Dundonald until now, there has never one day or scarcely an hour passed but I have thought of home and the dear ones who live there.'

as 'Ministering to clothing'. Ten years later the figure is 157. Many of these flowered or embroidered fine quality muslins put out by Glasgow companies. According to tradition the women of Dundonald and Comber flowered with unusual skill and as a result did the most difficult jobs, such as the finishing of christening robes; which meant long hours of delicate, painstaking work, for scant reward. By 1914 only the older women embroidered. Maggie Harris, who lived at the head of the Green (and in her youth had been a chambermaid at Stormont) was perhaps the last of the local embroiderers. She was still flowering in the 1920s, when in her 70s.

The parish became less industrial. In 1860, for example, it had two thriving quarries. 'Ballyoran Quarries' at Quarry Corner produced a rich brown sandstone that was used in some of Belfast's most prestigious public buildings, and some of Dundonald's (300 cartloads of it built the presbyterian manse). Some way downmarket, Connor, Harvey, McLoughlin & Co. quarried hardcore at Grahamsbridge (McKee's dam) until the market collapsed in the 1890s. 'Very little work . . . now', noted the Rates Inspector in March 1894, chronicling its death throes, 'Only 15 tons sold since oct.' Both quarries had closed by 1901.

The ill-starred barque 'Dundonald', photographed around 1891. This ship was a floating disaster area, and after a catalogue of misfortunes it was wrecked off Disappointment Island (to the south of New Zealand) in 1907. Twelve of the crew including the captain and his young son died. The island had no shelter, so the survivors dug holes and lived in the grimmest circumstances for nine months, until their rescue. (National Maritime Museum, Greenwich)

Scutch mills were also becoming fewer and mattering less. In the early 1860s George Allen reported that his Unicarval mill worked 'but four months' in the year. Likewise, Thomas Killops, who had a pair of mills in Carrowreagh, complained to the Rates Inspector that 'for (the) last two years out of 23 stocks in *both* mills only 6 are worked': and this was in what should have been the middle of a boom! Even given that both men are shamelessly angling for rates cuts, it is not a heartening picture. When the mills became idle in the mid-1880s our two proprietors were again quick to put on the poor mouth. Killops, now down to one mill, protested that he had work for 'only four of his 12 stocks', and Allen declared that his mill was 'largely at rest'. Farmers were no longer growing flax. 'Too many mills in the district', noted the Inspector in 1896. His remark was apt. By 1901 all had closed.

As some skills became obsolete, others took their place. Society became a little more diverse. In the 1880–90s, as well as farmers, labourers, weavers, saddlers, millers, merchants, smiths, scutchers, tailors, shoemakers, publicans, the citizenry included an engineer, a draftsman, two sea captains, an artist, and no less exotic, a clerk.

The captains were Robert and John Hawthorne, both of whom married into another nautical family, the Woods. Neither family had much to thank the sea for. Both brothers and the Woods' boy drowned; John Hawthorne, the captain of the barque 'Dundonald' (a square-rigged, four masted steel sailing ship of 2205 tons), being washed overboard on the journey home from San Francisco.[18] *Lloyds List* records that the ship ran into 'a fearful cyclone':

immediately afterwards the sea ran mountains high . . . the vessel broached to on the starboard tack, and was torn completely over on her beam ends. Volumes of water rushed down below. A heavy sea dashed against the port lifeboat and wrecked it while the force of the wind tore the sails to atoms.

When the cyclone had spent itself the 'Dundonald' was righted, and it

St. Elizabeth's Church c. 1910, looking towards the Gordon window. Note the oil lamps. By then the boxes had been replaced by more democratic pews.

somehow managed to limp into port four months later. It had been extremely lucky to survive.

The churches I: church and castle

Dillon died in 1851 and was succeeded by Andrew Cleland, who had been given the rectorship by his uncle John (the Rev. John having disposed of it along with his other possessions in 1834). Church and castle became firmly bound. The congregation had then under 40 families (against 800 today), and the rector could call on the services of a curate (Cleland went through at least four), so that while the job was not a sinecure its duties would have been extremely light. (Light enough to make you wonder how he put in his time: one suspects a grinding round of soirees and foxhunts.)

Cleland served for 28 years, steering the church through the disestablishment crisis of 1869–71. In a sense this came at exactly the right time, for the Cleland influence on the affairs of the parish was at its height and John did much to help his uncle Andrew pull through. The church embarked on a genteel fund raising campaign and its results starkly illustrate its dependence on the patronage of the big two:

John Cleland Esq. (Stormont)	£1,000
Miss Gordon (Summerfield)	£500
Robert A. Gordon (Summerfield)	£200
Dr. Cassidy (Ballyhackamore)	£100
The Revd Cleland	£50
Others (total)	£5

The Rev. White, rector from 1890–1913, and father of novelist Agnes Romily White.

This, plus what was due from the Church Commissioners, put the finances on a sound footing. However Dundonald did not become a good living until the death of Catherine Gordon in 1900. She left the church £1,000, and it had a further £2,000 from the estate, which it was hoped would enable 'the preaching of the gospel to be secured in perpetuity'. (Unfortunately the money was disastrously invested and this high hope came to nothing.)

Andrew Cleland retired in 1880 and was succeeded by his sometime curate Arthur Farrell, the son of a wealthy Dublin architect, who for 27 years had served as rector of Tullynakill, that is to say as vicar to the Gordons of Florida Manor. (This was as close as the job came to circulating.)

Farrell became rector at the age of 67, evidently a hale 67, and as we have seen, if he was a well man there is no reason to think that the job would have overly taxed him. On his death in 1890 he was succeeded by Robert White. The appointment proved extremely divisive. Leslie & Swanzy write that:

His election led to a bitter parochial dispute. A large number of parishioners wished to have a different man and set up a rival congregation in the Orange Hall.

This very presbyterian sounding occurrence took place around 1900. The reasons for it are unclear (the Vestry minutes barely acknowledge that it happened), however the date may be significant. Catherine Gordon died in that year. She was much revered and if White was her protegee it is conceivable that his opponents stayed their hand until her death. The rift was serious, and the splinter congregation worshipped separately for several years. Eventually, however, we are told that, 'Mr White by his gentle consistent Christian character won them all round.'

The churches II: hastening slowly

The presbyterian succession went scarcely more smoothly. The 'genial and gentlemanly' Rev. Martin retired in 1882 ('due to poor health'), and the Rev. James Bingham travelled north from County Cork to serve as his assistant and successor. Martin continued a while at Bessmount as Senior Minister, but the arrangement proved painfully uncomfortable and Martin moved to Belfast, where he set about writing a history of the congregation. (This invaluable document remained unfinished at the time of his death and was never published. It may now be lost.)

The Rev. E.T Martin, the son, grandson, and great-grandson of a presbyterian minister.

At first the Rev. Bingham did not make it quite as far as Dundonald. Nowhere could be had in the parish, so he was found a house at Knock, and walked in, until a place in Ballyregan became available three years later. In 1891 it was decided to provide the minister with a permanent home. The congregation had the option on two sites: an acre in Ballyregan, with a commanding and no doubt psychologically satisfying view over, amongst other things, the Church of Ireland rectory, or two acres on the Comber Road. In spite of the attractions of the former, the committee went for the larger site and a stately manse was built here in 1892.

The presbyterian community appears to have enjoyed a healthy religious life. Sandy Hanna writes that:

It was customary in the late 1800's for the Sabbath evening services in the Church to be suspended during the summer months so that meetings could be held at focal points of the parish, i.e. Ballymiscaw, Bethesda and Milltown. At Craigantlet crossroads large open air meetings were held on Sunday afternoons at 4 o'clock

Cottage meetings were held at Milltown, midweek meetings were held at

Ballymiscaw, Craigantlet and Bethesda, where there were regular summer schools. Visiting evangelists preached in the church. In 1888 a new choir box was added, but the builders reckoned without the infectious enthusiasm of the choirmaster, Robert Symington, and the bursting choir box had to be extended six years later.

Music then played a relatively minor part in worship here. However conventions were changing, and towards the end of the century presbyterians debated the ethics of including hymn singing and instrumental music in services. Progressive congregations did both. In Dundonald, however, where the old guard held sway, singing hymns was seen as tantamount to giving the devil a toehold. Here the choir sang psalms and no musical instrument darkened the doors. No hymn was included in the Sunday service until 1910, and no music was played at a wedding until 1919.

To the methodists, whose creed is often described as having been 'Born in song', this reticence must have seemed very quaint. The origins of methodism in Dundonald are obscure. Matthew Langtree, an early 19th century missionary and preacher wrote copiously about his travels in County Down, and while he mentions preaching in Craigantlet, he nowhere mentions Dundonald. Even so, in 1861 there were 28 methodists in the parish, holding cottage meetings and occasional services, and in 1873 the minister of Ballymacarret recommended holding a weekly gathering here.

As the methodists edged their way towards independence, the presbyterians were busy on stage two. Church based organisations proliferated. To the Sunday School and choir were added a fife and drum, and then a flute band, and in 1898 Robert Symington founded a company of the Boys Brigade, which folded eight years later he retired to Knock (taking with him the congregation's highest accolade, a purse of gold soverigns.)[19] The flute band became known as the Symington Memorial Flute Band on his death. (It played all round the district. In June 1904, for example, we read that they performed at a church sale in Gransha at which 37 cattle, 3 pigs and a pair of cartwheels were sold; torrential rain fell throughout.)

Sunday School excursions gave many children their first glimpse of the sea. The presbyterian church's Easter Monday excursions were one of Dundonald's most delightful rituals. The children met at the school in the morning, where they were formed into the inevitable crocodile and marched to the station, led by the band. At the station this colourful, noisy procession was met by parents and friends. All would then take the train to Donaghadee, or Millisle, where the strand was broad and the water safe. After games, tea and sweetmeats, the crocodile reformed and the parade set out for home.

12 Up to the present

'One of the loveliest valleys in Ulster'

When the city of Belfast pushed out its boundaries in 1896, it and Dundonald rubbed shoulders for the first time. It was was a significant moment, for as chance would have it, the city's arrival coincided with the departure of both of its wealthiest and most influential families, the Clelands and the Gordons. It was out with the old power, and in with the new.

The extension was followed by three unofficial annexations along the new border. The first came in 1905 when the Belfast Corporation bought 42 acres opposite Summerfield, which it planned to use as a cemetery. They cost the ratepayers £40,000, a price which led the *Northern Whig* to fulminate that 'it may be of some consolation to those who bury at Dundonald to know that they are depositing their dead in the most costly bit of earth in Co. Down.' Thereafter, Dundonald like heaven but a much surer bet became 'the place you went when you died'.

The others came after the First World War, when the Knock Golf Club took over Summerfield, and the government bought Stormont. Otherwise, the city's expansion took place purely on paper. Dundonald remained some distance from Belfast, and continued to go its own way.

It had now some six little centres of population, each with its own distinctive character. Three lay on the Comber Road. There was Daisybank Terrace, six parlour houses behind the Central Inn, home of the gaelic sounding Dochertys, Donnellys and Magowans. Then there was 'Navvy Row', a terrace of nineteen kitchen houses correctly known as Park Avenue which stood at the foot of the Whinney Hill (where the children rolled their eggs at Easter), and was home to shipyard men, dockers and the grave diggers from the new cemetery.

It became best known, however, as the home of the McDonald brothers, wild drinking men who held court in the Hole in the Wall in Belfast. Sam was known as 'The Wild Man', and his reputation was such that respectable houses pulled their blinds down when they saw him coming. His brother Willie John was 'Star McDonald', or more fully 'The Star of the Comber Road', and after a hard night's drinking he would roll home singing:

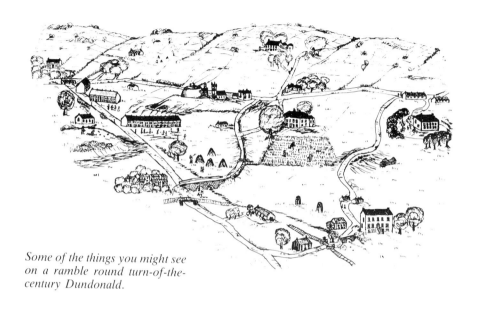

*Some of the things you might see
on a ramble round turn-of-the-
century Dundonald.*

The Star of the Comber Road
has got a job at last
along the railway road
between Dundonald and Belfast

And the people passing by the line
all rub their eyes and stare
and wonder who the navvy is
with the lovely curly hair

Heading on past water-meadows right and left we come to Ardara Avenue, a cul-de-sac of seven brick colossi situated just beyond the manse. Ardara was something new and alien: a stray fragment of suburbia, a place not quite of the parish and a pointer to what was to come.

Beyond it on Heathery Hill, or Heath Hill, stood Billy McKibbin's smithy[1] with its anvil, fire and oven, fed by a massive pair of bellows. On the walls hung the tools of the blacksmith's trade: hardies, fullers, swadges, sedges, wrenches, punches, chisels, drifts and tongs. Beside them were racks of horseshoes, individually tailored for his regular's horses.

The McKibbin's cottage stood next to the forge, behind a small garden '(where) flowers bloomed brightly in season and rambling roses surrounded the doors and windows.' It had a pleasant, sunny kitchen furnished with a stove, a

The view across the Comber Road water meadows to the moat c.1910. Note the dirty feet! (Green Coll., Ulster Folk & Transport Museum)

dresser, a wag-at-the-wall clock, a settle bed, a sofa, a big scrubbed table and a few hard chairs and stools, the lowest of them called a creepy: not everyone could have stretched to this sort of comfort.

Taking our leave of the smiddy, we might continue our tour by cutting down Mill Lane (now the Millmount Road) past Henryville, which would bring out near the railway gates, officially tended by Peter Connor but more often minded by his wife. Making sure that we don't meet the headless man who haunts the crossing, we come to a twist in the road and the ridge where the first Dundonalders made their homes, then its down a gentle slope through pleasant country to the Inler.

Being old Dundonalders ourselves, we might stop a while, and drink in the sounds of the stream and the birds, or gaze out over the cricket pitch and the mills, or beyond them to the two standing stones. We might admire the imposing frontage and manicured gardens of Millmount and get to chatting about the Galways, or about the night the three ladies from the tennis club got a little tiddly and fell in. Then, rested and refreshed, we might resume our ramble by walking down to 'the soda farl', the grassy triangle at the foot of the drive to Millmount, planted with three young chestnut trees: Faith, Hope, and Charity.

Millmount under John Meneely Galway was a model farm. The hedges were dressed, outhouses whitewashed, and ditches dredged every year or every other year. The yard was kept spotless and the stacks were roped and trimmed so neatly that one well-intentioned English visitor remarked it would 'put a home counties village to shame'. Galway was 'a hard but fair man', with an unpredictable temper. One Sunday, for example, a rook dirtied on his coat as the family were leaving for church; on Monday morning he went to the rookery and shot every bird dead. The Galways left in 1922 after John became crippled with arthritis. Ironically, given John's history, none of his sons wanted the farm it was sold.

But let us get out on the road again, and follow it to 'Milltown', the home of Galway's workers. Milltown was five whitewashed cottages, two of them thatched.[2] All had half doors and gardens, and a couple had donkey shoes (thought luckier than horse shoes) over the doors. Here lived Johnny Hare the ploughman, 'a wee low man and a great auld Christian', Robert Shaw, the gardener and beekeeper, and Johnny Walker the byreman who married Shaw's daughter Ellen. Their homes had little in the way of furniture: the adults sat on hard chairs and the youngsters on butter boxes. They cooked using the traditional crane, crook and crock; and slept on 'tick beds', with chaff mattresses refilled every six months or so at 1/- a time.

But let's not dally. We're off to Quarry Corner now, and as we don't want to take all day lets take a short cut over the cow track (now Culross Drive) past 'Spike Island' and 'the wilderness', with its eerie, roofless mills, onto the Newtownards Road, close to two long cottages set well back from the road, near the water-filled quarry holes. This is McRoberts country, and the cottages in front of us house the families of the men who work on McRobert's farm.

Johnny McRoberts. (Norah Gardiner)

'Safely gathered in'. Robb's stackyard c.1910. (Agnes Lawrence)

Ballyoran had by now become the very picture of gracious living; a fine house set about with lush parkland and beautifully kept gardens bright with dahlias, chrysanthemums and begonias. The lane had become 'the avenue', and in spring its borders were a mass of speedwell and daffodils, which were picked, tied with raffia, and sold by the dozen in May's Market. The farm produced beans, peas, potatoes and thick pink rhubarb, and before dawn on Tuesday and Friday mornings two or sometimes three carts stacked with vegetables set out to market.

Behind the house were racing and livery stables, a croquet lawn, a tennis court and greenhouses where peaches, nectarines, gooseberries and Victoria plumbs were grown; to be sold, turned into countless pots of jam or given in bucketfuls to the staff.

By 1900 Mary had become Ballyoran's undisputed mistress. She was strong willed and straight-laced, and as the family got older the parties became fewer, and the atmosphere became increasingly staid. However, while the ladies of Ballyoran became very proper, Johnny McRoberts remained something of a maverick. Released from the demands of the farm, cosseted by his sisters and free to pursue his passion for horses, he never quite grew up, nor was he required to.

Johnny hunted with the North Down Harriers and the County Down Stag

Hounds, and both hunts gathered here once a season, amid a great flurry of activity. In the kitchen cakes were baked, hams were cooked, tongues were pressed. Meanwhile the hunt gathered outside, the men in red jackets and hard hats, the women dressed in black and riding side saddle. There was laughter, conversation, the stirrup cup was served from a silver tray, then all clattered off, hounds yelping, to the slaughter.

Life was usually far more sedate. Mary liked to read and garden; Kate engraved in wood. Mary was active socially too. As well as managing the Dundonald Presbyterian sustentation fund, she taught at Bethesda and generally busied herself, in a ladylike way, with good works. She also set down her family's history, writing that:

It is true that it is not very much yet little and all as it is, I believe none of my brothers and sisters know anything at all about it, and I think that where one has an honourable, upright ancestry they ought to be proud of it.

This calm was punctuated my minor crises, most of them attributable to Johnny. Alec Robb liked to tell a story about Johnny McRoberts and a ghost, which had brought life on Dunlady to a standstill. One evening at dusk Johnny rode up the hill and hid near where the phantom had last been seen. For a long time nothing happened, then suddenly, an almost luminous white figure flitted past him. Johnny's automatic response was to set about it with his riding crop, whereon the beleagured spirit broke down and cried 'Aow! Stop hittin' me, Mr McRoberts, I swear I'll never do it again!'

Between Ballyoran and the village lay the territory of the Robbs. Sandy Robb died in 1910 and his son Alec took on the farm. A workbook has survived from Alec's first year in charge and it shows the daily rote in fascinating detail. The notebook shows us that in the week beginning July 9th 1911 the men were busy thinning and grubbing turnips. Tuesday was fine so they spent the day making hay. There followed a break for the glorious 12th, and then it was back to turnips.

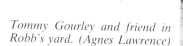

Tommy Gourley and friend in Robb's yard. (Agnes Lawrence)

	Mon	Tues	Wed	Thur	Fri	Sat
James Gourley	Byre	Byre.Hay	=	=	=	=
Al McKitterick	Coals	Potatoes	away	Potatoes	Thinning	=
Thomas Brown	Potatoes	Potatoes	away	Potatoes	Grubbing	Thinning
James Brown	Grubbing	Coll. hay	away	Harrowing	Thinning	Thinning
James Porter	Thinning	Building hay	away	Thinning	Thinning	Thinning
Hugh Fisher	Thinning	Leading horse	away	Thinning	Thinning	Thinning
Js Richardson	Ditching	Forking hay	away	Thinning	Thinning	Thinning

Four weeks later they were busy with the harvest:

	Mon	Tues	Wed	Thur	Fri	Sat
James Gourley	Byre	=	=	=	=	=
Al McKitterick	Tying corn	Building oats	Stooking	Tying	Stooking	Building
Thomas Brown	Sheaves	Carting oats	Stooking	=	Stocking	Carting oats
James Brown	Tying corn	Carting oats	Stooking	=	Drawing straw	Carting oats
James Porter	Tying corn	Carting oats	Stooking	=	Turnips	Carting oats
Hugh Fisher	Tying corn	Throwing sheaves	Stooking	=	Turnips	Sheaves
Js Richardson	Tying corn	Stooking	Guiding stack	Tying	Drawing straw	Stack

By the end of August the work had become more varied:

	Mon	Tues	Wed	Thur	Fri	Sat
James Gourley	Byre	=	=	=	=	=
Al McKitterick	Thatching	Thatching	=	Threshing	Building oats	Stacks
Thomas Brown	Drawing straw	=	Thatching	Threshing	Carting oats	Grubbing
James Brown	Bringing	Turnips		Manure	Carting oats	Carting manure
James Porter	in	Drawing straw	Thatching	Threshing	Carting oats	Cleaning stackyard
Hugh Fisher	oats	Turnips	=	Threshing	Throwing sheaves	Manure
Js Richardson	oats	Garden	=	=	Guiding stack	Garden

The first thing to strike us on our return to the village would probably be how little it had changed. As Agnes Romilly White wrote:

The village had flung out little shreds of streets here and there in an effort to expand itself, but Gape Row remained undeniably the principal thoroughfare. It saw the traffic from the city pass through on its way into the quiet distant spaces of the country: it gathered facts such as births, deaths, marriages, courtships, quarrels and flittings almost without thinking: it knew who had bought anything from a cow to a new hat as soon as the bargin was completed, and it took a devouring interest in politics. Its eyes roamed hither and thither after the manner of a searchlight, and when it was not intent on the world whirling past its doors, it was looking sideways at itself.

A visitor from the mid 19th century would at once have felt at home. Its only significant new adornments were the school and shoolmaster's house, completed in 1901. Compared to the old, the new school, with its big glassy eves, was a phantasmagoria of light and space. The pupil's verdict?

> Our wee school's a nice wee school
> Its made of bricks and plaster
> The only thing that's wrong with it's
> The baldy headed master

The much maligned master was Mr Weir, who taught for nearly 40 years, accompanied for most of them by Miss Waterworth who ran the girls' school (the sexes were mixed just before the First World War) and lodged round the corner at Pella Cottage. The boys' and girls' wings were divided by a slated wooded screen which could be pulled up into the ceiling when the hall was needed for evening meetings (often held when the moon was full, as there was no street lighting) and against which Mr Weir banged his head in moments of excitement; such as when a sack of mice was let loose one morning during the harvest. Maps and cautionary pictures lined the walls. One pair showed a boy smoking and looking pleased with himself, then showed him green and queasy. Unsubtle, and to judge from the number of smokers the school has produced, not very effective. Terrifyingly graphic temperance lectures were given after which the school en masse signed the pledge.

After class the children might spend a few coppers at Minnie M'Nall's, or Jinny McNeill's where they could get six Red Rose Caramels for a penny, or a Paris bun for ½d. If they were older and bolder they might try for a packet of five Woodbine.

Jinny McNeill ran the Iveagh Bar and grocery and during the day she could be seen out emptying the teapot, or resting her 18 stone weight on one of the barrels by the door. She sold snuff, clay pipes and bacon, a side of which hung from a beam by the counter. In the evenings she dealt more in beer; and on Saturday nights, whether he had an audience or not, James Gibson preached from the corner opposite, harangueing anyone who tried to slope into McNeills, and calling, 'There'll be no clay pipes in heaven!' after fugitive smokers (who usually gave as good as they got.) Inside, there was the usual warmth, laughter, chit-chat and rough talk. The beakers were washed in the well that fed the village pump and it was said that by biding your time on a Saturday night you could get 'a pint for nowt' at the pump.

Jinny McNeill and Mrs McConnell who ran the Moat Inn, were the latest in a long line of female publicans and spiritgrocers, traceable through Mrs Herron and Jinny Turner to Mrs Long, who was serving pints in 1852 when records began.

The village was something of a female citadel. In 1912 eleven of its 23 households were headed by women. This amiable matriarchy comes roaring to life in Agnes Romilly White's novel *Gape Row* (1934), which is set in the village on the eve of the First World War, and its sequel *Mrs Murphy buries the Hatchet*, which came out two years later. These 'stories . . . of Irish peasant life' were published to great acclaim: *Punch* described *Gape Row* as 'A book so fresh and unaffected that it almost seems to have grown rather than been written'. *The Observer* called its characterisations 'masterly', and said its dialogue 'goes to one's head like wine'. At last the local dialect had a champion.

Granny Bell, in later life, outside her cottage at the head of the Green, and to the left, the tree stump where she used to sit. (Ada Grange)

The star of both novels is the unforgettable Mrs Murphy, an easy-going, tyrranical, hypochondriac, who makes her entrance looking like 'a large animated parcel which had been tied somewhat carelessly in the middle'. She gives her all to her family and neighbours and when they are not interested consoles herself with endless cuppas, subterfuges and an imaginary past invented around an ancient teapot:

She had been a McSpeddan, and this was the McSpeddan teapot . . . With only the teapot for a start she had built up a romantic family history, in which silk dresses, calves, silver spoons, miskins of butter and stuffed chairs jostled each other recklessly and familiarly. Like a nest in which there are too many young birds, her imagination at times became overcrowded, and some of her brightest fledglings fell over the brim and were heard of no more. But although most people believed in the teapot, and in the teapot only, her artless and inventive conversation had the knack of leaving little wisps and tags of the McSpeddan glory sticking to her.

"Dear bless us, but them pink cups of the pedlar's would go with it lovely!" she murmured, holding the teapot from her and looking at it with almost tears of affection in her eyes, "maybe when I sell the chickens I'll be able to get them. Its well for them has money and no mistake."

Who was the real life Mrs Murphy? Maybe Minnie M'Nall. She was a big lumbering woman whose half door was usually open and whose kettle was

The Rev. Dr Bingham; 'for many years one of the outstanding personalities of the church'. (Dundonald Presbyterian Church)

rarely far from the boil. She sold sweets, and five miles from the smart city centre you could call into her Gape Row kitchen, a room 'that dark you could hardly see her and she the same colour', and be served 2d worth of brandyballs in a newspaper poke or get a 'lucky packet' for ½d. Then again she might have been partly Granny Bell, who lived at the head of the Green with her much put upon husband Tom, in a cottage coming down with mice and knicknacks. Granny Bell was wild for knicknacks. No-one could go anywhere without bringing her back one. Like Mrs Murphy, she thrived on frys and turned the scales at an uncompromising 20 stone.

The book's most easily identifiable character is the author's father, the Rev. White, who hovers about in the background, wrapping the village in a sort of saintly glow. Life, alas, was less charitable, and between bad health and congregational splits he had much to put up with. The book's most notable absentee is his brilliant presbyterian counterpart, the Rev. Dr Bingham who became Moderator of the Irish Presbyterian Church in 1914.

Bingham towered over the place like a colossus. He ran the church and managed the school, signing its cheques and fixing its holidays, which tended as a result to be short. Few dared cross him and his disapproval could be unendurable. (The McConnells were made to feel so uncomfortable about selling alchohol that they left Dundonald to worship at Bangor.)[3]

Dr Bingham was a minister of the old school. Before preaching, he inspected the pews to see who was absent, and as these were the days of 'pew rents', it was easy to see who had not come. If you were absent Bingham called to find out why. He expected to get a good answer and dear help you if you didn't have one. These journeys were known as 'the doctor on his rounds.'

Backsliders received individual attention. Sammy Brown kept the presbyterian stables (now the library and car park) and watered the horses while everyone was in church. This done he would nip into McNeill's for a surreptitious drink. Now Dr Bingham's preaching could be very pointed. He preached against particular evils, and while he did not name names the congregation was rarely left in doubt as to who he had in mind. On one occasion Dr Bingham prepared a sermon on temperance and asked Sammy Brown to make a point of attending. However, when the day came Sammy Brown was nowhere to be seen. Dr Bingham is said to have left the pulpit and plucked him from the snug during the 119th psalm.

Most of the village men were labourers, but there were also a smattering of traders and artizans, such as William John Kennedy the milkman and Hugh Bowman the saddler, who could not afford a horse, and roamed the roads on an ancient bicycle. His cottage was easy to spot, for his last saddle or bridle always hung on a nail by the door. William Kane the cobbler, 'one of the straight, honest old fashioned kind', (honesty was old fashioned even then) mended the neighbourhood's boots and shoes, mostly boots. Shoes were strictly for the nobs (even the Galway boys wore boots) and in the good weather many children, including his own, went barefoot.[4]

The village had no proper streets. Its plan was open. Gape Row faced 'the broad road' and the grassy slopes of Ballyregan, and Meetin' Street looked out over a field and the stables. Other landmarks included the Orange arch, put up at McNeill's, and Huston's slaughterhouse, said to have at times made Meetin' Street run red with blood. The police barrack was in the tall house facing the crossing. It overlooked the village from the north, completing, as Mrs Riddell noted approvingly , a powerfully symbolic landscape in which church, motte, rectory and barrack held the high ground, while the village, with its cheerful, put-upon peasantry, nestled obligingly below.

Many in the village found it hard to make ends meet.[5] Very little went to waste. Bundles of firewood (and hazel nuts) were picked in the glens, boys gathered skins, a cart toured its dry toilets collecting manure. Jack McKibbin writes that:

A favourite task of Mother's was washing letters out of flour bags brought from the grocers for a few pence. Mother had her own formula and these flour bags made excellent sheets or pillow cases. Flour came in four stone and eight stone bags. These were collected and boiled and turned out white as snow.

Though chronically poor, the villagers were not quite at the bottom of the heap. Even they had something to be thankful for, and they were constantly being reminded of this by the endless stream of travellers who waited on and courted them. The district crawled with small time traders and vagrants. Take the two Annies, for example. 'Cummer Annie' was a big sloppy woman with a beat up cart and an old jack donkey who toured the roads until the 1920s,

The Central bar, now the Elk, c.1910. Note the dozens of cart tracks. (Green Coll., Ulster Folk and Transport Museum)

selling whatever she could pass off, and coming out with memorable remarks like, 'When you come from Comber you can wee where you like.'

The other Annie lived under Grahamsbridge, when the bridge had two arches, one wet and one dry (later blocked.) She and her donkey lived in the dry arch, keeping the wind out with a board or a sheet of corrugated iron, and as a result the bridge became known as 'Annie's cuddy's bridge'. She survived by collecting junk and selling fruit and veg.

As well as such as 'Betty-fly-around', who begged or offered her labour, Jack McKibbin recalled the arrival of evangelists, gypsies, Punch and Judy shows, 'an old woman who smoked a clay pipe and always asked mother for a fill of father's tobacco', 'two women selling delph and a packman we loved to see displaying all kinds of clothes':

Singers made their appearance from time to time, and we had a one-man-band, to say nothing of the hurdy-gurdy man who sometimes had a small monkey with a red cap to collect the pennies. A man with a large performing bear arrived one day which rather frightened us.

More routine callers included the fowl man, who bought up chickens and ducks, usually after some spirited bargining; the delph man with his basket of crockery and 'an unfailing urbanity of manner, which no amount of bargining

could ruffle'; and best of all, the herring man. Agnes Romilly White writes that
when he turned up:

Gape Row came to life again, and the joy of the bargin palpitated from door to door . . .
By six o'clock the smell of frying herrings was everywhere. It met you in a solid body if
you walked down the street, and if you tried to escape round the corner, it was there,
waiting to embrace you. Men coming home from their work welcomed it on the breeze,
and hastened their steps.

Socially, it seems to have boiled down to making a choice between drink and
religion, though some managed both. Most respectable social activity was
organised by the church. At the other end of the spectrum there were regular
Sunday cockfights in Killarn Glen, which galled local Sabbatarians intensely
but drew big crowds and were accompanied by much drinking, betting and
lounging around. The entertainments put on by the Orange Order fell some-

Signing the covenant in 1912. (Mrs McConkey)

where in between. Home Rule pushed the lodges into the centre of local life,
and by 1900 the Orange Hall had become one of the parish's liveliest social
centres.

On the theme of Orangeism, it is perhaps worth noting that the schism which
led to the founding of the Independent Orange Order touched Dundonald, for
Tom Sloan and his cronies (who felt the official Order to be too liberal) held
their first twelfth in Dunlady, in a field donated by Thomas Killops. However
the 'MONSTER MEETING AT DUNDONALD' as it was billed, was not an
entirely unqualified success. The parade was to begin at the city hall. However
very few turned up. The *Irish News*, suitably tickled, reported that:

The little knot of supporters who clung to . . . (Sloan) presented a woe-begone appearance as they started for Knock . . . As regards the "great democratic protestant" himself it must have been indescribable torture to his sensitive feelings to see how he was deserted at the eleventh hour.

The *News Letter*, annoyed at the lack of unionist unity, was scarcely more charitable, and so the tiny, friendless band wended their forlorn way to Dundonald, where further humiliation awaited them. As the *Belfast Telegraph* reported:

At the village of Dundonald a handsome arch spanned the roadway and it was interesting to observe that one of the inscriptions on it was "Long live Colonel Saunderson" . . . Portraits of the late Wm Johnston . . . etc, were also suspended from the arch.

This was perhaps the sharpest cut of all, for Saunderson was one of Sloan's bitterest opponents. When they got to the field, however, matters improved and an estimated 4,000 turned out to enjoy themselves and hear (as the *Irish News* put it):'the hills and valleys of Knock (one Orange village was evidently very much like another) resound in vigorous challenge to the papacy'.

Though colourful, Sloan's invasion was a sideshow. The issue that mattered was Home Rule. On 'Ulster Day', September 12th 1912, most of the male population signed the covenant. After a service in the presbyterian church, 133 men signed in the old schoolhouse. 130 women associated themselves with the menfolk. 140 signed in the Orange Hall. Others signed in Belfast. The Ulster Volunteer Force organised here, and Steyr rifles and ammunition were secreted in many of the district's farms.

The War

At first there was great enthusiasm for the war and 'a tremendous number' joined up. As Jack McKibbin recalled:

A poster with Lord Kitchener was displayed everywhere . . . with the words "Your King and Country need you. Enlist to-day." Dundonald gave a goodly number of men and six women volunteered as nurses . . . Some of our ladies went to work in Belfast making munitions . . . working parties of women were set up for knitting socks scarves and gloves.

Recruitment was better in the valley than in the hills. Making the sort of mistake that characterised the war in general, the authorities asked Sir Robert Kennedy of Cultra Manor, a stern and unpopular RM, to recruit at Ballymiscaw school. Only one man, Thompson Gray, joined up. Outside, however, some men who had suffered under Sir Robert took his pony and trap from the blacksmith's where it had been stabled. The trap was abandoned in the middle of a ploughed field, its lamps were impolitely quenched, and amid great hilarity his pony was given a slap and sent home. The mischief-makers then threw pepper into the schoolhouse and tied the doors. Sir Robert made a great fuss, but 'the top of the hill' closed ranks and no-one was caught.

Johnny Walker enlisted, in spite of a weak heart, and became a machine-gunner. Tommy Bell, Jimmy Johnston and Harry Reynolds found their way

German prisoners photographed around 1917 by John Robb, who served with the Ambulance Unit of the Ulster Division. (John Robb)

into the Royal Ulster Rifles band. Willie Johnston served on HMS Pembroke. Sam Caughey tried to join up at 14. He was refused so he walked to another recruiting station and said he was 16, and went on to win the Military Medal. Edith McRoberts went nursing in Flanders with her friends Kate and Margaret Carruthers. Nurses had to pay for their training so this was only an option for the monied. Kate was wounded, and awarded the Military Medal for bravery; her brother William was killed.

Dundonald lost at least 19 men. Johnny Walker was killed at the Somme. He is said to have been running into no-mans land with a machine gun in one hand and a box of ammunition in the other when a shell landed blowing him to pieces. He left a wife and five small children. Fred Sands was gassed and left with chronic bronchitis. Mrs Thompson, lost three sons in one day. Thompson Gray was killed. Bryson Robb was shellshocked. Willie Meharg of Ballyrussell lost a leg. Jim Galway died storming a German machine gun post; he was twenty.

The late casualties were perhaps the worst. Robert Marshall was wounded in 'the last big push'. He was being carried off the field when a shell exploded killing him and both stretcher-bearers. When the telegram reached Ballystock- art his grandmother's hair is said to have whitened overnight. John Ireland died in September 1918, aged 18. Rabbie Gourley from Robb's Corner (whose life-line was the parcel of soda bread soaked in margarine and sugar which he was sent every week from Robb's Corner) was wounded twice, and was due to be shipped to the front on the day the war ended.

The war transformed the local economy. The army bought hay and horses from local farms. There was a huge increase in ploughing. Gardens were put in potatoes, outhouses were converted to take extra men. There was plenty of work in the shipyards and foundries. It was a time of prosperity: 'People ate butter, and went back to marg. after the war.'

Members of the 108 Field Ambulance Unit at play. (John Robb)

Even so the Armistice was greeted with relief and delight. The church bell rang out and when the troops marched back to Newtownards there was a big, flag-waving turn out. On Armistice Day wreaths were laid on the Green at the foot of a small wooden cross, painted white, and veined to look like marble. Dr's Bingham and Burton delivered powerful valedictory addresses, and recited the names of the dead. These were intensely melancholy occasions, for almost everyone knew someone who had been killed or maimed. (The memorial tablet in the presbyterian church shows that 75 enlisted and 11 died. The Church of Ireland congregation lost six.)

The Northern Acropolis

When it became clear that Northern Ireland was to have its own parliament, no-one was at first very sure where to put it. The sub-committee appointed to make 'urgent private enquiries' as to a suitable site considered all the large Belfast demesnes and came up with three options: Belfast Castle, which the cabinet were not keen on; Orangefield, already seen as desirable building land and thought likely to be expensive; and Belvoir Park, 650 acres then let to Sir James Johnston, who had intimated that he would leave, if the price was right. The cabinet were attracted to Belvoir and negotiations were opened with its owner, Lord Deramore. It was only when these became deadlocked that the Prime Minister, Sir James Craig, considered siting the new parliament at Stormont, which he had been informed could be had for a very reasonable £20,000.

Stormont had been omitted from the original shortlist not because it was considered inferior, but because the Government of Ireland Act had stated that the parliaments of Eire and Northern Ireland 'shall be in Dublin and Belfast respectively', and Stormont, of course, lay in Dundonald. Craig inspected Stormont and liked it, and within three weeks its purchase had been

The building of Stormont, 1924. Note the mini railway. (Stormont Library)

ratified by the British government (who were to pay), and an amendment
passed permitting building outside the boundary.

Attention now focused on the buildings themselves. What should they look
like? Where should they go? Two sites, a lower and an upper terrace were
considered, and though the upper would be more expensive to develop, it was
agreed thet there was 'no comparison . . . from the point of view of dignity and
grandeur'. It was decided to build high.

Though Craig had urged that work should begin 'as rapidly as possible', it did
not start until February 1924. The government's embarrassment was intense
and it was decided not to invite the Prince of Wales to cut the first sod in case
this drew attention to the delay. The excavation of the terrace began around
April. Unfortunately the summer of 1924 was one of the wettest of the decade
and the navvies, many of whom were ex-servicemen, spent it floundering about
in glutinous mud. It was a little like a re-run of Flanders, all that was missing
was the barbed wire and the thunder of the guns. Even so the job went to
schedule. The foundations and the main steps followed, however work on
these went slowly, giving the cabinet a chance to deplore the delay and hold the
English-staffed Board of Works responsible. Things were working out nicely.

In spite of Craig's declaration thet there would be 'no gorgeous waste', and
the practical consideration that, though the buildings were to be a gift from the
imperial parliament, the expense of keeping them would fall on the people of
Northern Ireland, the original plans were shamelessly palatial. It was initially
planned to raise three buildings on the hill (a domed parliament, flanked by
impressive departmental offices), however shortly after the completion of the
foundations, the imperial parliament took fright and insisted that the scheme

be scaled down, with the result that the architect Sir Arnold Thornley was given the unenviable job of putting a single building on the tripod's foundations.

The result was Stormont, solitary, scrupulous, almost virginal in its simplicity. The Portland stone gives the building a bleached effect, making it look as if it had been cut out of linen and draped from the surrounding trees.

It is not by chance that it impresses the eye. The hillside was carefully moulded to display the new parliament to its best advantage. Two terraces were cut, one for Stormont and one for the circus around Carson's statue, and the spoil was used to make the approach to each more sheer, artfully amplifying their impact. For though it looks very grand, Stormont is neither especially large nor opulent, and depends for its effect on honest seeming proportions, clean lines and decorative restraint.

The key to it is the ¾ mile Processional Way (won as a palliative in the 1925 package of cuts), which more or less guarantees that none of this ingenuity will go to waste. It rises through rows of lime trees to an immense flight of steps, which extend the building downwards, and the portical columns which lift the eye to the pediment and its frieze capped by Brittania, which further inflates the impression of mass, and incidentally raises the building into the form of a cross. Its most powerful subliminal message, however, lies in its classical form and the unfortunately wishful allusion it makes to the democratic traditions of the Greek city states.

The foundation stone was laid in May 1928 by the Governor, the Duke of Abercorn, as the Prince of Wales was not available. In the light of this disappointing circumstance it was decided not to declare the event a public

'Hey ho, and up she rises'. The new parliament building takes shape; Stormont side view. (Stormont Library)

holiday. The building was completed almost a year ahead of schedule and, after a bill was passed taking the place out of the jurisdiction of the Intoxicating Liquor Act, Stormont was opened amid great ceremony in 1932, giving life to a building that, like perhaps no other, has been viewed through an emotional camera obscura, and evaluated using criteria that are quite extraneous to it.

Stormont's arrival bore only marginally on the life of the parish. Prime Ministers desported themselves around Dundonald, and Brookeborough became president of Knock Golf Club. The grounds became a public park, popular with ramblers and picknickers. There were few economic benefits. Stormont was largely self-sufficient, it had its own bank, post-office, police station, telephone exchange, canteen, garage, bars, joinery and bakery, so in terms of services its coming made very little difference. More importantly, the estate became the headquarters of most of the main departments of government. In came large numbers of civil servants.

The old estate became lost in the new. Its showpiece, the castle, was consigned to the margins and has since become built about with departmental offices. Though demoted, the castle was given an important place in the new scheme. It became the Prime Minister's official residence and the home of the cabinet office, and Craig declared that it would become known 'in much the same way as the Americans talk about the White House.' But several days before praising it in public, he had privately considered knocking it down. Soundings were taken, however:

Captain Herbert Dixon, our Chief Whip, who is very shrewd in such matters, agreed with us that public opinion might misunderstand the Castle being pulled down.

The Craigs moved in in June 1922. Their arrival was not without incident. On the night of the 19th shots were fired at the castle. The sentries returned fire, and according to the *Belfast Telegraph*, 'fleets of cars laden with police hurried to the scene'. The plantation was searched but the atackers had slipped away, and Craig moved in without fuss three days later. The castle was then in the throes of refurbishment and Craig's biographer St John Ervine writes of Craig coming back from work to find his wife and an official arguing about furniture, 'and almost (leaving) again to meet the Republicans who were, he thought, the lesser evil'.

This anecdote, intended to remind readers that Craig's concerns were manly, greatly misrepresents his attitude to the estate. Craig made Stormont his home and his hobby. He became engrossed in the detail of its management, and took an almost obsessive interest in the building of the new parliament, drafting long, passionate memoranda on the subject of its gateposts: leading one unsympathetic biographer to call Stormont 'the only issue' on which he took a consistent and informed interest.

For fifty years the government of six counties was conducted from John Cleland's castle. After Craig, however, it was not lived in until 1969, when James Chichester Clarke had an apartment made on the first floor, and a toilet cut into the thickness of the outer wall. Brian Faulkner and his deputy Gerry Fitt met here during the life of the power-sharing executive in 1974. (If walls could talk . . .)

With direct rule in 1972, a new breed of political mogul moved in. The Secretaries of State worked at Stormont and the Northern Ireland Office, successor to the old cabinet office, continued to be based here. Secretaries of State came and went: Whitelaw, Pym, Mason, Rees, Atkins, Prior, Douglas Hurd, the talking plank, Tom King (who must at times have wished that the castle was genuinely medieval; complete with vats of molten lead), and their successors. By then of course the symbolism had altered, and the vacant Stormont had become, in Sam McAughtry's words, 'a visible reminder, to Loyalists . . . of high ground lost to the foe.'

'the quaint little old-fashioned village of Dundonald'

Summerfield also changed hands in 1920. It was taken on by the Knock Golf Club, which, oblivious of the outrage felt in the village, set about turning the thickly wooded demesne into an 18 hole golf course. This was a very unsettled time, and the disturbances in Belfast had an echo on the golf course, where catholic workers were told to 'prove their loyalty' by attaching orange lilies to their spades. They declined to, and for good measure chopped up the lilies. For this gesture of defiance they were run off the course.

The club had very little to do with its adopted parish. Dundonald provided occasional members, such as Bryson Robb, but it mostly provided skivvies, groundstaff and an endless stream of caddies. On tournament mornings 50 or 60 men and schoolboys would gather hoping to be hired, for a shilling a round

View of the village from The Beeches, c.1930, showing Gape Row, and to the right, Tom McConnell's. Tom McConnell was licenced to sell alchohol to 9.00pm, however the Belfast bars could stay open till 10.00pm, so at 9.15 there was usually a mad rush from McConnell's to Paddy Lambe's at Ballyhackamore, inside the Belfast boundary. (Kathleen Robb)

plus tip. 3d tippers were avoided. 6d bought cigarettes and a trip to the pictures and 6d tippers like McDermott, manager of the Alhambra, were dearly prized.

Meanwhile, back at the half empty schoolhouse Mr Weir decided to put a stop to the mass mitching. He waited for his moment. On the occasion of a big club tournament in 1924, 15 boys were mysteriously absent. At least ten were known to have been caddying, so the governors sent the club a sharp letter threatening to prosecute it if this happened again. This brought matters under control, however even in the late 1920s there are instances of caddies suddenly flinging down their clubs and fleeing the course, hotly pursued by the school inspector.

By the early 1920s, in spite of mitching, the school had become badly overcrowded and classrooms had to be improvised. So an arc of brass screws were driven into the floorboards towards the corner of the room. The children then sat behind it, and the teacher taught from the corner.

The making do came to an end with the building of the present school in 1923. It was built on a six acre site, and the Board's decision to buy what was then deemed an extravagant amount of land was to prove far sighted. The schools became known as the 'new school', the 'middle school' and the 'old school', and with the 1923 Education Act the management of the school was

Stanley Wright, headmaster 1927–44. (Noel Wright)

'Baldy Wright's a funny wee man,
washes his face in a frying pan,
combs his hair with a donkey's tail,
scratches his belly with his big toe nail.

taken out of the hands of the presbyterian church. On his retirement in 1927, Mr Weir was given an enormous armchair, a hint that he could at last put his feet up. His place was taken by Stanley Wright ('Baldy Wright'), an enthusiastic headmaster, and reputedly one of the best water diviners in the county.

The Rev. Dr Bingham also retired in 1927, and was succeeded by James McQuitty, the youngest of four brothers, all of whom became ministers. His position was in many ways unenviable. Bingham's was a hard act to follow, and McQuitty's first years cannot have been easy. Bingham's counterpart and rival, the Rev. Dr Burton had also retired by then, after a short but colourful reign.

In his time Burton had been a boxer, a missionary with the Bush Brotherhood, and a forceful opponent of Home Rule. He was also a man of means. His wife Anne, the daughter of a well to do Lurgan JP, was known as 'the doctor's old guinea hen', because it was said that she had a guinea a day from her capital. They lived in style, keeping a manservant, a cook and a gardener, and unlike Bingham, who walked everywhere. Burton travelled by pony and trap and later by Bath chair, tapped folk with his cane by way of greeting, and tossed handfuls of coins to the children who gathered about his trap. He is remembered as 'a dear man', with a big tummy and a full white Santa-like beard, who strode around radiating good spirits.

His successor, John Beresford Cotter, faced the same difficulty as McQuitty only in a less acute form, mainly because Burton's ministry had been so much shorter, but partly because the two men were so different. Where Burton was ample and flamboyant, Cotter was meek and slight. Where Burton was wealthy and a trifle vulgar, Cotter was gentlemanly and poor (and got about in an 'old tumbledown shack' of a car.) However, he soon became liked and trusted, women mothered him, and as R. Taylor-Nobbs has written, he 'ministered with great piety and dignity until his death in 1950.'

The Ballystockart tug of war team in action on the Cricky Field in 1921. (Mrs Cairnduff)

The big two were joined by a Methodist minister in 1937. This had been in the offing for some years. At the turn of the century there had been some 40 'swaddlers' in the parish and in 1904 Wesley Guard of Knock preached in 'a Hall' here, probably the Orange Hall (the district's third church), which hosted fortnightly services in 1925. Numbers kept rising and twelve years later a church was built at Grand Prix Park.

This was also the heyday of the Bethesda summer Sabbath School, and its annual fete was one of the highlights of the summer. When the grown-ups weren't looking, however, the children got up to all sorts of tricks. Down in the village it was 'all mischief, all divilment!' Endless jokes and pranks were played: gates were switched, windows were blackened (so that people would sleep in, thinking it was still night-time), and carbide was exploded in the schoolyard. (One figure who stood out in bold, black Victorian relief against this tide of mischief was Granny Bell, who was not a bit fussy about who she guldered at or took the rod to.)

Most of this youthful energy was directed into games. Football was popular, and on summer evenings needle matches between Navvy Row and the village were played on the site of the Co-op. If no ball could be found a pigs bladder was begged from Smith's farm on the Stoney Road.

In the late 1920s two veterans from these games started a 43rd B.B. old boys team. The 43rd's deadliest rivals were the 10th from Cherryvalley. Absolute solidarity was required in the face of the 10th, and one player who switched allegiances (after a row) found his name was mud for years after. One of the 43rd's most memorable games was played against the 33rd from Legoniel in the Neill Cup. The Dundonalders had allegedly been hacked off the field at Legoniel the previous week, and the re-match was awaited with great trepidation. In spite of the presence of Sgt. McFadden and all three constables, and Alec Robb's frantic attempts to calm everyone down, the match ended before it had properly begun, with scrapping on the pitch and melees on the touchline, when some Dundonald supporters, who had sticks under their coats, set about the Legoniel men, who turned out to be equally well prepared. Dundonald were disqualified.

Teams came and went. 'Dunedin', Dundonald's oldest known team, began before the First World War and lasted until about 1925. Then there was 'Dundonald Central', run by Johnny Bell of the Central bar, 'Ashmount', 'the Saints' (St. Elizabeth's) and 'Millmount'. Millmount played all over the Ards peninsula, and when they played Kircubbin or Ballyhalbert, 8–10 busloads of friends would come along for the trip. Their needle matches were with Comber, and the rivalry could be traced to Dundonalders chatting up Comber girls after the game. On the way home the team were showered with stones from Stone's plantin'. The same thing happened after the next match, and from then on the team sneaked home along the railway line.

It was not all football. Cycling, fishing (poaching), sledging, ferreting and quoits (played on the Green with horseshoes) were popular, as was golf, but not at posh Knock. Golf was whacking balls from the moat into Kirkwood's farm, using sticks cut from Mather's or Grey's Glen, and balls cribbed from 'Auld Goldy's' farm at Bessmount. The 11th was then a dog leg around

Going home from school through Dunlady, c.1930. (Mrs Gourley)

Bessmount. Big hitters tried to cut the corner and so the balls rained in on Bessmount, and the youngsters poured in after them. Mr Goldthorpe would lie in ambush behind the hedge when he had wind of a raid, then chase trespassers half way to the village.

Being chased was a sport in itself. Geordie Stevenson of Gape Row was another reliable chaser (children tied thread to his door and rapped it from the other side of the road), as was Gibson the dairyman, who prowled the moat field looking for trespassers and is said to have once set a hedge on fire to smoke out a courting couple.

Another game involved walking the gutter under Gape Row, an underworld of eels, rats and slime, which the bravest negotiated barefoot. Other popular games included 'kick the tin', catching smicks, gathering nuts, spinning (with a whip and pirrie), or seeing who could hit their wooden 'piggy' furtherest. Everyone had a hoop and cleek, and the idea was to see who could spin theirs longest. 'Easter houses' made of branches were built on Easter Monday. Eggs were boiled on a fire at the door and dyed with whin blossom, tea, or onion peel, to make them look like marble.

Racism aside, one of the nicest customs of the time was the children's 'Queen of the May' celebration, which took place on May 24th at Navvy Row. A queen was chosen and dressed as a bride, complete with veil and bouquet. The other girls took her train and they all went down the Row, getting a penny at each door. At the far end they were met by the boys, who were dressed as 'darkies', with blackened faces. The girls sang:

Oh the darkie said he'd marry her, marry her, marry her,
the darkie said he'd marry her, she's the Queen of the May.

They recited this twice and the second time sang 'but we'll all run away!', then scattered and were chased. Afterwards everyone had a picnic on the footpath.

In summer a circus set up on the green in front of Navvy Row. It brought with it a smattering of technology (swing boats and chair planes), but the main bill was a very traditional combination of clowns, novelties (such as a sheep with three horns) and horses, including a clapped out nag trained to nod its head in front of an elderly woman when asked the question, 'Who takes whiskey in their tea?'

The big race
The biggest event in the calendar was the Tourist Trophy race. After the almost
unexpected success of the 1928 T.T. (which drew 44 cars, and would have had
45, had one Frenchman not boarded the wrong ferry), race day became *the* day
in Dundonald.

It is easy to forget just how spectacular an event it was. On the morning of
Saturday 17th August, 1929 the village woke to find its pavements and small
front gardens full of people. A vast procession of cars, bicycles, trams and
busses beat its way out of Belfast, jamming the road all the way to Knock.
Others arrived the night before, making their way over fields by the light of
lanterns, and camping where the Ulster Hospital now stands. Ferries and a
transatlantic liner provided a round the clock service from Britain, and special
trains ran from Dublin and Cork. In all some 500,000 people, including
contingents from the U.S.A., Australia, India and all over Europe, came to
watch the race.

*The Central bar gets ready for the
invasion, c.1929. (Welch Coll.
Ulster Museum)*

The preparations had begun weeks beforehand. The track was tarmac'd,
scaffolding was erected, advertising billboards were nailed into place. The
circuit became a charmed place. Charabancs and busses toured it exploring its
every nook and cranny, while guides explained its subtleties and dangers. The
drivers and the international press arrived with two or three days to go. Some
crews lodged at local farms, from which they could drive out and test their
mechanic's latest modifications. Nuvolari stayed at Glencovitt. The Fergusons
of Ballyrogan put up Prince Beara and Prince Chula. Here, the drivers slept in
the bedrooms, the family slept in the outhouses and the mechanics slept with
the cars. As Mrs Ferguson put it 'For weeks we lived, ate and breathed T.T.
races.'

The village on T.T. day. The race was a great social occasion. Villagers suddenly found themselves popular with remote in-laws. Women baked for days ahead and familys gathered. (Ulster Folk and Transport Museum)

However, not everyone's thoughts were on the race. Every huxter in Ireland seems to have put in an appearance. Nor were our local entrepreneurs caught napping. From her shop at the foot of the Granaha Road, Mrs Moore sent out fleets of youngsters armed with trays of Nestle's chocolate. Others sold programmes, official and otherwise. Farmers let out their fields, and Dick Warwick ploughed one of his into parking spaces, selling them at 1/- a time. Others, whose land had been trampled last year, tried just as hard to keep people out. Gates and fences were pasted with pitch and 'Beware of the Bull' signs were posted.

The big day began at dawn, whether you wanted it to or not. This was the last chance the drivers had to practice, and superchargers screaming, they hurtled round the still open roads at 5 and 6 o'clock in the morning. At 10.00am, amid mounting excitement, the steward closed the course. By now the atmosphere was festive, flags and bunting hung from poles and buildings. Kites and light aircraft hovered overhead. Dance music blared from the grandstand speakers. Some people climbed trees to get a better view. Others commandeered the flat roof of Fleming and James, dancing and whooping it up, to the partner's despair.

Activity centred on the R.A.C. grandstand near Quarry Corner. Beside it was the Ulster Automobile Club's exclusive enclosure, and an impromptu village of marquees and beer tents, plus the scoreboard, the finishing line and

Signing autographs. In spite of the amount of money involved, the race was an amazingly innocent affair, with petrol being poured from milk churns and drivers sticking chewing gum into their ears to blot out noise. (Kathleen Robb)

the pits, scene of many great dramas, such as when Hamilton lost the race in 1933 by reducing his mechanic to such a state of nerves that he set himself on fire.

    The race started at 11.00am, and the 1929 Tourist Trophy race was one of the greatest of them all. Under a blazing sun, 65 cars – Lagondas, Rileys, Lea-Francises, Bentleys, Alfa Romeos, Mercedes, Bugattis and a pair of privately entered family Fords – joined the mad scramble at the starting line.

August 1928, ready for the off. (Billy Galbraith)

One driver got so excited he forgot to turn and ploughed straight into Quarry Corner. All the big cars started well and Carricola took an early lead, hotly pursued by Birkin in a Bentley.

Half an hour later an almighty downpour changed everything. The heavy tourers skidded everywhere. 'Passing another car became an art in itself', wrote one driver. 'Ahead would be the rival machine thickly veiled in flying spray . . . we would just get by without knowing quite how close the two cars had been.' None of the cars had windscreen wipers, save one. Carricola had fitted his white Mercedes with an extra windscreen equipped with wipers, and as the others eased off, he took his lap speed to below 11 minutes, crossing the line just before 5.00pm, two minutes ahead of Campari.

The next year Nuvolari and his Alfa Romeo team-mates took 1st, 2nd and 3rd, encouraged no doubt by a telegram from Mussolini, instructing victory. This was the last clash of titans. In 1931, amid bitter complaints about the handicapping system and disparaging remarks about 'small fry', the heavy metal withdrew, leaving the field to the MGs and Rileys. If this took away from the glamour, it did not detract from the excitement, and the race continued until 1936 when eight spectators were killed at Newtownards; and the circuit reverted to horses, bicycles and the occasional Morris Cowley.

Goodbye Gape Row, Goodbye
It is hard today, perhaps, to imagine Dundonald as a beauty spot or the village as a tourist mecca, but in the 1920s and early 1930s it was both, and its admirers were legion. The *Belfast Telegraph* called it 'The rambler's paradise'. The French writer Victor de St. Helme set the first chapter of his novel *Ruby Laure* here in the delightful 'Tombeau de Donald'. This was also the age of J.J. Marshall's history *The Romance of Dundonald*; and when the Rev. McQuitty wrote of 'the quaint little old-fashioned village of Dundonald' in 1932 he was not exaggerating or being sentimental (at least not very).

With its unpresumtuous churches, inviting whitewashed cottages and friendly, characterful people, plus curiosities like the moat and the mausoleum, Dundonald was a beguiling little place. Best of all, this state of grace was the result of natural evolution. It had come about quite casually, almost by chance. Dundonald's setting added further to its charm. It lay in rolling farmland, criss-crossed by narrow dirt roads that existed courtesy of the landscape and in spite of the best efforts of the roadmen, were constantly threatening to return to it.

The bulk of its visitors were day-trippers from Belfast, who took the tram to the end of the lines at Summerhill and spent the day strolling the high and by ways, finishing off with a slider from Sam Johnston's: large wafers 2d, small ones a penny. Then came the obligatory stroll along Gape Row, which might have been sealed in a time capsule for all it had changed since the 1860s. Peering into the first cottage you would still find Minnie M'Nall, now Granny M'Nall, supping tea or poking the fire. The sweets were still there too, on the table, 'with *everything* crawling over them'. The McKeags lived several doors down, under a big black boot, for John McKeag was a shoemaker by trade. He also practised folk medicine, spending his evenings in the fields picking herbs,

Looking towards the Green, c.1935. (Sammy Perry)

and as the village had no doctor his potions circulated widely.[6]

The nearest doctors were Dr Irvine of Knock, and the gnomic Dr Henry of Comber, 'a coarse old stick' with a big paunch and a no-nonsense manner, epitomised by his remark: 'You've enough manure in you to cover that garden', delivered to a man in agony with constipation. It is said that 'You didn't need to be in your last throes' when you called Dr. Henry. (Stories about Dr Henry abound. On a visit to Millmount he is supposed to have come on a man repairing a cart. Peering over his half-rimmed specs, Dr Henry was quick to notice a mistake and point it out to the carpenter, who calmly replied, 'I can paint out my mistakes, Dr Henry. It takes more than a lick of paint to cover yours.')

The Symington Band and entourage on the Newtownards Road in the late 1920s. The then police barrack is in the background. (Mrs Hunter)

But to get back to Gape Row. Harry and Lizzie Boyd lived in the last cottage with their eight children, Billy, Tommy, Harry, Acky, Lilly, Jean, Sadie, and Ann. Big Harry Boyd was the ploughman at the Beeches, and played the Lambeg drum in the Star Flute Band, the local kick-the-pope band who operated from the Orange Hall. The Boyds loved a singsong and every so often friends would call, the accordian came out, the drink would flow, and the Row would get no sleep until the wee, wee hours.

The Star was a one key flute band and its members were mostly rough diamonds, renowned more for their drinking than their musicianship. Even so, it usually managed to look the part on the twelfth, thanks mainly to a squad of dummy fluters, who materialised at moments of crisis. The Star folded in the early 1930s leaving the field clear for the rather more respectable and professional Symington Band.

As cities have orchestras, Dundonald had the Symington Memorial Prize Flute Band. It was a part band, and a good one. As well as being hired for the twelfth (for £14 plus expenses), they played at almost all Dundonald's set piece occasions, turning out for services, fetes, galas and the coronation of George VI; commemorated with a fete on the Cricky Field, and a bonfire on the moat, built from dozens of empty tar barrels kicked and rolled from Quarry Corner.

The McConnells were now the village's publicans, Tom at one end and Sam at the other, propping it up like a pair of bookends. Tom McConnell ran the Moat Inn. He was an easy going landlord and too free for his own good with credit. It is said that he 'kept half of Dundonald' during the depression. As well as a publican, Tom was the local grocer, coalman, petrol seller, banker and undertaker's agent, arranging funerals for Browns of Belfast. The grocery was run from what is now Tom's Cabin, and had you called during the '30s you might have been served by Tom's brother in law, a shy young man named Jack McKibbin; weekly orders delivered by pony at no extra charge.

If anything Sam was even more easy going than Tom, but he fell out with people easily. The harder type drank here. Like Tom, Sam did a bit of everything. He started a chippie, frying up in a pig feeder in the basement until it went on fire and he doused it with water and was lucky to get out alive. Sam

The new police barrack in 1938. It has since been turned into a fortress.

turned the grocery into a sweetshop and tobacconists, and began a sort of haulage business involving his brother in law Tommy Murphy and an old second hand truck. The rickety hall he built behind the bar became 'the Iveagh Club', the biggest centre of entertainment in miles. In it were held boxing matches and dances, which women of reputation on the whole did not attend.

If these too turned into boxing matches, as they sometimes did, Sgt. McFadden or one of his constables, such as John Duke, known as Lord Kitchener on account of his handlebar moustache, could usually be relied upon to keep order. McFadden's style of policing was low key and unflustered. It is said that his idea of a raid on the Central was 'to push the men out and take their place.' This starkly contrasted with the style of his successor, Sgt. Reid who hid behind bushes so that he could catch cyclists riding without lights. Not surprisingly, under Sgt Reid, the McFadden era became remembered as a golden age.

The constabulary were not the only ones with time on their hands. Many of the men of the parish were regularly out of work, particularly during the depression, when they were sometimes undercut by unemployed shipyard workers from Belfast, who offered themselves at £1 per month. Farm workers were not then allowed unemployment relief, and many families suffered great hardship.

When idle the men of the village met at 'the wee wall' or 'the corner' at the foot of Church Road, where they chatted and joked to pass the time of day, or for entertainment got youngsters to race round Robb's Road, giving a few coppers to the winner. In the evenings they would loll on the bank opposite, or walk 'round the course', or into Holywood.

As a meeting place the bank and the corner were the equal of the pump, with the difference that while both sexes gathered at the pump, the corner was a male preserve. (Only men were allowed to go out specifically to loiter!) Anything that would relieve the boredom was eagerly seized on, and when Tom McConnell had the idea of setting up a marbles tournament, he triggered a six month marbling epidemic.

Greyhound racing on the Harefield (now the new police station) was another popular diversion. These meets drew hundreds, including dozens of bookies

It wasn't just the children who got up to mischief. (Mrs Moore)

and all manner of spivs. Everything about these gatherings was highly irregular. Races were rigged and favourites were allegedly painted so that they could
slip in again at long odds; and on one infamous occasion a fancied front runner,
who was partial to fish, is said to have been lured off the track by a plate of
herrings. The bookies made a killing.

Just about everyone had a nickname. There was 'Beef Conkey', 'Psyche
Dempster', 'Trout Gilmore', 'Spider Harris', 'Boxer Brown', 'The Dude
McIlvenny', and his brother 'The Shark', and 'Grub Gray' (who 'had the
whola' Bangor blocked', when he went round it on his trap and pony). This was
also the era of vanished landmarks like the dungstand that stood near the Old
Dundonald Road at Tullycarnet; the Co hayshed, irresistible to courting
couples; and the Quarry Lane style, where Dundonald took on the might of the
B&CDR in 1938.

In spite of the depression the number of shops in the village steadily
increased. Along came Shaw's 'wee huxter shop', the Miss Leech's drapery,
Joe Cordner's bicycle shop, and the grocery which sounds as though it should
have been a west end tailor's, Fleming and James, run by Victor Fleming, a
small, busy hunchbacked man, who 'kept his ear close to the ground', and the
always gentlemanly Mr James.

Fleming and James was something of an oddity in that it was a purpose-built
shop. Hitherto shops had tended to evolve. They usually began with someone
selling from their kitchen for a bit of extra cash, were added to gradually as,
say, the Calor man or the Gallagher's rep. called.

Many never passed the first stage. Mrs M'Nall's shop in Whiteman's Row (as
opposed to Mrs M'Nall of the village) was one of these. She sold sweets
potatoes, cigarettes and meal. She dressed in an old flat hat and a potato bag
tied with string, and she would close the shop to feed the goats which grazed at
the back.

But the old style was in retreat in the 1930s, and nothing brought this home to
people more than the demolition of Gape Row. It was levelled in 1934 and five
characterless semi's were raised in its place. The Row disappeared not because
it had reached the end of its useful life (though this cannot have been too far

*The end of Gape Row in 1934.
Everything was pulled down but
the post office. It went a few
months later. (Rosemary Caruth)*

off), but because there was no profit in it. Its tenants were scattered to the winds and not all of them stayed in the district. That it was superannuated, cramped and barely sanitary was soon forgotten: Gape Row passed into legend.

Goodbye Gape Row, Goodbye

They're tearin ould Dundonald down
They're tearin' down Gape Row,
The kindly dacent folks are gone
And scattered to and fro.
There's something aches inside o'me
That niver ached before,
For niver more the ould folks lean
Across the ould half-door

They're tearin' ould Dundonald down
They're tearin'down Gape Row,
That ould White Row held hearts of gold
We'll miss them when they go.
It makes me sad to pass there now
There's no-one there to say,
'Just sit up tae the fire
While I make a cup o'tay.'

They're tearin' ould Dundonald down
They're tearin down Gape Row,
And why they tear it down at all
Bates a'the De'il will know.
It didn'ae look sae ill a'tall
As everybody knew
It seems that something dear must go
To make room for the new.
They're tearin' ould Dundonald down
They're tearin' down Gape Row,
The ould folks left their hearts behind
Their ghosts now come and go.
If you should dander down that way
You'll hear the soft winds sigh,
'They're tearin' ould Dundonald down
Goodbye Gape Row, Goodbye.'

Did its residents feel this lyrical about its passing? We can only guess. However there is no doubt that the Row was widely mourned, and that the significance of its passing was not lost on people. It stood for the old ways, simplicity, neighbourliness and an unpretentious rural way of life: everything that was under threat. Its demolition not only robbed the village of much of its magic, it heralded its end as a country hamlet. Dundonald was to be reploughed and replanted.

The housing boom
The newcomers were townies, of all classes. Between the wars the population doubled, and for the first time the parish began to fail to assimilate its new

arrivals, mainly because of the unprecedented numbers. Galway and Reaville Park (named after Galway the landowner and Rea the builder), were the biggest interwar developments. Their residents were policemen, insurance agents, mechanics and civil servants; living in houses with names like Parusia, Sirius, Gwynn Lea and Lynkview. And as Ardara Avenue owed its existence to the train, this island of 80 or so bungalows and semi's was made possible by trams and busses.

Some 45 houses were built on and off the Old Dundonald Road, near the station. Between 115–20 houses were built piecemeal along the Comber Road.

'Ah hannie them done yit.' Jack (left) and Geordie Whiteman outside their bootmaker's shop in Whiteman's Row on the Comber Road, around 1935. It later became the Northern Bank and is now a Chinese takeaway. (Mrs Gourley)

These included wooden chalets, tall seaside terraces, parlour houses and a wooden house built by a stager in the shipyard; which is also said to have supplied most of the raw materials!

Then there were the shanty towns, 'Tintown' on Quarry Lane, and 'Timbertown' on the Gransha Road, wooden cabins with tin-hat chimneys that looked like a stage set for a western. These housed the families of shipyard, mill and foundry workers, plus a quota of entrepreneurs like Anthony Robinson 'the tea man', who sold plotted tea door to door, and Rabbie Courtney who wrote poems and carted dung. (He may have been the author of 'Goodbye Gape Row, Goodbye.')

The only resident (landowners apart) to profit in a big way from the property boom was John Boyd the builder. He began by converting old houses and ended up building the Burton Hall, Burton Avenue, part of Burton Drive (all named after old Dr Burton), Boyd's Avenue, and 'Laurelvale', nicknamed 'Clabbercastle', where he made his home.

Next door in Cherryvilla, lived someone even more renowned than he. She was Mabel Jacobs, a woman of easy virtue, and Cherryvilla was Allybrook House, the former home of the rector's wife. Though no beauty, (she is said to have had a 'hook nose and a big red face'), Mabel Jacobs was a well rared, well-spoken woman. Her nose gave her a vaguely patrician look, which fed the rumour that she was connected to the fig roll people, from whom she was supposed to receive an annual retainer.

Mabel Jacobs solicited in red lipstick and an off-white coat (important when there were no streetlights), and it may have been this which gave her her nickname, 'the White Knight'. She walked the roads with a dog on a long lead, in which she would ensnare passers-by and so strike up a conversation. This small piece of disingenuousness aside, Mabel was quite open about what she did. She talked to folk, and folk talked to her (indeed you did well to speak, for she could be sensitive to imagined slights), and she excelled in light hearted banter: 'How's business, Mrs Jacobs?' 'Not so good since your daughters went on the road, Mr Boston.'

She did not have the field to herself. Other women (who 'done it behind the hedge for half a crown'); and men, who tended to be younger and daintier than the women, could also be found walking their dogs at odd hours. They shared the roads with tramps and travellers like 'Auld Fortycoats', 'Old Hardegg' and Joe Blake, who wore skirts and had long hair. There was also a kindly big man who would slip into farmyards and break into song. He was well liked and some had him in to tea at Christmas, the feeling being that 'there but for the grace of God go I.'

The most novel sights on the roads, however, were busses. McCartney's blue busses were first, then came the red 'Millisle Queen', and the yellow 'Imperial', which ran between Belfast and Donaghadee.[7] There was fierce competition for passengers, which brought out the best and the worst in the free enterprise system. The busses were immaculately kept. However on the down side, if you were alone waiting for a bus, and there were four people waiting up the road, the driver might ignore you and pick up the others, in case a rival whisked them off.

Bringing in the hay at Ballyoran, c.1930, looking out over Carrowreagh and Killarn. (Agnes Johnston)

Sammy Brown carting turnips at Robb's farm. (John Robb)

While the west of the parish began to fill up with houses, the rest stayed much as it had been. Quarry Corner is a case in point. If anything, the pace of life here slowed, for when Johnny McRoberts died the big livery stables were closed, all but a couple of horses were sold, and in time Kate got a Morris Cowley. This made life difficult for Joe McKeown, who now manned the Quarry Corner smithy. But this was perhaps not the greatest of his worries, for he believed witches haunted the forge, and every so often stuck a red hot poker through the roof, just to let them know he wasn't someone to mess with. When he fell out with one of his neighbours, he made a mud likeness of him and stabbed it with a golden pin, muttering darkly, and going into transports of delight when the man complained of pains.

Perhaps he was spending too much time with old Mrs Brown, the custodian of the local fairy lore. She lived partly in this world and partly in another. She heard fairies sing and play the fifes (Dundonald's fairies are Scottish, of course), saw the will o'the wisp in Carrowreagh and swore that a woman in gray haunted Millmount.

In spite of the influx, Dundonald's business, as ever, was farming. Every corner that was not built on was farmed. Stormont was farmed until the opening of parliament. Sheep grazed on the golf course (until the club reluctantly bought a mower in 1927.) Hay grew in the grounds of the primary school, and rucks were forked on what is now the football pitch. (Eddie Ferguson had them for the work of cutting them, however the hay got badly trampled by children, and when he fed it to the cattle he complained that the milk yield went down!)

Farms ran on horsepower. For example Eddie Ferguson, who farmed 40 acres in Ballyregan, usually kept three horses, two for ploughing and one to get about on. They were shod for 8/- a set by Thompson of Chichester Street. Sometimes they were taken to McKeown's, and once they went to the smith at Craigantlet Cross, but his shoes came off so they never went back.

The number of horses in the parish halved between the wars, not because of the arrival of cars and tractors, but because less land was being ploughed. In 1925 about half the parish was in pasture. By 1939 this had risen to two thirds. Dundonald was becoming cattle country; in terms of land use it was reverting to its economy of a thousand years before.

World War Two

The Second World War turned Dundonald into a sort of international shanty town. Nissen villages were built at Rosepark/Ardcarn, the Stoney Road, Cumberland, Coronation Park, Greengraves, Camperdown and the Comber Road.

Buildings of every description were requisitioned. The Air Ministry moved into Stormont evicting several hundred civil servants. The British Legion Hall, built on stilts near the river, became a military police billet. The middle school became the N.I. Radar Control Centre, much to the concern of one old lady, who is said to have spent half the war fully clothed, rather than undress and be seen by the prying radar.

The place bristled with military installations. The hills buzzed with morse messages. A top-secret signals station was built on the golf course. Trans-mitting stations that looked like oil wells were set up in Ballykeel and on Swain's hill. The R.A.F. took over the G.P.O. communications centre in Ballyhanwood. Bunkers were built on Swain's hill and Ballyrogan. Mock infantry battles were held on the Cairn Hill.

Then there were the A.A. defences. These involved some extraordinary deceptions. Imaginary villages were built in Ballymenoch, and on Carro-wreagh Hill. (Where three families were put out to make way for it.) Artificial lakes (aircraft tracking systems made of netting wire, intended to shimmer like water from the air) were constructed at Ardcarn and Camperdown, where the 'lake' covered a four acre meadow. Stormont acquired two A.A. machine gun nests (on the roof), rifle positions on the doors, concrete blockhouses and barbed wire entanglements. Two barrage balloons were raised at Rosepark, and a light A.A. gun, thinly disguised as a haystack, was set up across the road.

A small balloon was put up at Camperdown, and the Belfast area barrage was added to until at one point 42 balloons could be seen. They did little good but it was reassuring to count them as they rose in the evening. Two A.A. guns and a pair of searchlights were set up near the Kempe Stone, and a battery of two, then four, then six, then eight A.A. guns were sited at Camperdown. Most of the guns were installed *after* the blitz; indeed two of Camperdown's guns were built after the war, (contracts are contracts). Few saw action.

People then feared air raids in much the same way that we today fear nuclear attack, however civil defence preparations were similarly woeful. Four air raid shelters were built on the Green. Two were built in the primary school courtyard. Two were built on what is now Burton Avenue. Several were put up at Camperdown. Stirrup pumps were distributed. Sirens were installed.

These were to protect the military. Civilians had to fend for themselves. The Civil Service Association asked for shelters at Stormont. As they were not mandatory in Northern Ireland, the government declined to provide any, 'lest other employers react badly.'(!) The idea that civil servants might build their own was blocked by the unions, with the result that no precautions of any kind were taken.

It was the same all over. When the worst came you hid under the stairs or below the kitchen table, and there was a big run on basements, especially Dugan's basement on the Comber Road. Half of Navvy Row (the prudent half) sheltered under the railway bridge. They had read the advice and sneaked down the Comber Road wearing pot-lids and saucepans, keeping well in to the verge, and ssshing one another quiet in case the Germans were listening. Joe McKeown dug a 'scoot hole', where he sat lit by a candle.

Children carried gas masks to school and collected books for the forces. Badges of rank (private, sergeant, colonel, etc.) were awarded according to the number of books collected. Some children were luckier than others. Agnes Gourley and her friend were given half the Robb library, and became instant Field Marshals.

The war upset routines. The B.B. and C.L.B. were suspended. The Sunday School made its excursions to the Polo Field. The Band closed 'for the duration of the War', which by its calculations lasted 3½ years, for it reconvened in 1943 in time for 'Wings for Victory Week.' In June it was planning route marches, and at the A.G.M.:

One pound of sugar was auctioned and knocked down after very keen bidding to our Highly Esteemed President Mr Thos McConnell. The results of which the Funds of the Band profited by over £3.

The Stormont estate was stripped of its iron railings. All but the ornamental gatework and frontage disappeared, never to be replaced. Castlereagh Council asked the golf club for the use of an outbuilding as a morgue. The Home Guard were given part of the course as a bomb throwing range. The club even took the grave step of rationing the bar to six bottles of whiskey on a Saturday night. Things were clearly getting serious.

It had no less of an impact on the land. Pasture was ploughed, the cultivated area was extended. Oat production doubled, large scale barley and wheat growing began. Grain was planted on the 10th and 11th fairways. They were now so fertile it is said to have grown over 2m high, then fallen over before it could be cut. The club then grazed sheep, to the delight of local gardeners, who gathered their droppings for tomatoes. Part of the Stormont estate was turned into allotments, and potatoes, cabbage and carrots were grown in lazy beds (the ribs of which can still be seen.)

Lives changed too, of course. Over eighty men and women enlisted. Some, like Alec Long of the village and George Hosford of Church Road (who was

Mrs McConnell's geese. As you can see it didn't take Guinness long to get in on the act. (Mrs Johnston)

awarded the George medal for rescuing a man from a burning plane), lost their lives. Others joined part-time organisations like the Auxiliary Fire Service (A.F.S.) led by Davy Kane; the Air Raid Precautions Unit (A.R.P.); the Women's Voluntary Service (W.V.S.); and the Home Guard, the black uniformed Local Defence Volunteers (known as 'the Dundonald army'). It had some forty members ('the aged and the infirm'), and fortunately never saw combat.

The W.V.S. did the military housekeeping. They ran small stores of blankets and rations, and knitted socks and scarves for the troops. A First Aid Unit was set up under Stanley Wright's son Noel (a student doctor). From it sprang a Mobile Gas Decontamination Unit (which drove around in an old Buick lorry fitted with a shower, looking for people to wash with carbolic), and an Anti Mustard Gas Squad, which painted letter boxes with a yellowy paint that changed colour on contact with the deadly gas.

The most active body was probably the A.R.P., which enforced the blackout. It had about 20 members and four or five posts, including one on the golf course and a sandbagged hut on the moat. And while its members were doubtless as dedicated as anyone, it was widely known that its big attractions were the blue serge uniform (considered very dashing), and the chance to play billiards in the presbyterian stables (until the Kirk Session found out and called a halt).

The population doubled or trebled. Canadians, English, Welsh, Poles, Belgians and Americans flooded in. The Rev. McQuitty asked his people to invite servicemen into their homes, and some, such as Hans Woods did. Soldiers attended dances in the Burton Hall and parties in Navvy Row. 'The darkies' on the Stoney Road (black and white G.I.'s were separated), fraternised with the local girls, pushing gum to them through the fences, and the W.A.A.F.'s tried to coax the village's bashful menfolk to their dances at Ardcarn (with mixed success). Soldiers courted and married local girls.

People also mixed through sport. The Home Guard lost 13–0 to an army football team (not bad, considering). What are now the Boy's High football pitches resounded with public school accents, for this is where the English officers played polo, and as a result the field became known as the Polo Field.

The invasion did wonders for business. Service personnel filled the tea rooms and the bars. Mrs Sloane's cafe on the Comber Road was popular with G.I.'s, who would sit over tea and 'baldy cake' until 11.00pm, and then be reluctant to pass the graveyard, after hearing spooky stories about a luminous headstone, and the early death that was supposed to follow seeing it. Cakes and buns were at a premium, and on a Saturday morning there was always a queue outside the Wendy cakeshop. Mabel Jacobs prospered, and the chip-shop did a roaring trade.

The village also managed to make a small contribution to national morale, courtesy of Mrs Sam McConnell's geese. Before the war Mrs McConnell was given a present of geese, but had not had the heart to kill them. Instead she let them do as they pleased, and they became utterly spoilt: when they crossed the road traffic stopped, and if the bar door was shut the gander rapped the window until they were admitted. This picture of them traipsing home appeared in the *Picture Post*.

Enter the dragon
On Easter Tuesday 1941, David Galway and his young cousins were out ploughing when they heard the hum of an engine, and saw a single plane flying

With Belfast turning out ships, tanks, artillary pieces and aircraft parts by the thousand, it is perhaps hardly surprising that the parish briefly found itself in the front line. Dundonald was one of the dozen or so Irish towns and villages to be bombed.

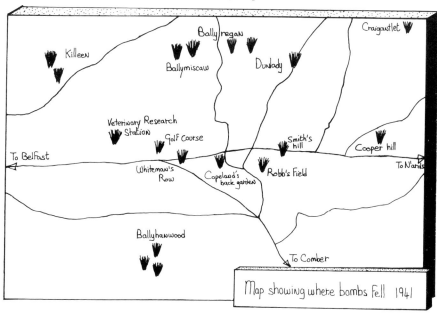

Map showing where bombs fell 1941

high overhead. It was a Junkers 107 reconnaisance plane, a so-called Angel of Death, and its visit heralded Dundonald's worst night of the war.

Around midnight, about 180 Heinkel 111's, Junkers 88's and Dorniers swept in over Divis, flying just above the barrage. Parachute flares lit the sky as if it were day, and almost four hours of slaughter followed.

A number of bombs fell in and around Dundonald. While terrified refugees sang hymns in Dugan's basement, eight or nine exploded on the Cairn Hill. Others landed on the golf links and in soft sand off Church Road. Another went off behind Whiteman's Row. It demolished most of the Row and blew the walls out of a nearby house, leaving the roof on the debris with hardly a slate out of place. A man was killed and several were injured. And so the Luftwaffe knocked out two key economic targets, Sadie M'Dill's grocery, and Mrs M'Nall's wee shop. None of the other bombs caused serious damage.

The next morning Mrs M'Dill, weeping, picked over the pieces of her house. Children inspected the giant craters and examined the charred paper that littered the Holywood Hills. (Stock sheets, and bill-heads from York Street were found in Carrowreagh and on the top of Dunlady.) Friendly fire nearly did as much damage as the Germans. Fire from H.M.S. Furious cut the tops off trees on the Cairn Hill, and a lot of shrapnel fell on the golf course. Other pieces fell on Mooretown Terrace, Robb's yard and McMillan's lane.

In Belfast nearly 900 died. Another 1,500 were injured. There was a spontaneous and uncontrolled exodus from the city. Almost everyone took in refugees. 26 slept on straw and mattresses in the old blacksmith's shop at Robb's Corner. At Ballyoran they slept head to toe on the drawing-room floor, in the sitting room and in two outhouses, and cooked on fires and primus's using pots and pans brought with them. Dozens slept at Millmount, and a baby is said to have been born in its hayshed. Sandy Dickson filled every outhouse with people, and is said to have charged them for the privilege. Cotter opened the Burton Hall, for free. Others, the famous 'ditchers', slept in the fields, pocketing their weekly homeless allowance.

Some stayed for weeks, going in to work and coming out at night. By the summer's end most had drifted back, however some got billeted and stayed for years, sending their children to Dundonald primary.

But this was a move from the frying pan to the fire. Three weeks later Dundonald was attacked again, in the course of another raid on Belfast. Incendiaries fell on Jim Anderson's farm in Dunlady, but he put them out with manure. Others exploded in Ballyhanwood, but no-one was injured. Belfast, however, was mauled. Viewing it from the hills was like watching a giant transistor short-circuit, then ignite. After school the next day, children watched it blazing from the moat and saw the tired, blackened faces of Davy Kane's auxiliary firemen as they returned from town, after fighting the conflagration with everything at their disposal, including the Connswater River.

That summer, somewhat belatedly, the government decided to camouflage Stormont. The Camouflage Office recommended blacking the windows and painting the building green and brown. But the government hoped that the Air Ministry might be persuaded to foot the bill, so it dawdled as a succession of ever more extravagant schemes were brought forward. However, by Septem-

Black Stormont. In the summer of 1941 it was planned to camouflage Stormont by draping it with artificial grass. A scheme to hide it beneath something very like a giant hairnet was also considered. In the end, however, it was painted with bitumen. (P.R.O.N.I.)

ber it was felt that something had to be done urgently, so in lieu of a decision on a more ambitious scheme, Stormont was painted with tar. The Camouflage Office proclaimed this a great success, and declared, with characteristic oiliness, that Stormont 'now melts into the background'.

Equal priority was given to masking the grounds. The Camouflage Office looked with horror at the symmetrical roadways and suggested that all inessential roads be sown with mustard. However it was thought that this would take too much soil, so it was instead decided to spray the roads with tar and cover them with 'cleaned furnace clinkers', at 7/6 per ton. The rows of lime trees were blurred with dumpwire and brushwood. Then there was the delicate matter of Carson's statue. Should it be left out to face the might of the Luftwaffe? The cost of 'bringing in' the great man was estimated at £300, so he was left to take his chances.

The war's end, when it came, was gratefully celebrated with an End of the War dance, a Welcome Home Concert, and a Victory Sports, not to mention many smaller, and far more private celebrations. There was a lot of adjusting too. The military left, and the land was de-requisitioned, however promises to restore fields were not always kept. Farmers auctioned their nissen huts. (Squatters settled in the huts at Coronation Park and on the Comber Road.) Sometimes the forces were reluctant to let go. The golf club wrangled with the Air Ministry for over 20 years before it got back the Ministry's part of the 13th fairway.

Then there was the tricky business of removing Stormont's warpaint. No-one was very sure as to how this could best be done, but it was eventually decided it should be scrubbed clean with wire brushes, like a big tooth.

Relics from the war are now rare in the parish. The makeshift camps have been built over or returned to grass. However, faint traces of distemper can still be found in nooks and crannies at Stormont. The Ballyrogan and Swain's hill bunkers, recognisable by their periscope-like ventilation shafts, can still be explored, and parts of the tracking station (now a cowshed) survive at Ballykeel. Camperdown's crumbling gun emplacements and its concrete arsenal survive. But as with so much else before, in terms of the landscape, it is almost as if the war never happened.

As you were

The next forty years were to see the end of one Dundonald and the building of

Cutting hay on Robb's farm, c.1946. This is now part of the Ballybeen estate. For a while after the war things were pretty much as they had been, and Dundonald's business continued to be farming. (Kathleen Robb)

another.

To put the building into some sort of perspective, before the war four farms or estates were sold for purposes other than farming, but only one was built on. After it at least 15 farms ceased to be worked. All were built on. The green fields went, and the landscape's remaining kinks and foibles were evened out to better carry housing. These were the most far-reaching changes since the plantation, and the losers this time were the 'old residenters', who like the wilde Irishe, gathered in knots and bewailed their disposession.

In 1945, however, most people were blissfully unaware of what was in store. Countryfolk and countrified townies were still in the majority, and though much added to, Dundonald had not quite lost the sense of itself as a country village.

The kernel of the village was now the area around the foot of Church Road, with a small shore running along the Newtownards Road from Laurelvale to the post office. Here lived the likes of 'Boot Stevenson' the roadman, Sammy McNeill, who played the accordian at Legion dances; the Whitemans, whose porch folk sheltered under as they waited for the bus; Harry Mateer, the barman in Tom McConnell's; and lame Minnie Carlton, who lived in the pink, sash-windowed terrace that ran up to the presbyterian church. Polio had left her with a withered arm and impaired speech, but this did not stop her from getting her buttermilk from Kirkwood's every Tuesday, and bringing back a pint for her friends the McDowells. Her useless limbs, tiny beard and dated dress frightened children, who teased her mercilessly and called her a witch.

Davy Kane now managed the post office. He piled everything everywhere, and constantly amazed customers by putting his finger on exactly what he wanted. This was just as well for he smoked an unremitting tobacco called Gallagher's Warhorse, which meant the place 'smelt like a stable', and it was very much in the customer's interest to keep the transaction brief. Davy was also an agent for Brown's the morticians, and would have taken a corpse away at any hour of the day or night, a service for which many were grateful.

After hours, he was a member (and ex-president) of 'The Hooks Club', a select circle who met on Saturdays in McConnell's back kitchen, where under the watchful eye of their president (solemnly attired in a chain of Guinness corks), and with the help of a crate of Guinness and a bottle of whiskey, they chewed over the ills of the world.

No group or family monopolised trade. Meat was had from Miskelly's on the site of the T.S.B. Occasional slip-ups aside (one man remembers complimenting them on their flavourful sausages and reading a few weeks later that they had been prosecuted for doing washing in the sink), they served the district well for over 30 years. Joe Docherty and the ever affable Ernie Boston now ran Fleming and James, competing with Bell's up the road, in the murky, fly-blown hole-in-the-wall that had once been McConnell's spirit grocery. Sammy McKittrick, known as 'Jawblades', mended shoes. There were two bicycle shops, however there was only trade for one so Sammy Johnston also sold 'High Class Confectionary', and his rival Joe Cordner sold models.

Joe Cordner was a 'droll auld boy, . . . a long-headed boyo', (a wit) who besported himself in a soft hat and plus fours. His great loves were bicycles and inventing and he is said to have been the first man to have cycled up the river Bann. He had also addressed himself to the problem of unaided flight, and was widely supposed to have become airborne over Portrush strand, again using pedal power. He lived in Jinny McNeill's dream home by the river, the bungalow she had begun but not had the money to finish. Sam McConnell lived alongside. The Church Road culvert and the river ran between them, and when it flooded each would loudly blame the other for letting the culvert block.

Sam had more to worry about than the river. Because he had married a catholic some of his customers no longer used the bar. The business came near to ruin, giving a bitter twist to the story that when he was asked for something out of the ordinary, Sam would slip out 'to get it from the store', then sprint down to collect it from his brother.

Another business in a gentler and rather more inevitable decline was that of Mabel Jacobs. Her fame, however, had by now spread far and wide, indeed Dr Wright remembers arriving in Melbourne, mentioning where he was from and being greeted with a hearty 'How's the White Knight?' Mabel's regulars aged with her and this led to some curious incidents. Once an ambulance had to be called to attend to a Bangor man. By then a crowd had begun to nosy round, and there was laughter when the man was carried out on a stretcher. This increased when he saw the crowd and asked to be taken back inside. (The ambulancemen had never met such heartless people, and were happy to oblige.) Mabel finally had a fall on the road and was taken, cross and crabbed,

The Beeches, c.1950. It is now part of the Ulster Hospital. (Billy Kirkwood)

to Downpatrick Hospital. She is buried in the churchyard.

Gradually the village lost what remained of its rural character. The pump and the 'wee wall' were removed. Shops replaced houses along the main road. By degrees the 20th century registered its arrival. Electricity, water, and sewage pipes, which had reached the village shortly before the war, were sent up into the hills. Two doctors, Leslie Goldring and Desmond Wright, set up practices in the village, ending seven virtually doctorless decades. The half dozen street lights (switched off during the war) were lit again, (and promptly switched off every night at midnight.)

Dundonald also experienced electricity in its rawer form. One May evening in 1948, not long after John Cruise had locked up the church, lightening struck the tower of St. Elizabeth's, sending one of the spikes crashing through the roof, and blowing out the vestry door. A rain of earth and stones fell, and a woman was knocked over by what was described as a ball of fire. Windows were broken, fuseboxes melted and Mrs Miskelly the butcher's wife fainted at her ironing. The storm was as brief as it was bizarre; it lasted for under five minutes.

Though the village changed fast, the most furious commercial growth was on the Comber Road. Its rise began with the coming of the Co-op. A row of shops was built opposite it in the late 1940s, and along came congenial places like Mrs Smith's sweetshop, where the smallest visitor was made to feel like visiting royalty. For a decade the Comber Road had the stir and the bustle.

The village struck back in the 1960s with the arrival of the Spar and eight new shops. The Comber Road replied with a bigger, brasher supermarket, and another clutch of shops. Not until the brightly lit acres of Wellworths descended on the village like a giant spaceship in 1985, did the village recover its leading place. The division scuttled the prospect of Dundonald developing anything like a town centre.

The Comber Road, (still 'the meadow road' to a dwindling band of old residenters) became built up from the Elk Inn to the station, and a more motley set of houses would be hard to imagine. They ranged from large detached villas through respectable semi's and terraces to one roomed cottages, nissen huts and tiny shacks. Virtually all human life was here. There were Romany gypsies, who lived in brightly painted caravans on the waste ground behind the Orange Hall (and in the Church Road sandpit), squatters, navvies, civil servants, traders like Mrs Brown 'the tick lady', and skilled men such as Thompson the piano tuner, and 'Tattoo Jack' the tattooist, who lived with his wife, a tattooed lady, beside Navvy Row.

The road's most exotic feature was McKee's dam, said to have filled in a night, drowning the quarrying machinery. In summer the dam looked almost Amazonian. Its yellow, cloudy waters were overhung with vegetation, so that even though the rubbish of Dundonald went into it, it retained a certain sinister romance. (Some said it was bottomless, and pearls were said to lie in its murky depths.) It was also the scene of several horrific drownings, the last of them in the 1940s when a boy who had fallen from an overhanging branch got caught in submerged tree roots.

'Straight as a ruler'; Lawrence McMillan of Dundonald on his way to winning the World Ploughing Championship in 1959. (The McMillans)

The road has since lost much of its charm. Two graceless road widenings, the idiotic demolition of Grahamsbridge, the filling in of McKee's dam, the building on the sandpit, the closure of the railway station, the demolition of the manse, the nissen huts, Navvy Row, the wooden house and the blacksmith's cottage (in spite of an adventurous plan to take it to the Folk Museum), have robbed it of much of its interest.

For a time after the war most of Dundonald's old country cottages were still lived in. Mather's mud walled cottage was still occupied, as was the thatched cottage which stood in front of the Ulster Hospital. Mrs McKelvey and her sons Harry and Sam lived in another mud and thatch cottage on the Greengraves Road. Harry would knot ropes for an ounce of tobacco, Mrs McKelvey sewed, Sam trapped hares and all spat as they pleased on the floor. There is a story that Johnny McRoberts once visited the house; seeing something on the pan he sniffed around and asked what was cooking, only to be told 'Nothin'a yours Mr McRoberts'! All loved music, and they had some great sessions courtesy of a wind-up gramophone; old Mrs McKelvey, who liked a drop of whiskey and a pinch of snuff, taking a full part in the proceedings.

Lizzie Bell was another old stalwart. She lived beneath what is now Miller's Forge, in a tiny thatch and tin-roofed cottage, with an old scrub table and a few black crocks, and had gin parties on Sunday nights. These old folk are long gone, and their homes have since been demolished.

'Mrs Hugh Edgar's budgie laid an egg last Saturday'

Socially, the options had widened greatly. Dundonald now had pigeon, airgun, tennis, bowls, darts, badminton and table tennis clubs; cricket, football and athletics teams; the golf club (afloat in whiskey), a ploughing society, the band, the masons; one Black and four Orange lodges – the older lodges having been joined by a junior lodge (The Rising Sons of Dundonald), a ladies lodge, and The Dundonald True Blues – two drama societies (the Moat and Village Players), a Unionist Association, and branches of the British Legion, the Mother's Union, the Woman's Institute and the Business and Professional Woman's Clubs.

Football was played on almost every dry, flat surface, including the Green, and the Rev. McQuitty cannot have been the first presbyterian minister to catch boys playing against the church walls. 'I'm surprised to find you, H____ N____, playing football against God's house', he chided on one occasion, only to be innocently told, 'I'm in goals sir, I'm trying to stop them.'

The older boys played for the Saints or the 43rd. The Saints played on what is now the green in front of Davarr Avenue, and every Saturday their manager Psyche Dempster marked out the pitch with sawdust. The team changed in a tin hut lit by a tilly lamp, and when the game was over the kits were flung onto the floor in a steaming heap, and taken back to the team's real hero, Mrs Dempster, who had them clean by Monday. The cricketers met here too, for leisurely derbys in which townlands like Ballybeen, Ballylisbredan and Ballystockart played teams from the new estates.

At the golf club it was a case of Whiskey Galore. In May 1947, in a spirited reaction to post-war austerity, the club bought £4,000 worth of Irish whiskey. But the whiskey did not sell, so it was taken to an expert for blending. Even this did not move it, and only when the price was cut to 5/- per glass did the problem disappear.

As the evenings drew in the drama societies met to consider their forthcoming productions. Hugh Longridge and Davy Kane produced the Moat players, and their repertoire included country favourites like *The Kye amongst the Corn, Boyd's Shop*, and *Too Young to Marry*. Both companies toured widely, avoiding only the Group Theatre, Belfast, in case their work would attract unflattering comparisons. Their most ambitious venture was an adaption of *Gape Row*, in which the off stage dramas were every bit as interesting as those on stage, for the Whites refused to allow the production, and when they at last relented it was to allow only three performances. These played to a packed Burton Hall. The Village Players disbanded in the late 1940s. The Moat Players folded in the mid 1950s, and a recent attempt to revive them was unsuccessful.

Meantime the Symington band was flourishing. 1946 and 1947 were years of 'unprecedented activity', full of music making and good times. Even so, the

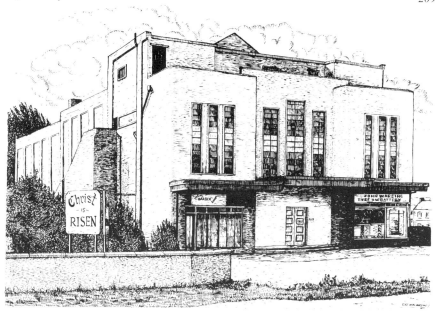

The Metro cinema, victim of a very unfortunate piece of timing. It closed just before Dundonald's great expansion. The interior was extremely plush, probably too plush, and notable for its 'coortin' seats' (doubles).

band found it hard to shake off its self doubts. Success came as a constant surprise, and it is endearing to read in the minutes that such and such a concert proved that the band 'was still a popular local organisation'; sentiments that weren't perhaps easy to feel on a wet Monday evening when nobody had come to rehearsal. A Ladies Committee was formed after the war. Its activities revolutionised the band's finances, and in 1952 the Symington took the plunge and became a Silver Band.

The Unionist Association met in the Orange Hall. This is where prospective party candidates were interrogated, and they needed to be on their mettle. One member would patiently bide his time through the candidate's views on education, etc., and then spring the following questions: 'Are yan Orangeman?', 'Dya attend your lodge regularly?', 'Dya walk on the twelfth?'. For most candidates, however, such questions held few perils. Dundonald remained emphatically unionist, with unionist candidates regularly taking over 90% of the poll, and the only point at issue being the shade of unionism it would support.

This unionism was in the fibre of the place, and in spite of any impression given above, it was not normally bellicose or intrusive. It was simply there. And its presence was reflected in a thousand small ways, for example, the district's only dances were held in the Orange and the Legion Halls, where people swung and jived to the accompaniment of an accordian, or bands like 'the ever popular maestro Mr Tommy Kirk and his Ambassadors.'

There were other more private and more exclusive entertainments. There was the bridge club, held in sixteen of the district's larger houses. There was also an elegant high tea circle, whose membership included the remnants of the parish's gentility: the Miss Robbs, Mrs Greeves, the Miss Jacksons of the Old Dundonald Road, and of course the Miss McRoberts, without whom no such gathering could be considered complete. When the circle met at Ballybeen House, the brass was burnished, the steps were scrubbed, everything had to be just so. On good days the ladies sat on the lawn, and had freshly baked scones served hot on silver trays. For all their apparent formality the teas were relaxed affairs, conducted with great style (hats and gloves were *de rigeur*), and with a minimum of one-upmanship: the ladies were much too sensible for that.

And when the 'Dundonald Pars' column began later that year Reggie Harpur wrote up all its goings on for the *Newtownards Chronicle*. Little escaped his eagle eye: 'I saw a furniture van heading for the Gransha Road the other day', he wrote and immediately set off in hot pursuit, eventually winkling out the news that the Cairnduffs of Moatview had bought a house there, so he published an item wishing them happiness at their new address. Recoveries from sprains and falls were celebrated. Nothing was too small for him to 'slip in' here or 'pop in' there to record it; and when he missed something he could usually be depended upon to make the necessary imaginative leap: 'Mrs Hugh Edgar's budgie laid an egg last Saturday. I am sure it caused excitement among the children.'

The 12th July parade at the foot of Church Road in the 1950s. (David Cruise)

As Reggie was D.M. of The Dundonald True Blues there was no shortage of Orange news. Installation dances got good coverage, as did Unionist party socials, which offered Reggie a chance to get in a friendly dig at Jim Milligan, the Worshipful Master of the rival lodge and 'the biggest blow in the hall'! Worthy tradesmen, such as 'our good friend Mr Thompson', were recommended. Newcomers were welcomed, particularly when they were clearly made of the right stuff. Greeting the arrival of two new families in 1953 Reggie hoped that they would be very happy, and noted with satisfaction that 'both these young men (have) joined the local platoon of the Ulster Special Constabulary', of which he was also a member.

The main force behind the phenomenal growth in organisations was the church. Most of the societies listed above had at least an informal church connection. Many were direct offshoots. In 1961 the Church of Ireland had some eight associated organisations, most of them youth related. The presbyterian church had even more, and of course there was considerable duplication. The drama societies are a case in point. Each congregation had to have its own, and partly as a result, both folded.

Relations between the big two improved greatly with the arrival of Thomas Frizelle as rector in 1951. The key to the improvement lay in his personality. Frizelle was direct, plain spoken and completely without airs. 'He hung his coat on the floor', as the phrase goes, and would have gone to almost any lengths to help his parishioners. One widely known story about him involves his returning to the rectory in his bare feet, because he had given his shoes away earlier that day; and his reputation is such that no-one will confidently deny that it might have happened.

Combined services and joint Sunday School excursions were held as a result of his bridge-building. This may sound like very little, but it would have been unimaginable a few years before. Of course it did not prevent the occasional spot of polite aggro. For a time the Church of Ireland service clashed with the end of the presbyterian Sunday School, and there was chaos on the Green as everyone tried to drive away at the same time. As the presbyterian church lay between them and the road the Church of Ireland people parked their cars at the foot of the Green, where the presbyterians were accustomed to parking. Needless to say, this did not go down well with the Kirk, and had relations been less fraternal there would probably have been a complaint. As it was the matter was settled amicably in the traditional manner (a Church of Ireland climb down.)

'Unconditional surrender to the builders'

During the period 1951–71 some 3,770 houses were built in the Dundonald area. About 320 were put up by the Castlereagh Rural District Council, some 2,420 were built by the Housing Trust, and the remaining thousand or so by private contractors.

Most were contained within some ten estates. The first, Ardcarn, was begun by the Housing Trust in 1951. It was followed by two privately developed estates, Cumberland and Cherryhill, begun in 1952 and finished in 1954, during which time the C.R.D.C. began Moatview, Mawhinney Park, and Coronation Park, built on the site of the wartime camp. After a three year lull these were followed by Wanstead and Brooklands. In the late 1950s Mount Regan Avenue, Ballyregan and Canberra Park were built around Cherryhill, creating a solid block of houses to the north of the village. Houses and bungalows were built along the main roads.

The developers were a very mixed bunch. Cumberland, for example, was mostly built by Lee and Lowry, an ex-breadserver and an ex-baker, who largely learned their trade as they went along. Most of Cherryhill is the work of McCready, a respectable builder who intended to build it using experimental materials, however the first houses of the new type nearly collapsed, so the rest were built along conventional lines.

Not everyone who settled in these houses was new to the district. Brooklands attracted people from Timbertown, and a smattering of country folk. Old residenters like the Whitemans and the Boyds settled in Moatview; and the new council estates inherited Navvy Row's reputation for toughness, hard drinking and mayhem.

Being housed by the council was very different to being housed by the Housing Trust. Whereas the council took in whoever needed housing, the Trust selected its tenants and made sure that they kept its properties up to scratch. Miss Frazer, who collected the rents from Ardcarn, kept the place in cowed subjection. If the rent was not forthcoming when she called, she would be back at 6 o'clock, by which time it was expected that arrangements would have been made; and it is said that they usually were.

All this changed with the advent of the Housing Executive. Trust style paternalism became unacceptable. However, the biggest change came with the advent of public housebuying. One-third of Brooklands and almost half of Moatview was sold, and in many places it is impossible to tell public from private. Ardcarn and Moatview, with their broad greens, have a graciousness completely lacking in the private estates, particularly the shoehorn developments of the 1980s.

All these estates have since become very much part of the fabric of the place, indeed the district has developed so quickly that some now represent aul' dacency itself.

This period also saw the arrival of the district's two big public buildings. In 1956 the Hospital's Authority purchased 'The Beeches' and set about building the new Ulster Hospital for Children and Women. It was built in stages, which

The Ulster Hospital, as seen by Michelle Davies of Euston Street Primary School, Belfast.

gave it a continually half-finished appearance, so that as the successive skeletons of girders rusted there were complaints that it was an eyesore and a disgrace. In 1962, however, the hospital was opened by the Duchess of Gloucester, who though its facade looks like a ransacked chest of drawers, found it in her heart to describe it as a building 'not only of functional excellence but also of distinctive beauty'. It became a general hospital in 1967.

Work on Dundonald House began in 1960, in the grounds of what had been Daniel Blow's house, Primrose Park. (Enough, one imagines, to make that ardent United Irishman turn in his grave.) When it was opened in 1963, this thin, glassy building was one of the biggest office blocks in Northern Ireland, and its statistics are accordingly impressive: over 70,000 tons of earth were moved during its construction, it has 5½ acres of floor space, and accomodates some 1600 civil servants: who dine in 'Belfast's only skyline restaurant, offering staff a dizzy view across the rooftops of the city.' Like Stormont, it is finished in pieces of Portland stone, which were cut and numbered in England and put together on site, in what the *Belfast Telegraph* called 'Ulster's biggest jigsaw'.

The backlash

In September 1960 the *Belfast Telegraph* sent a reporter to what it called 'the great sprawling district known as Dundonald' to ask how it felt about the recent building. Not great, came the reply.

When the building of Ballybeen was proposed in 1960, some of this discontent was translated into action. Two Church Road housewives, Yvonne Friers and Joan Farbus (who were careful to emphasise that they were 'not militant feminists') lodged a petition of 200 signatures with the C.R.D.C. charging it with failing the people of Dundonald by not keeping them informed or giving them any say in the proposed changes. It was fairly meek and mild, but it was a start.

The protest movement combined several strands of thinking. There was an innocent, moral/environmental element, summed up by Mrs Farbus' remark that 'It is wicked to kill the living beauty of the countryside by pouring cement on it.' There was also a strong class element. Many of the protesters were newcomers who had paid a lot of money for their houses and were worried about the likely erosion of property values. The group's opponents seized on this, and the Labour councillor Robert Bingham (who represented Cregagh, and could say what he liked) called the protesters snobs, and dismissed their environmental arguments as a smokescreen. This tactic was effective. The protestors were marginalised and their arguments went largely unanswered.

They fought a civilised, hype-free, unsensational campign. There was no picketing. Nobody lay down in front of J.C.B.s. Meetings were held, a Ratepayer's Association was formed and a committee was set up to co-ordinate opposition. It called for greater public consultation, and registered the 'strongest possible protest' against random building.

Not everyone was against Ballybeen. There was a strong pro-development lobby within the council, and both local councillors, Reginald Taylor-Nobbs and Sally Cuthbertson, favoured the proposed scheme. In January 1962 there was a fiercely contested debate on the question of whether Dundonald should be included in the proposed Belfast Urban Zone. The pro-incorporation (and to some extent pro-development) motion was narrowly defeated.

Realising that Ballybeen could not be halted, the Association attempted to influence its character. And in this they won a small concession. The Housing Trust undertook to make the houses in the buffer zone, Ardnoe Avenue, compatible with those in Church Road, so the protest was not entirely in vain. And it may be worth noting that of all the areas affected by Belfast's resettlement, only Dundonald mounted a sustained campaign of opposition.

Tullycarnet and the 'been

Ballybeen was begun in 1963 and was mostly in place by 1971. Perhaps the most striking thing about it is its size. It is absolutely immense. It consists of some 2,400 dwellings, half of which are houses (of approximately eight types), and a quarter of which are flats, and is the second largest estate in Northern Ireland, and reputedly one of the half dozen biggest in the British Isles. It has a reputation to match. No impressionable newspaper reader would dare set foot in it. They would anticipate a life expectancy of about 10 seconds, and picture it as a decaying, sprawling ghetto where everything that moved got knifed or robbed, or both. However, Ballybeen the housing estate and Ballybeen the legend have very little in common.

The estate's main problem is its vastness. (Ambulances are not able to find emergencies, hearses get lost going to funerals.) The planners undoubtedly have a lot to answer for in this regard, for they anticipated the problem, and in their confidence thought it manageable. In an attempt to encourage neighbourliness they adapted an American style of design called Redburn, which was then fairly novel in the U.K., and grouped the houses into intricate patterns of cul-de-sacs. However, these proved a mixed blessing, and their lifelessness often enhanced people's sense of isolation.

The second important planning mistake was in area of providing amenities. Little attempt was made to cater for people's everyday needs. The Housing Trust created what in effect was a town the size of Comber without churches, banks, pubs, clubs, doctors, dentists, or a proper community centre, and without any variety of shopping.

But the infastructure came. The churches were quickest off the mark: Ballybeen has now five, and as the phrase goes 'a drunk man couldn't fall here but he'd hit the railings of a church.' Schools were built at Carrowreagh and Ballyoran. The council provided a community, an activity, and a woman's centre; and the opening of Wellworths has eased the shopping problem.

Ballybeen was mostly settled from east Belfast, which was then being redeveloped. In came protestants from the Newtownards Road and catholics from Short Strand. The east Belfast connection took time to weaken, and for years Ballybeen, like Tullycarnet, continued to shop, work, drink and worship 'down the road'. Ties have recently begun to loosen, and as Joe McCullough, chairman of the East Ballybeen Resident's Association, puts it, 'we're always talking about down the road, but don't ask us to go back there.'

The estate took a long time to settle. Initially, problems were few, but as the houses rose, wave after wave of new people arrived and left, keeping the place in constant turmoil. For many, Ballybeen was a journey into the unknown. The quiet was eerie. The space was strange. There were prolonged problems of adjustment. While most people tried to make a new start, for some Ballybeen was a sort of transit camp, somewhere to be endured until the contractors had rebuilt the Newtownards Road. Others tried to make a go of it, but missed the hustle and bustle. By the late 1960s about 20% of the estate had moved back down the road.

Just when things were beginning to settle the Troubles arrived and there was a second exodus. Ballybeen was about 20% catholic, and in the early 1970s this group left. Perhaps 4–500 families went – a staggering number. Their places were taken by protestants fleeing west Belfast. Some 100 newly completed houses in the Valley were settled from Ardoyne and Suffolk in a U.D.A. organised squat. There followed a further winnowing out, for perhaps 20% of the newcomers also left. By the mid 1970s, however, the people who lived here were largely those who wanted to. Though some 25 years old Ballybeen has had only ten or twelve settled years.

Though it perhaps seems formless to the outsider, the estate is made up of strongly contrasting regions. The central area (Bute Park, Morven Park, the dismal, shuttered shopping centre, and Ballybeen Square) is the least stable. Its flats, maisonettes and bedsits form an itinerant zone. The Valley lies further east, on what to its imported cityfolk feels like the edge of the known world. It got off to a shaky start, and its reputation is only now beginning to recover. It has the estate's only Resident's Association, notable for several successful environmental campigns, and for its regular 'Jolly Nights'.

Enler Park (which would have been Inler, had the 19th century cartographers been able to understand the local brogue), and Ardnoe Avenue are the oldest and by reputation the most sedate parts of the estate. (Baffled callers ask, 'Where's Ballybeen?') They also have the strongest links with the rest of Dundonald. Since the introduction of home ownership some 400 homes have been sold, and parts of this westerly area are moving rapidly into the private sector. As the estate has matured, it has become better integrated, better balanced (two generation family units have grown up), and more attractive, and it can only be a matter of time before its reputation catches up.

Tullycarnet's story is in many ways similar to that of Ballybeen. The prosperous years have been unsettled, and the settled years have been poor, and characterised by mass unemployment (recently estimated at c.60%). Like Ballybeen, Tullycarnet was mostly settled from east Belfast. 'I saw the shipyard and foundry workers arrive . . . in their thousands', wrote Sam McAughtry, who lived in nearby Cumberland;

They boasted about the new furniture . . . and fittings in their spanking new homes:'That woman of mine has the place carpeted wall to wall,' husbands would say, trying to hide their own pride in three piece suites, colour T.V.s and chandeliers that tinkled when the door opened.

The estate was built between 1964–73 and has some 850 houses and flats. The east of Kinross Avenue came first, and for several months it sat on its own, like a mistake, in the heart of the country. Cattle from Hutchinson's grazed in the

Tullycarnet by Andrew Coombes.

front gardens, and on several occasions the police were called to shoo them off. The rest of Kinross followed in 1965, and building above the road began in the same year.

In many ways Tullycarnet is two places. The Kings Road, which cuts it in half, is a psychological as well as a physical divide. Both Melfort (above the road), and Kinross (below it), have been indifferently served by the planners. Though it has magnificent views over Stormont, Melfort has some 80 poorly heated, split-level houses, arranged in bare, barrack-like rows separated by bald wastes. Kinross has the dreaded sector block, a tenement of 120 dwellings. The block (allegedly chosen from a catalogue) is of the same design as the notorious Divis flats. In spite of a recent face-lift, most of its tenants are reluctant, and while some 140 of Tullycarnet's houses have been sold, none have been sold here.

Meanwhile, private building continued, but on a much reduced scale. Between 1967–9 some 180 houses and bungalows were built at Dunleady Park, Moyra Crescent, Willowvale and Rosepark, and in the grounds of the manse, where 23 houses and a road were crammed into two acres. During the first phase of building, the private-public ratio had been approximately 2–1. During this second phase the ratio was dramatically reversed. For every house built by a private developer, 20 were put up by the public authority, with the result that Dundonald lost its middle class bias almost as soon as it acquired it.

Unfortunately, the village was too small and too meagre a provider to enable the new development to cohere into a town. Little was done to help it do so. The Belfast Urban Area Plan recognised Dundonald as one of thirteen 'townships' (the South African analogy is appropriate, townships were labour pools, places where people slept), but contrary to its avowed aim, did nothing to encourage its independent development.

Dundonald's growth was reckless and anarchic. No great thought was given for the consequences, probably because no-one with influence particularly cared. When the government finally called a halt in 1969 the valley had been transformed. A horizon, the Matthews Stop Line, was drawn around the existing and projected estate boundaries, and building was forbidden beyond it.

As a result, the building of the 1980s has largely been a matter of filling in the spaces. This has led to some grotesque excesses. When the King's Inn closed, Frazer Developments squeezed 41 houses onto the site, some of them so flush with the hill that their tiny gardens rise above their rooftops. 23 sheltered dwellings were built behind the Orange Hall; and when two adjacent houses were demolished, quick as a flash 18 houses and five shops were crammed onto the site. Bungalows mysteriously appear in people's gardens. No spare quarter acre is safe. This catalogue of minor outrages has in a creeping way done more to change Dundonald than the much publicised arrival of the big estates.

In came a crop of new place names, few of which have much to do with Dundonald.[8] Ballybeen is said to owe its place names, (Gleneagles, Inchmarnock, Drumadoon, Craigleith, etc.) to the homesickness of its Scottish architects. Likewise Tullycarnet, where hard, unmusical and historically meaningless street names like Lothian, Govan and Kinross predominate. Private street names err on the lush side. Here it is all grandeur, and pseudo-pastoralism, as for example at Miller's Forge, which evokes the timeless country picture of the miller busy at his anvil.

Ferment and change
The influx sent local institutions reeling. The primary school was swamped with children. In the the early 1950s it had seven classes 'in' and seven 'out' around the Green. It was extended but this proved no more than a stop gap, and by the early 1960s the school was again bursting at the seams. New building was clearly required, and primaries were set up at Carrowreagh (1965), Ballyoran (1970) and Tullycarnet (1972). However the abrupt rise was followed by a sharp fall in numbers and a painful period of contraction followed, culminating in the closure of Ballyoran and the demise of the old national schools at Ballystockart and Ballymiscaw.

A similar thing happened at secondary level. Dundonald acquired its first intermediate in 1967 and as numbers rose it expanded. A grammar school was planned and a site earmarked but fashions changed and the new school was built as a boys' comprehensive. The intermediate became the Girls' High and Dundonald acquired what were designed to be Northern Ireland's first comprehensives. However they never quite got there. When numbers fell the older school closed and the Boys' High went co-educational. It is ironic to note that had the grammar school been built, both schools might still be in action.

The life of the churches was also transformed. The presbyterian congregation rose to a nominal 800 families and in 1964, with the incorporation of eleven new Session members, power passed from the more established families to the newcomers. Today less than a quarter of the members of the Session could be described as members of old Dundonald families.

Mothers and babies outside the Burton Hall, c.1960. The population rose dramatically between the 1950s and early 1970s. (David Cruise)

However the transition was not completely painless, and the tension between old and new expressed itself in some curious ways. In 1966 for example, at the behest of its new members, the Session banned smoking on church premises. This decision went down particularly badly with the members of the men's bowling club, whose members included old timers like Sammy Perry and Tommy Gourley, men who were very partial to a pipe of tobacco. But the matter went deeper. The Gourleys and Perrys were amongst the families that had raised the hall: who did these imports think they were, coming along and telling them how to use it?

The club protested and the matter went to Presbytery. A commission was set up under Dr John Barkley and the smokers hopes rose considerably when, at the commencement of his deliberations, Dr Barkley took out his trusty pipe and tobacco. The commission recommended that smoking be tolerated, and grudgingly, the Session set aside a room ('hardly bigger than a toilet!') for smoking. The smokers were not overjoyed, but they recognised that to push it would be to risk all, so there the matter ended. (An attempt to heal the rift by holding a social evening nearly made matters worse for the moderates and hardliners could not agree on whether the festivities should include non-sacred music, or that arch-corrupter, dancing.)

The balance of the congregation changed in other more subtle ways. When ill health forced the retirement of the Rev. McQuitty in 1956 a new minister was sought. The Hearing Committee did the rounds, but could not agree on who should succeed him. Its fundamentalists wanted Craig of Portadown, and prayed together and canvassed furiously on his behalf. The liberals opposed him and when Craig heard that the call was not unanimous he withdrew his candidacy, and as the crucial vote approached the 'tenters' turned to their second choice, the Rev. Jenkins of Loughgall.

The congregation met in an atmosphere of complete confusion, and voted in the Rev. Jenkins, a result that was something of a fundamentalist coup. However the fundamentalist's position did not become secure until 1964. Most of the elders elected in that year were radical conservatives: the Session took a lurch to the right.

As the fundamentalists extended their authority within the church it gradually became clear that the Rev. Jenkins would not be enough for them. Though he leaned towards fundamentalism Jenkins was not a crusader. He was kind and unassertive and uncomfortable with church politics, and he had a strong and constantly thwarted desire to please and reconcile his congregation. But these qualities were not in vogue. As time passed the fundamentalists came to the view that the situation needed a strong, charismatic figure. In time the Rev. Jenkins moved to Donacloney and in 1975 he was replaced by the Rev. Roy Magee.

By then however a much larger battle was in progress: the campaign to woo the two big estates. The General Assembly's Church Extension Committee took sites in Ballybeen and Tulycarnet and moved in energetic ministers in the hope that new churches might take. These churches were frontier posts: mission halls. They had to overcome not only apathy and irreligion but the efforts of other churches, for the building of the estates was followed by an unseemly evangelical free-for-all, and on Sundays their roads were thick with busses spiriting the faithful back to the Newtownards Road.

Ballybeen took first. Christchurch in Miller's Lane became a fully fledged congregation in 1974, serving some 400 families most of them from Ballybeen, plus the odd refugee from its factious neighbour. Its style is charismatic and it is no coincidence that two of its three ministers have been missionaries.

Tullycarnet, with its smaller catchment area, has had a much more difficult time. In the 1970s the Committee proposed uniting it with high falutin' Knock but Tullycarnet would have none of it, indeed the congregation were so stung by this awful possibility that donations rose by some 27%. Like Dundonald around 1700, Tullycarnet is struggling gamely for independence.

St. Elizabeth's too faced problems of absorbtion, but as it had less of a core of established families it had not the same capacity for conflict. In flowed energy, talent and money. The older families were deluged and the townie takeover was virtually unopposed.

As resources increased, St Elizabeth's embarked on an ambitious programme of new building. An improved Burton hall was built in 1956. Ten years later a big new church was built (in 'Celtic' style) in the shadow of the old at a cost of £80,000, raised mostly in a whelter of jumble sales, beetle drives, raffles and rectory garden parties.

As numbers continued to rise two new parishes were formed, St. Molua's, in the no-man's-land between Dundonald and Knock, and St. Mary's in Ballybeen, where a hut was built on a site bequeathed by Alec Robb. St. Mary's is an unconventional church. Its services are vivid and joyful, as one parishioner put it 'our church isn't like a church.' It took some 600 families and St. Molua's took about 50. This took the pressure off St. Elizabeth's, leaving it with around 800 families.

The immigration broke the presbyterian hold on Dundonald. In 1981, for example, for the first time, the parish contained roughly equal numbers of Anglicans and presbyterians, and presbyterians formed a minority in the big estates. The influx was both good and bad news for the methodist church. It could not, and did not want to ignore its new constituency, yet it was not big enough to set up a daughter church. Its problems were the most acute, and its solution was the most drastic: it moved its entire Dundonald operation to Ballybeen.

The religious options widened. Two baptist churches, two pentecostal churches, several gospel halls, the Assembly of God and the free methodists have all set up here. During the enlightened 1960s there were even plans to build a catholic chapel. Amazingly, the C.R.D.C. did not oppose the application. After a 28 minute discussion in private councillors emerged to tell the waiting press that 'our resolutions in support of Captain O'Neill's bridge building policy are not just sanctimonious humbug'. However the county council advanced various dubious objections and planning permission was refused.

In the course of these changes the natural environment was savaged. Roads were widened and a dual carriageway was laid through the village turning it into a grimier, less companionable place. In 1974 the dual carriageway was carried on to Newtownards. In the process the landscape was completely homogenised: rock was blasted, earth was moved and the old road's fierce plunges were persuaded into gentle curves. The Old Dundonald Road was broadened to Ballyhanwood and Dixon's Hill, the bane of generations of carters, was surgically removed. Bramble hedgerows were uprooted, trees were felled, gardens were shortened, streams were paved. The needs of traffic were put first as a matter of course.

This accompanied a revolution in the local economy. Dundonald became a service/industrial as opposed to an agricultural component of the regional set-up. There was also a revolution in scale. Whereas the biggest pre-war employers had been farmers regularly employing 7 or 8 men, in the 1970s 1450 worked at Rolls Royce, 1600 in Dundonald House and 1200 at the Ulster Hospital. Thousands travelled in and out daily.

Dundonald attracted two multi-nationals. Ulster Hosiery, a subsidiary of Berkshire International, set up in Carrowreagh. At its height the plant employed 300 in the manufacture of 'seam-free stretch panti-hose and stockings'. Rolls Royce built a large, glass faced factory in Carrowreagh. This produced steel components for aircraft engines until the mid 1970s when, in what might be seen as a classic example of the fickle character of muli-national investment, the company thought better and pulled out.

The site did not go to waste. In 1979 it was taken over by Fisher Body, a subsidiary of General Motors (the world's largest manufacturing company), who produce car seat belts, locks and window winders. The company doubled the manufacturing area and now employs about 1000 people, many of them local.

The biggest local paymaster, however, is the state, through the civil service, the Ulster Hospital and more recently, the D.H.S.S. Even by Ulster standards Dundonald is unusually dependent on the state. It is also unusual in that its big concerns mainly employ women, with the result that in many homes, particularly in Ballybeen, women are now the breadwinners.

Just about the only thing that did not expand was the social life, with the result that Dundonald became considered very tame. Still, it had its moments. In 1974 it was planned to have a medieval fair in the Moat Park, the highlight of which would be a 're-enactment' of King John's arrival in 1210. There were to be jugglers, tumblers, a fortune teller, a fire eater and horsebacked jousters (to be bought at great expense from England). Mead, hot chestnuts, pancakes, sheepskins and tallow candles were to be sold from draped stalls under the careful eye of the Ulster Medieval and Historical Society.

King John, in the guise of the suitably bearded Brian Willis of Ballyregan, would arrive on his charger followed by a rabble of footsoldiers (equipped with binlids and broomhandles, and supplied by the Boy's High School). They were to approach from the Stoney Road direction as they had in 1210. Two key scenes would then be enacted: the storming of the moat (which probably didn't happen, but so what) and the theft of King John's soldier's clothes (which probably didn't happen either). Then everyone would tuck into the food. But it didn't quite work out like that. The pageant clashed with the first week of the U.W.C. strike, and was posponed and eventually abandoned.

Troubles

The present Troubles have brought unhappiness to a number of Dundonald families. Five policemen have been killed, and at least nine civilians have died as a result of sectarian and paramilitary feuding.

Some 30 Dundonald men have gone to prison, mostly for posession of firearms, and about 60 rifles etc, have been found in houses fields and garages. Bombs have exploded outside the police station, and there have been innumerable scares and hoaxes; several suspect cars have been blown up, and on the introduction of internment two men from Ballybeen and one from Tullycarnet were were taken to Long Kesh.

During the sectarian 'purifications' of the early 1970s catholics flitted from Ballybeen, Tullycarnet and Ardcarn. The exodus involved perhaps 500 families. Some were petrol bombed, some had their houses stoned or received

Tullycarnet funeral, by Andrew Coombes.

threatening notes, however the vast majority moved because they no longer felt secure, and once the migration began it proved unstoppable. Their places were taken by protestant families leaving catholic areas for the same reasons. Lorries stacked with belongings came and went. Empty houses were opened and taken over.

Vigilante groups began here as elsewhere in 1971, and for several months ran a sort of extreme form of neighbourhood watch scheme. It was a nervous time. The catholic flight left Ballybeen feeling vulnerable to random sectarian attack, and in 1972 parts of Ballybeen aped the Bogside and became 'No-Go' areas. The Square was blocked off for over a week, Davarr Avenue and Drumadoon Drive were closed, and admission was refused to strangers. The barricades came down by arrangement with the start of Operation Motorman.

Though a belated attempt was made to protect Tullycarnet's remaining catholic households from teenage gangs, in general the atmosphere was poisonously sectarian. Sam McAughtry remembers drinking in the Elk Inn when a group of men arrived:

They called the manager, pointed to a member of the bar staff: "Is he a wrong one?" The manager could only nod. The barman, a Catholic who had formed many friendships . . . over the previous two years, took off his apron, threw his jacket over his shoulder, and walked out, white-faced.

McAughtry writes that when the paramilitary Ulster Defence Association was formed in 1971: 'Tullycarnet men well known to (me) threw up permanent and sometimes pensionable jobs, and assumed field rank with the paramilitaries.' Dundonald became an important cog in the U.D.A. machine, providing the organisation with its leader Andy Tyrie of Ballybeen, and a batallion of men, the G.B. batallion (c. 300 men), mostly recruited in local halls and bars.[9]

When the Ulster Worker's Council strike began in May 1974, this group, together with a fringe of older teenagers (who kept the 12–16 year olds in line) enforced it in Dundonald. Barricades went up around Ballybeen and Tullycarnet. The Newtownards and Comber Roads were blocked sporadically, and the Kings Road was cut at Tullycarnet. No-one tried to open the roads. The strikers could hardly believe what they were being let away with, and the mood on the barricades was euphoric.

This was all too much for the chief executive, Brian Faulkner:

I went straight in to the Secretary of State's office (in Stormont Castle) and demanded angrily that something be done to remove all the barricades, but he insisted . . . that roads were in general clear. I ended the argument by taking him to the window and pointing to the barricade at Dundonald House, and in some agitation he hurriedly instructed his officials to have it cleared. Shortly afterwards a bulldozer arrived and pushed the obstruction aside, but an hour or so it was up again at the same spot.

Dundonald was far from unanimous in support of the strike. Large numbers of people attempted to go to work. Queues formed at the barricades on the main roads. Canny drivers got in by the back roads. Bill Maguire, the headmaster of Regent House, Newtownards, took his school's crestfallen Dundonald contingent in over Craigantlet. The Girl's High School walked out, but the U.D.A. didn't want children on the streets, so they were marched back in again.

After initially wavering Ballybeen and Tullycarnet went overwhelmingly pro-strike, but the village and the Comber Road remained equivocal. Many here supported power-sharing. Others had no love for the strike's leaders, and feared that thuggery and lawlessness would follow.

Dissenters had to suffer in silence. Shops and businesses were asked to close. Cecil Carson, however, was able for them: 'Just closing. Just closing', he said, as his visitors appeared, and when they had left again he opened up shop and continued trading. In case anyone missed the point Michael Brooks regaled the village through a loud hailer on the same theme – until he was sent packing by an irate woman passer by, who told him he should be ashamed of himself. Nonetheless, by lunchtime on day two the village and the Comber Road were pretty well at a standstill.

What of industry? Again circumstances varied. The Dundonald U.D.A. closed the Shorts plant in Newtownards. The two big local factories reacted very differently. Rolls Royce shut down at midnight on day one. (Its workforce included L.A.W. committee members, so its response was not in doubt.) Berkshire, staffed by women, carried on working until forcibly closed on day six. (This operation was frought with domestic difficulties. The wife of one U.D.A. man refused to stop working, so he was excused picket duty in case of an embarrassing scene.)

The atmosphere on the big estates was extraordinary. There was much camaraderie and in some areas the strike was supported with passionate intensity. Two strike committees governed, and the estates developed their own seige economies.

In Tullycarnet the procurement system worked beyond its organisers' wildest dreams. Ten tons of coal ('a gift') arrived from Tyrone. Potatoes and vegetables were picked from the fields and sold at cost price from the community centre. People with gas cookers heated food for neighbours. Others cooked on fires, in back gardens. Soup was dispensed from catering urns. Pensioners were brought tea (and some refused it.) 'Essential services' were allowed to open during the afternoon, the shops being 'supervised' to prevent panic buying. Bread and milk supplies were not interrupted. Lorries removed refuse. During week two, when workers became eligible for strike pay the D.H.S.S. operated from Vionville farm. The money slushed about and there was widespread fraud.

In Ballybeen the strike got off to a confused and shaky start. However, when people saw which way the wind was blowing opinion swung, and by day five the strike was pretty solid. Harold Wilson's famous 'spongers' broadcast helped bring the waverers into line. The following morning people wore pieces of sponge on their lapels, and the committee were inundated with offers of support.

If it was the men who enforced the strike, it was the women who sustained it, mainly through U.C.A.G. (the Ulster Community Action Group), the welfare wing of the U.D.A. Pensioners were served with soup, stews, and cups of tea. The church halls served tea and coffee. Bread and milk (from Craigantlet) were

People on their way to the rally at Stormont which followed the resignation of the executive in 1974. (Newtownards Chronicle)

sold at purchase price. The was almost no profiteering. The bins were lifted and the rubbish was disposed of. Workers in emergency services were issued with passes and supplied with petrol. People helped one another with cooking and food, and as the weather was good and the pubs were closed, folk came out to chat and do their gardens.

The Ballybeen barricade was the last to go down around Belfast. The army were told that it would go down at 2.00pm and not before. It did and so the strike here ended with a flourish. From the organiser's point of view all had gone smoothly. Key roads had been blocked, the estates had been supplied, and most importantly the potentially lawless teenage fringe had been kept in check. (This was the era of tartan gangs, such as the Ballybeen Riot Squad and the Ardcarn Boot Boys.)

Unbelievers found the fortnight a trial. The Dundonald section of the *Newtownards Chronicle* called it 'a serious, difficult and for many, frightening time', marked by 'several ugly incidents'. It achieved its aim. The power-sharing executive resigned, and the strike was followed by a huge celebratory rally at Stormont, addressed by the Rev. Dr Paisley.

On the eleventh night the D.U.P. hierarchy, which had more to celebrate than most that summer, held a bonfire party in the hills near Craigantlet. It was an evening rich in symbolism, not all of it intentional. One of its highlights was (what else?) a tug-o-war, and the *Chronicle's* correspondent was there to record it:

> Everyone gathered round while the D.U.P. team took their places opposite the Vanguard team . . . Both teams pulled with all their strength and it seemed as if neither side was gaining any ground when suddenly the rope broke. The roar of laughter from the spectators was deafening, while the 'muscle men' of D.U.P. and Vanguard struggled sheepishly to their feet.

With darkness gathering, Ian Paisley lit an enormous bonfire, crowned by an effigy of Lundy. Lemonade and buns were served, and as the fire spat and sparked the crowd sang Orange favourites, concluding with hymns and the national anthem.

Nothing since has compared with the events of 1974. The barricades rose again in 1977, but this time the 'crisis' was patently synthetic. It did not have the same paramilitary backing and obstructions were promptly cleared. 1982 saw the celebrated incident in which the Secretary of State, Jim Prior, was hissed as he took his seat in Dundonald presbyterian church, at the funeral of the Rev. Robert Bradford. Pictures of him being jostled outside the church were published and broadcast nationally.

In the wake of the Anglo-Irish agreement contingents from Ballybeen and Tullycarnet were prominent in the various seiges of Maryfield, home of the Anglo-Irish secretariat. 22 police families were petrol bombed or threatened from their homes (14 from Tullycarnet). The culprits were mostly 'kids', whom the U.D.A. could have stopped but chose not to.[10]

In February 1986 the *Irish Times* published an article by Sam McAughtry on Tullycarnet's reaction to the agreement. The message came across loud and clear: its denizens (as the paper chose to describe them) were having none of it. McAughtry detected plenty of heat, 'but, so far, no crackle'.

It came. On March 3, 1986, the 'Day of Action' there was a brief re-run of 1974. The roads were blocked at Ardcarn, Ballybeen and Tullycarnet. Businesses and most schools closed. However, apart from some scuffling at Ardcarn, where an unruly crowd barracked police, all was fairly quiet.

B.B.C. cameras arrived in search of sensation, but it was so thin on the ground that they had to make do with a car being kicked at Ardcarn, a protest so inconsequential it was almost touching; and Dundonald again appeared on national television. Unsatisfied, the cameras moved to Stormont. Here a Union Jack had been laid on the ground at the main gate, and traffic was being defied to drive over it. This was more promising, so they waited for something to happen, and recorded the following sorry exchange between a van driver and an overweight, publicity-seeking councillor, the gist of which ran:

> Councillor: Don't you realise what this has done to your freedoms? When will you stand up and fight for your country?
> Van driver: I fought for it during the war. What did you do? (Silence.)

This too was broadcast to an uncomprehending nation.

The real mischief began after dark when a police family was intimidated, and Dundonald's makeshift chapel was burned down. The campaign continued with a string of protest meetings held by various Unionist groupings, and an intensive fly-posting campaign. In 1986 almost every lamp post, pillar box and telephone kiosk in Dundonald carried an 'Ulster says No' poster, in glorious red, white and blue; followed by an 'Ulster still says No' poster several months later. This met with an equally strong reaction, and in the 1987 council by-election many people repudiated the events of the previous 18 months by registering a 44% vote for the Alliance Party.

Dundonald's Disneyland

The Dundonald International Ice Bowl, rather like, say, Knock International Airport (though the comparison might not be welcome), is very much a result of one man's vision and commitment, and like all such projects something of a triumph over the conventional wisdom. The person in question is of course Peter Robinson M.P., mayor of Castlereagh, deputy leader of the D.U.P. and since 1984 a resident of Dundonald.

The saga of the Ice Bowl (or rink to its early opponents) began when Castlereagh Borough Council decided to build a recreational centre at Dundonald. The obvious, almost automatic option was to put up a leisure centre, but the council had important practical and philosophic difficulties with this idea. Leisure centres are unglamorous loss makers, and Castlereagh Council, a very forward-looking body,[11] was then ripe for a prestige project. The idea of setting up something so routine and financially unattractive went right against the grain. In particular the prospect was inimical to the ruling D.U.P. group, and largely on their initiative the council decided it would go for something more experimental.

When the plans were at a formative stage Peter Robinson visited the United States, touring pleasure parks and speaking to businessmen involved in the leisure industry. The visit was to play a critical part in giving the scheme its final shape. Shortly after his return the council announced imaginative plans for an American-style theme park, which as the borough already possessed a Robinson Centre, was to be called the Dundonald International Ice Bowl.

As well as an ice rink the complex was to include a fairground, a 3D theatre, bowling alleys, a turn of the century Ulster street, a grass ski slope, an assault course, log cabins for tourists, a lake, a mini golf course, activity trails and sports pitches. There was even talk of reconstructing the Ballyhanwood cashel. The scheme had something for everyone. One paper called it Dundonald's Disneyland. The bill was estimated at a cool £4.8 million, the price of a top grade leisure centre.

The D.U.P.'s job now was to sell the idea to the council and the electorate. The Official Unionists and the Alliance Party opposed the plan. Torville and Dean were then all the rage and when news came in that Belfast and Bangor also planned to build rinks many councillors took cold feet. However, at the end of the day their attitude was irrelevant, the D.U.P. had an outright majority and the plan was railroaded through.

The electorate were similarly blitzed. Brochures explaining the 'Low Cost and Logic' of the plan were sent to every home in the borough. A cuddly ice bowl character (called Donald) toured the schools winning children. Astonish-

Artist's impression of activity around the Ice Bowl, when the theme park is in place.
(C.R.D.C.)

ing accounts of the likely impact on the local economy appeared. Was
Dundonald about to replace the Giant's Causeway as the province's number
one tourist attraction? You could certainly be forgiven for thinking so. As the
East Belfast News put it:

The future looks rosy for the people of Castlereagh for tourism figures are set to rocket
following the completion of the council's impressive Ice Bowl and Leisure Park and
unemployment in the area will plummet.

The wild speculation went uncountered. The cautious were kill-joys. The
council's attitude was upbeat: 'We expect to be inundated with visitors', said
one official, whose optimism was based on some scarcely scientific market
research, the results of which were not published. And this is about as much as
the public were told. A call for a referendum on the matter was ignored. There
was no public debate. There was no time for one: the first sod was cut within
three months of the plan's announcement.

Work proceeded at a furious pace and the Ice Bowl (known in some quarters
as 'Robinson's folly') was opened in September 1986, less than ten months after
construction started. This ended the debate. The dissenting parties acknowledged the Ice Bowl as a *fait accompli* and gave it their backing.

In the meantime, however, the scheme received several blows. The government decided not to grant aid it. An application to the European Regional
Development Fund was also declined. The project had to be pared down and
temporarily lost most of its exotic features. In March 1986 an unprecedented
rise in the rates was announced. However the confusion resulting from the

council boycott, and uncertainty as to how much of this was due to the Ice Bowl meant that the rise was less damaging than it might have been. Work continued. (Even this had important ramifications. The fact that Ice Bowl business continued to be conducted irked councillors elsewhere and hastened the end of the province-wide boycott . .)

The strangest twist in the saga, however, came in July 1986 when in order to preserve the 'serenity and peace of the traditional Ulster Sunday' Alderman William Ward proposed that the Ice Bowl be closed on the Sabbath. This put the cat among the pigeons. Sunday was one of the Bowl's busiest days, and it was estimated that closure would add 8p to the rates. The proposal was acutely embarrassing to the priest-ridden D.U.P., which had an instant attack of moderation, and suddenly became very particular about not forcing its Sabbatarian views on other people.

After a three hour debate and much professing of christianity, Alderman Ward's motion was rejected in favour of an ammendment promising to hold a referendum on Sunday opening if 25% of the electorate asked for one. This new-found interest in the wishes of the ratepayers sat ill with the council's earlier, cynical refusal to give subject a proper airing, a point not lost on the residents of the borough.

The Rev. Roy Magee championed the cause of Sunday closure and sent petition sheets to every church and mission hall in the borough. Addie Morrow of Ballyhanwood, the deputy leader of the Alliance Party, led the seven day openers. Though the 25% figure was widely regarded as unreachable, the quota was matched and a referendum now seems likely.

In the meantime the Ice Bowl flourished. It was imaginatively marketed and drew almost 750,000 visitors in its first year. The project received another fillip in 1987 when the E.E.C. offered 50% funding. Time will tell whether its popularity will endure, but at the moment the Ice Bowl shows every sign of confounding its critics.

'The most objectionable people in Ireland'

In May 1987 the Department of the Environment published a new draft Belfast Urban Area plan. The proposals came in an elegantly vacuous booklet, full of pleasant pictures and completely lacking in hard information. It was an astonishing document. Even the Department's Community Technical Aid unit were moved to declare that it 'does not constitute a document upon which . . . the public may base an informed response.' Its sub-text was clear, and more than a little insulting: 'Relax', it said 'We're nice guys. Leave it to us, we know what we're doing.'

The reality alas, was rather different. The plan was in many ways a profoundly backward looking document, based on ideas which many planners, particularly across the water, would consider to be discredited and out of date. It contained only one genuinely innovative feature, the proposal for the Laganside. The rest was the familiar story of precious areas of green belt being given to developers.

The proposals relating to Dundonald were particularly alarming. The valley was to be turned into a giant building site. Housing was to be allowed to Quarry

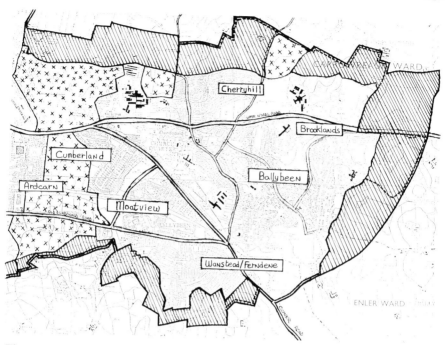

The area zoned for development in the draft version of the 1987 Belfast Urban Area Plan. If the proposals are enacted Dundonald will almost double in size.

Corner and up the hills to above Dunlady House. Furthermore, it became clear that the land to be 'rezoned', i.e. turned into mock Georgian villas, had been chosen in a slapdash, arbitrary way, taking very little account of the local geography, and using environmental standards far below those set by Matthews. Prominent drumlins were to built over. Six historical sites, including the Carrowreagh ring barrow, were to disappear. Dundonald's few remaining unspoilt roads were to be replaced by dismal access roads. But worst, all this would occur not to meet genuine social need, but to satisfy the demands of speculative builders, whose input into the plan remains one of the most intriguing and deeply mysterious aspects of the whole ill thought out saga.

The plans met with great hostility. On July 28th a protest meeting was held in the Burton Hall. The packed hall heard Sam Noble call for a complete revision of the plan. Dundonald's dead were summoned in its defence. Mr Noble outlined Dundonald's history of protest, going back to the crooked road campaign of the 1750s, and there was laughter when he described Dundonalders as 'the most objectionable people in Ireland'. It was decided to form a Green Belt Association to fight the proposals, and Mr Noble was elected chairman.

The Association published articles, set up support groups in the estates, and floated the idea of drafting an alternative urban plan based on holding the stop line. Posters and car stickers were published, and their efforts were complemented by the work of the Dundonald Community Association and the East Ballybeen Resident's Association, both of which firmly opposed the plan.

This is one tale, however, which it is not possible to follow to an end. Looking backwards, it would now seem that Dundonald's inclusion in the Belfast Urban Area Zone in the 1960s was extremely unfortunate, for it has been treated as something of a dumping ground, and while much has been said about preserving Belfast's fine setting, no acknowledgement has been made of Dundonald's, which is in its way equally splendid. It would be a tragedy if Dundonald were to be handed over to the profiteers. The mistake would be unrectifiable, and we can only hope, for the sake of our children and their children, that the Green Belt campaign is successful.

Appendix 1

Presbyterian ministers

1645–70 Thomas Peebles
1670–78 Gilbert Kennedy
1678–1702 Thomas Cobham
1709–48 James Stewart
1754–58 James Hamilton
1761–65 William Ray
1766–71 Hugh Smith
1772–1814 James Caldwell
1810–34 William Finlay
1835–42 William Graham
1843–91 Edward Thompson Martin
1883–1930 James Bingham
1927–58 James A. McQuitty
1957–74 Ian Alexander Jenkins
1975- Roy J. Magee

Church of Ireland rectors

1619-? John Lowthian (Leatham)
1634-? John Kynier
1636-? James Hamilton
1668-? John Fineau
1670-? William English
1676-? James Hamilton
1713-? James Hamilton
1730-? Bernard Ward
1758–66 Edmund Leslie
1766–1810 Jacob Hazlett
1810–51 Roger Moore Dillon
1851–80 Andrew Cleland
1880–90 Andrew Thomas Farrell
1890–1913 Robert White
1913–22 Joseph Grundy Burton
1922–51 John Beresford Cotter
1951–80 Thomas H. Frizelle
1980- Eric Crooks

Appendix 2

Townlands
Dundonald parish
(Showing present and 17th century spellings; O'Donovan: John O'Donovan's 1833 translation.)

Ballybeen (1623, Ballebeine): the town of the peaks.
Ballylisbredan (1644, Ballelisdrumbraden): the town of the fort of the salmon.
Ballymiscaw (1623, Ballelisnescra *alias* Ballehugh): the town of the fort of the whitethorn tree, or the town of Nasc's fort.
Ballyoran (1620, Balliorane): the town of the cold spring.
Ballyrainey (1644, Ballenerany): the town of the point.
Ballyregan (1620, Ballinregin *alias* Ballinregny): O'Regan's town.
Carrowreagh (1605, Balleinecarrowreagh; also associated with Carow-Kilnevagh: the quarter of the church of the ravens): the gray quarter.
Castlebeg (1623, Ballecaslanbeg): the little cashel
Church Quarter (1644, Balledundonell: the town of Domnal's fort).
Dunlady (1333, Dunleth; 1630, Balledimlady; coll. Dunladdie): the fort at the fork of the rivers.
Killeen: the little glen.
Unicarval (1623, Ballewynnicarwell *alias* Ballemonycarwell): the town of the bog of the sacred tree; O'Donovan: O'Carroll's pillar

Neighbouring townlands
Ballycloghan (Knock): the town of the stepping stones.

Ballyloghan (Comber): the town of the stepping stones.
Ballyhanwood: de Hanwude's town.
Ballymagan: O'Mahony's town
Ballymaglaff: unknown.
Ballymagreehan: the town of the summer house.
Ballyrogan: O'Regan's town.
Ballyrussell: de Rossal's town.
Ballyskeagh: the town of the whitethorn tree.
Ballystockart: the town of the high stook.
Craigantlet: the rocky hill of the plague grave.
Gilnahirk: unknown
Gortgrib: unknown.
Greengraves: (nee Ballycloughtogal: the town of the raised stone, or the stone of the
   strangers) Grainne's grave, or the sunny thicket.
Killarn: the church of the sloes.
Mount Alexander: Mount Alexander, after Mount Alexander house.
Tullycarnet: the field of the little cairn of stones.

Appendix 3

The trial of Henry Ferguson of Ballyrogan, farmer.

The 1798 rebellion was followed by a purge. The following is the record of one of the
numerous trials conducted in Newtownards.
CHARGE: Acting as a Traitor & Rebel and endeavouring to excite Treason &
Rebellion in Ireland.
PROSECUTION: Advocate John Cleland.

Witness 1: *Samuel McMeekan of Killarn, mason* Saw Ferguson commanding a large
party of rebels assembled in Ballyskeagh, Sunday, June 10th. CONTRADICTS
HIMSELF, EVIDENCE DISMISSED.
Witness 2: *Samuel McKann of Ballycullen, mason* Equivocates, can identify Ferguson,
but not sure if he saw him bear arms.
Witness 3: *Michael Campbell of Ballyalton, stonecutter* Saw Ferguson between
Cairngaver & Conlig on June 10th, with a great many armed men. Heard him issue
commands like 'Shoulder your pikes'.
Witness 4: *William Logan of Ballycullen, labourer* Considered Ferguson his leader. Saw
him with a sword at Conlig and marched with him to Ballynahinch.
Witness 5: *William Wallace of Ballycullen, labourer* Saw Ferguson at Cairngaver with
numerous armed men, Sunday, June 10th. Ferguson marched them to Ballynahinch
Witness 6: *Isaac Fenwick, member of the York Fencibles* Taken prisoner on the morning
of June 10th and marched to Conlig. Says Ferguson was a company commander.

DEFENCE: Prisoner throws himself on the mercy of the court.
VERDICT: Guilty.
SENTENCE: To be transported to New South Wales.

Notes

Chapter three

1. The Irish Mesolithic (middle stone age) is usually thought of in two parts, the Early Mesolithic, (c.7,000–6,300 b.c.), when sophisticated, high-tech tools were the norm; and the Later Mesolithic (c.5,800–3,500 b.c.), when people went in for bigger, cruder tools and weapons. In between comes a mysterious 500 year blank. No sites used during it have yet been uncovered, and as a result it has been suggested that the last true Irishman became extinct around 6,000 b.c.

Chapter four

1. Two of them are in the townland of Ballygraffan, Comber. However one of these is collapsed, and the other is barely recognisable as a dolmen. There seem to have been at least two more: there is strong evidence for a dolmen on Scrabo, which seems to have been destroyed around 1854; and Knox (p354) mentions 'Massive stones, evidently the remains of what was once a cromlech', in the graveyard of the former parish church at Knock.

Chapter seven

1. There may have been lands attached to the chapel. Gortgrib and large parts of Ballyhanwood were in church hands at the time of the disestablishment. If it had lands during the Early Christian period it would also have had tenants (manaig) to maintain it. The chapel at Castlebeg may not have been so fortunate. If it had developed, say, a hole in the roof, its bishop (if such he was) would have had to call on help from one of the nearby ranches.

2. The origins of the Ui or Hy-Blathmac are unclear. Likewise the root of their name. Reeves suggests that it is a contraction of 'baile ata', the town of the ford. O'Laverty, evidently unimpressed, suggests that they are descended from Blathmac, a 7th century king of Uladh.

3. This may once have been a royal residence. The 1620 Letters Patent identify it as Ballisnesca, which may translate as the town of the fort of Nasc or Nesc, a 6th century petty king or noble, and the father of Laisren, who founded the monastery at Holywood.

4. There has long been a supply of stones on the hill. (There is a story that the 17th century rectory stood near the church, and was surrounded by a walled garden, the remains of which can be seen near the primary school gates. One of the cottages that stood here until recently had a long drystone wall to the rear.) Even so, this seems a strange claim.

5. The name Dundonald has only recently become fixed. En route it has had Latin, Irish and Scottish elements. Originally it was probably 'Dundonnell' or 'Ballydundonnel', acquiring its final 'd' when it was first written down in the 12th century. However its people would have continued to call it 'Dundon(n)el', as it appears on the 1625 maps. As there was virtually nothing but a church here in 1600, the planters came to know it as 'Kirkdonnel', or 'Curdonnel' in everyday speech. By 1800 'Dun' had displaced 'Kirk', and the Scots 'Donald' had replaced the Irish 'Domhnall'. By this quirk the final 'd' returned, giving the name its modern form.

Chapter eight

1. According to tradition John tied his horse to an elm tree (which grew near what are now the village traffic lights), and watched his men storm the motte. Afterwards they are supposed to have had their clothes stolen while bathing in a nearby stream.

2. At the time of the Dissolution the townlands of Ballyoran, Ballylisbredan, Ballyrainey and Unicarval were grouped into a mini-parish called the Rectory of

Ballyoran. Its boundary may be that of the Norman estate.

3. Roger probably lived here. He and Richard de Dundoenald (who had fought together, and would have known one another well) may have been neighbours.

4. Glasscock (*Irish Geographical Studies*, p165) tentatively associated two rectangular sites in Ballymaglaff with the Normans, but these have since been found to be clipped raths.

Chapter nine

1. Cusacke adds that 'an honest companye of horsemen would doe much good for the quyett and staye of the countrye there about', implying that Hugh had difficulty in keeping the peace.

2. Smith was one of England's leading intellectuals. He had been much influenced by the Utopian ideas of Sir Thomas More and planned to found a model community here. His biographer characterised the locals as 'mere Irish or Irish Scots and natural haters of the English'.

Chapter ten

1. Salary as quoted in Hamilton's will of 1616. The true figure may have been lower. The 1657 Commission of Enquiry records the rector's income as £4 in 1640 and 'about the same' in 1657.

2. This date is uncertain. The 18th century plaque on the church tower reads 'ERECTED MDCXXIV', however the 1625/6 map shops the church as roofless, as per the 1622 Visitation. Church histories use the date 1634, a convention followed here.

3. This force cannot, initially, have inspired confidence. The *Hamilton Manuscripts* describe it as weakened by 'unseasonable Jealousies', and a chronic shortage of arms.

4. Peebles was Clerk to Ireland's first Presbytery. Adair described him as 'a man learned and faithful, eminent in the languages and history'. He may also have been a little hot tempered. Adair writes that the Presbytery's records were lost through his 'tossings and distemper'.

5. He is said to have travelled along the Stoney Road. Marshall says that the road, (which he says was known as 'King John's road' in Norman times, and 'the monk's road' under the O'Neills, when it linked religious houses in Holywood and Comber), then became known as 'the minister's road'.

6. Though well-born and connected (Hamilton was a nephew of Claneboy, and his wife was either a niece or daughter of Bishop Echlin) he was clearly no spineless placeman. The *Hamilton Manuscripts* describe him as 'bred in the University learning; a man of good parts... and temper... a peaceable man, very civil to all'.

7. This is a guess. Uncertainty as to what the 'Census' counted makes estimates based on it somewhat unreliable.

8. The townlands do not quite constitute Dundonald as we know it. Unicarval is missing. Ballyrussell is now part of Comber, however its inclusion is interesting, as several other sources name it as part of Dundonald. On a similar theme, the Raven maps show Ballymiscaw to be two townlands, Lisneskeagh and Bally Clohan Upper, suggesting that the parish contains not 11¼ but 12¼ townlands. Perhaps even 13¼, for Carrowreagh may also be two townlands, Carrowreagh and Carrowcallyduffe, a townland name which also falls out of use during the 17th century. Early 17th century sources show the district's townland base to have been relatively fluid.

9. Ross is as likely to have lived in Killarn. The 1663 Subsidy Roll mentions a John Rosse of Kilcarne.

10. On a wider scale, community relations seem to have been less than cordial. In 1610 Chichester wrote that the Irish 'hate the Scottyshe deadly', however nature took its course and the Session Book records some four marriages between the bearers of Scots and Irish surnames. This animosity was if anything exceeded by the warmth of feeling

between Anglicans and presbyterians, or at least between their representatives. In 1619 William Lithgow lampooned the 'warbling mouthes (and) empty sculles' of the Anglican clergy. Chichester in turn deemed the Scots 'hot-spirited and very griping'. The extent to which these feelings were general is not clear. Latimer writes that Peebles' successor Gilbert Kennedy was at one point reduced to preaching 'in the glens near Comber by star-light', to avoid the military, however on what may be a reconcilatory note McQuitty mentions that he was eventually buried in the aisle of the parish church.

11. Unfortunately the Session Book contains only one page of Session business (more fornication). Thereafter the minutes were entered in another volume, which, alas, has been lost.

12. This note issued to a couple moving to Carnmoney is typical:

> Dundonald. Aprile 8th, 1725: That David Cook and Margaret George his wife were orderly persons while with us and were... free of scandal and Church censure. All of which are certified by me. Jas. Stuart.

13. Cobham is believed to have fled to Scotland, however McQuitty mentions his having been in Derry at the time of the seige.

14. Only one piece of 'folklore' from the period survives. King Billy is sid to have spent a night in a cottage that stood below Dunlady House on the old road to Belfast. This cottage was rather disloyally demolished in 1985.

15. These include the interesting observation that Comber had 'hitherto peaceably suffered Dundonald to enjoy Balyrussel tho it lies very near the meeting house of Comber (it does not), and its inhabitants are in other respects members of the parish of Comber.'

16. To an extent the village made its own adjustment. By the mid 18th century it had detached itself from the motte and crept down to the shelter of the meeting house.

17. This 'spaw well' was by all account an extraordinary phenomenon. In his *Briefe Description of the County of Antrim* (1683), Dobbs writes that it was:

> discovered by one Gregg, a presbyterian minister in a dream,.... and for some years after it was frequented by multitudes of people some forty or fifty miles off, and the water carried some ten or fifteen miles to people who were not able to travel, for all sorts of distempers, and many people received ease and benefit by it – at least thought so; but now it is little used, either by reason it is common, or as some say the man's ground where it is, being oppressed with the people and horses that in the Summer time lay there day and night, it is enclosed as they have not the freedom to come to it.

It appears on the county map of 1743.

18. The roadway, a magnificent example of its type, ran from Short Strand over the hills to Newtown, running like a rollercoaster up hill and down dale almost without deviation or regard for gradient. The desolate, efficient dual carriageway which replaced it follows a sanitised version of the same route.

19. This in spite of the departure of certain families to form a congregation at Gilnahirk. Caldwell apparently possessed a 'most amiable and engaging gentleness of manner' On his death in 1814 he is described as 'an Israelite indeed in whom there is no guile'.

20. Their relationship seems to have been affectionate. In his will Blow left the indigent Caldwell ten guineas 'to purchace a suit of mourning'.

21. They were not the first residents of Dunlady. Its earliest occupant may have been the John Hamilton of Ballydunladie, mentioned in the 1663 Subsidy Roll. He seems to have been succeeded by the Archibald Hamilton who appears as owner of the townland in the 1670/81 Rent Rolls, paying a nominal rent if £1 p.a. However the first person who can be unequivocally associated with the house is 'John Hamilton of Dunlady, gent',

who left Dunlady to his youngest son Gilbert in 1698. The estate passed out of the family shortly afterwards, for reasons unknown. The first storey of the house is said to contain a stone inscribed 'R Lambert 1709'. Dunlady House may have been raised or rebuilt in that year.

22. The parish had at least three turf bogs.

who left Dunlady to youngest son Gilbert in 1698. The estate passed out of the family shortly afterwards, for reasons unknown. The first storey of the house is said to contain a stone inscribed 'R Lambert 1709'. Dunlady House may have been raised or rebuilt in that year. 22. The parish had at least three turf bogs.

23. Allybrook House, the village's oldest dwelling, stands behind the bookkeeper's at the entrance to Wellworth's. In the early 18th century it was a pleasant country house, and the hub of a prosperous 130 acre farm. During the last century it was the home of Mrs Dillon, the rector's widow. Allybrook was last occupied by Mabel Jacobs, 'the White Knight'.

24. Dundonald was on the fringe of the windmilling region. This centred on the Ards peninsula, where there was little water power.

25. The murder appalled the district. The Newtownards and Comber Cavalry, of which Cumming was a member, pledged a prodigious 320 guinea reward for the capture of the killers.

26. Innkeeper Hamilton Thompson died in 1813, 'in the happy enjoyment of an approving conscience.'

27. The government was better informed about the rebellion than most of the rebels. Its principal agent in these parts was the rector of Newtownards, John Cleland, who seems to have run a network of spies.

28. Dundonald's casualties are unknown, however Ballywalter may provide a useful analogy. According to the *Freeman's Journal* this 'trifling village' (another trifling village) had 9 men killed and 13 wounded.

Chapter eleven

1. From 1845 on the record includes a list of father's occupations. This shows the church to have been made up of all classes. The listed fathers were labourers, farmers, servants, grooms, coachmen, weavers, carpenters, roadmen, blacksmiths, gentlemen, merchants and millers, and included a flax dresser, a quarryman, a policeman and a shepherd, Samuel Graham of Carrowreagh.

2. One of Ireland's first horseless carriages is said to have been invented to get round the toll. 'The Bullock Wagon', invented by Bradshaw of Milecross, is said to have been partly pulled by cattle and partly driven by steam, which escaped through a chimney. Bradshaw had studied the toll schedule and was sure that his creation was untaxable; however he was turned back at the bridgehead and the schedule was made 'more full'.

3. In attacking Cleland, Byrne may have had the object of demonstrating that the very ground the hated Stormont parliament stood on was somehow deeply tainted.

4. There were alterations. The 1758 road was broadened and bad hills were avoided at Brooklands and the village, where the road was cut along its present line. This paved the way for the building of Gape Row.

5. These events have two curious postscripts. On Samuel's death it was realised that the family had no likeness of him, so a sculptor was fetched, and a cast taken of his head. A marble bust was made and the cast was forgotten. However, during the rebuilding of the 1850s Barney Telford accidentally came on the life-like, whiskered mould in the basement, whereon he had the fright of his life.

It is said within the Cleland family that Eliza had a premonition of disaster that morning, and begged Samuel not to go out.

6. David Gordon was also the inspiration behind the founding of the Belfast Banking

Company (1808), which went on to become the Northern Bank. In its early days it was known as 'Gordon & Co.'; and it is interesting to think that much of the planning that preceeded its launch was probably undertaken at Summerfield.

7. The origin of Gape Row (or the White Row) is unclear, however it would seem to have been built by Cleland around 1815. It was squeezed in between the road and the hill, as with a shoehorn, because this was the only point near the village at which his land bordered the main road. Though the Row became a symbol of 'Old Dundonald', like the 19th century village as a whole, it was in fact a young and relatively fleeting feature on the landscape

8. Probably the oldest of these stood on the old road to Newtown near Quarry Corner. It was knocked down around 1900. There is also said to have been an inn near the Old Mill Kennels. McQuitty (1932) mentions an 'old Inn called "the Dolphin"' opposite Summerfield, however this had yet to be built.

9. The Cummings were the last to go. When they lost Unicarval in the late 1820s it passed to James Ralph, an old batchelor who had a tannery in Comber. He tried to leave it to a local doctor, John Allen, but various remote relations came out of the woodwork and once again Unicarval became the subject of a celebrated court case.

While the case took in Allen's relationship with Ralph (which was strange to say the least), it hinged on whether or not Ralph was sane enough to make a will. The prosecution asserted that he was far from it. He was, they declared, 'an unaccountable being', a violent, painfully shy man who read the bible compulsively and was very vain when sober. This was only the beginning. They also contended that he had 'strange delusions about women, and fancied every pretty woman who looked at him was in love with him':

> This was harmless – but he had other delusions of a wicked and vicious character; he actually believed that every woman in Comber from fifteen to sixty, except his own mother and an old maiden servant was a prostitute, and that every man and woman in it had a certain disgusting malady. He also laboured under delusions respecting tombs; he had an apprehension that the old church of Comber might fall, and *break the bones of his brothers*, and prevent them from getting out *at the day of judgement*

It was decided that Ralph's mind was probably sound, and the Allens kept Unicarval until about 1930, building two fine stone yards and greatly adding to the farm. The Allens were Comber people and with their arrival the southern tip of the parish effectively became a part of Comber.

10. It provided much needed work, and local farmers are said to have hired out their carts for carrying soil. On the debit side, the disruption is said to have cost Dundonald two of its standing stones.

11. Whatever the politics, by the 1870s Dundonald had one of the lowest illiteracy rates in the county (7.4%, 5+ pop. 1871).

12. Brown's *Ireland in Fiction* (1919) remarks that her characters are 'drawn from a rather uninspiring and unsympathetic type of Ulster folk.'

13. *The Year of Grace*. Parts of Givan's narrative were found so gross that they were omitted from the second edition.

14. This anecdotal view is to an extent supported by the following extract from a letter sent to Stormont in 1870 by a tenant who had emigrated to Pittsburg:

> My dear and beloved Sur Mr Cleand – We landed all well hoping theses fue lines will find your oner and her ledship In good heth and all the her litel wans.
>
> We trust that the yung Ere is in good heth and All the femely We trust that he will be as good til the tenens as his forefathers Was We hope god Will bless you and your femely

15. He was greatly admired in the Lindsay household, Francis McRoberts named his

seventh daughter Catherine Gladstone and Tom Morrow hung a picture of the great man in the hall.

16. As a result, when Belfast spilled out along the valley floor, it pushed out long established families, and much of Dundonald's folklore was lost.

17. John Rainey, the last Dundonalder to have been hired at a hiring fair, died earlier this year at the age of 92. He had taken his 'half a crown of earl's' at the age of 16 and gone to work at Killinchy; however he did not much like the look of his master, and ran away.

18. There were at least two other, smaller *Dundonald's*. One was a two-decked barque and the other a steamer. Neither can with certainty be associated with Dundonald, County Down.

19. There was no comparable Anglican outgrowth, indeed with the closure of the Church Quarter School, the parish church ceased to have any out organisations.

Chapter twelve

1. McKibbin was one of a dwindling band of smiths. Teddy Young's smithy, behind the Central Inn, closed around 1900. Perry's, at the foot of the Dunlady Road, closed during World War One.

2. They were thatched for the last time just before the Great War, the thatch being fastened with scobes from the previous year's ditching.

3. William also collected the rents from Gape Row. In contrast to Charlie Allen's £418.2.10 p.a. for Stormont Castle, Gape Row brought in 1/- and 2/- per week per cottage. Records show that the Row had a large turnover of tenants.

4. Bingham was widely deferred to. For example, on hearing that Dr. Bingham had embarked on a D.D., Mr Weir the schoolmaster dropped his own, so as not to take the shine off the minister's achievement.

5. Catherine Gordon's £350 bequest to the parish poor helped some of the worst off to get by. In 1907, for example, Mary Montgomery was given a ton of coal and a handkerchief. Mrs Gilmore was given half a ton of coal, a blanket and a pair of combinations.

6. Traditional remedies were also used. Jack McKibbin writes that 'the kink' (whooping cough) could be cured by receiving 'a slice of bread and butter from married people of the same name.' Another cure was to pass the patient under a donkey. Warts could be cured by smearing them with slime from the blacksmith's trough.

7. The Comber Road had the 'Iona' and the 'Myona', however, by and large the southside of the parish took the train. When the 6.10 pulled in every evening the Old Dundonald Road became black with people, many with two or three miles still to walk. The closure of the line in 1953 left Grahamsbridge in a kind of limbo.

8. Some names are apt, for example the moat can be seen from Moatview, and Cherryhill once had cherry trees. Others are less so. Hanwood Heights is not in Ballyhanwood. Dundonald Heights is at the bottom of a hill. The King's Road has never had a king near it. Dunleady Park (while it commendably uses the 18th century pronounciation of Dunlady), is not in Dunlady. Ballyoran Primary is, or rather was, in the townland of Carrowreagh, as is Ballyoran Lane and half of the Ballybeen estate. While Tullycarnet is by some fluke in Tullycarnet, Vionville is on Beech Hill. (Vionville farm was on the other side of the road.)

9. In the early 1970s U.D.A. detachments trained on the Cairn Hill, posing as scouts on outward bound courses. Vionville is built on a former paramilitary rifle range.

10. Something similar had happened before. In the early 1980s six police families left Cumberland after receiving threatening letters.

11. Castlereagh Council has an impressive roster of firsts: first smokeless zone, first Woman's Centre, first council funded archaeological excavation, etc., all on one of the lowest rates in the province.

Bibliography

1 Books

Adair,P. *A true Narrative of the Rise and Progress of the Presbyterian Church in Ireland 1632–70* (in Killen,W.D.,Belfast,1886)

Ancient Monuments in N.I. not in state care (Belfast,1952)

Anon. *The County Down Election of 1805* (London,1805)

Archdall,M. *Monasticon Hibernicum* (Dublin,1873)

Armstrong,R. *Through the Ages to Newtownabbey* (Antrim,1977)

Arnold,R.M. *The County Down* (Whitehead,1981)

Bambrick,W.D. *Historical Development of Dundonald* (unp.thesis Q.U.B.,1952)

Barkley,Rev.J.M. *Short History of the Presbyterian Church in Ireland* (Belfast,1959)

Bassett,G.H. *County Down. Guide and Directory* (Dublin,1886)

Beckett,J.C. *The Making of Modern Ireland* (London,1966)

Belfast & Ulster Directory (Belfast,1852–1966)

Belfast Urban Area Plan Vol.1 (Belfast,1969)

Benn,G. *History of the Town of Belfast* (Belfast,1823)

Benn,G. *History of the Town of Belfast* (Belfast,1877)

Bigger,F.J. *Four Shots from Down* (Belfast,1918)

Blake,J.W. *Northern Ireland in the Second World War* (Belfast,1956)

Borlase,W.C. *Dolmens of Ireland* (London,1897)

Bowsie,G.A. *Carryduff Presbyterian Church* (Belfast,1985)

Brown,L.T. *A Survey of Turf Working in County Down* (unp.thesis Q.U.B.,1967)

Brown,S.J. *Ireland in Fiction* (Dublin,1919)

Buckland,P. *James Craig* (Dublin,1980)

Burgess,C. *The Age of Stonehenge* (London,1980)

Burke's Landed Gentry (London,1886)

Byrne,F.J. *Irish Kings and High Kings* (London,1973)

Camblin,G. *The Town in Ulster* (Belfast,1951)

Canny,N.P. *The Elizabethan Conquest of Ireland* (Sussex,1976)

Carmody,Rev.W.P. *History of the Parish of Knockbreda* (Belfast,1929)

Charlesworth,J.K. *The Geology of Ireland* (London,1953)

Charlesworth,J.K. *Historical Geology of Ireland* (London,1963)

Chart,D.A.(ed) *Preliminary survey of the Ancient Monuments of N.I.* (Belfast,1940)

Clarke,H.J.StJ.*Thirty Centuries in S.E. Antrim* (Belfast,1938)

Clarke,R.S.J. *Gravestone Inscriptions County Down Vols.2 & 4* (Belfast,1968,1971)

Cleland,J.B. *The Ancient Family of Cleland* (London,1905)

Colgan,J. *Acta Sanctorum Hiberniae* (1645)

Connell,K.H. *Irish Peasant Society* (Oxford,1968)

de Paor,M. & L. *Early Christian Ireland* (London,1978)

de St. Helme,V. *Ruby-Laure* (Paris,1919)

Davies,G.L. & Stephens,N *Geomorphology of the British Isles & Ireland* (London,1978)

Devlin,P. *Yes We have no Bananas* (Belfast,1981)

Dickson,C. *Revolt in the North* (Dublin,1960)

Dolley,M. *Anglo-Norman Ireland* (Dublin,1972)

Dugdale,W. *Monasticon Anglicanum IV, pt 2* (London,1886)

Ervine,St.J. *Craigavon, Ulsterman* (London,1949)

Evyns,E.E. *Irish Folk Ways* (London,1957)

Evans,E.E. *Prehistoric and Early Christian Ireland* (Batsford,1966)

Evans,E.E. *The Personality of Ireland* (Cambridge,1973)
Faulkner,B. *Memoirs of a Statesman* (London,1978)
Ferguson,Sir S. *Hibernian Night's Entertainments* (Dublin,1887)
Fulton,J.T. *The Roads of County Down 1600–1900* (unp.thesis Q.U.B.,1972)
Flanagan,L.N.W. *Ulster* (Heinemann,1970)
Forman,H,B *Collected letters of John Keats* (London,1895)
ibson,W. *The Year of Grace* (Edinburgh,1860)
Green,E.R.R. Industrial Archaeology of County Down (H.M.S.O.,1963)
Griffiths,R. *Valuation of Tenements* (Dublin,1861)
Hanna,A. *These 340 Years of Witness* (Dundonald,1985)
Harbison,J & J. *A Society under Stress* (Somerset,1980)
Harris,W. *A Survey of the County Down* (Dublin,1740)
Harris,W. *The Antient and Present State of County Down* (Dublin,1744)
Herity,M. & Eogan,G. *Ireland in Prehistory* (London,1970)
Herries-Davies,G.L. & Stephens, N. *The Geomorphology of the British Isles* (London,1978)
Herring,I.J. *History of Ireland* (Belfast,1937)
Hill,A.R. *An analysis of the spatial distribution and origin of drumlins in N. Down and S.Antrim* (unp.thesis Q.U.B.,1968)
Hill,Rev.G. *The Montgomery Manuscripts* (Belfast,1869)
Hughes,K. *Early Christian Ireland: an introduction to the sources* (London,1972)
Hughes,K. & Hamlin,A *The Modern Traveller to the Early Irish Church* (S.P.C.K.,1977)
Jones,E. *Belfast in its Regional Setting* (Belfast,1951)
Jope,E.M.(ed) *Archaeological Survey of County Down* (H.M.S.O.,1966)
Joy,H. *Historical Collections of Belfast* (Belfast,1817)
Joyce,P.W. *The Origin & History of Irish Names of Places* (London,1912) Joyce,P.W. *Irish Local Names Explained* (Dublin,1979)
Kennedy,L. & Ollerenshaw,P. *An Economic History of Ulster 1820–1940* (Manchester,1985)
Killen,W.D. *History of Congregations of the Presbyterian Church in Ireland* (Belfast,1886)
Knox,A. *History of the County Down* (Dublin,1875)
Lamplugh,et al *The Geology of the country around Belfast* (Dublin,1904)
Latimer,W.T. *A History of Irish Presbyterians* (Belfast,1902)
Lawlor,H.C. *Ulster, its Archaeology and Antiquities* (Belfast,1928)
Leslie,Rev.J.B. & Swanzey,Rev.H.B. *Biographical Succession Lists of the Clergy of the Dioceseof Down* (Enniskillen,1936)
Lewis,S. *Topographical Dictionary of Ireland* (London,1837)
Lindsay,J. *The Normans and their World* (London,1974)
Logan,P. *Irish Country Cures* (Belfast,1981)
Lowry,T.K.(ed) *The Hamilton Manuscripts* (Belfast,1867)
Lyttle,W.G. *Betsy Gray* (Newcastle,1968)
McCabe,A.M. & Hirons,K.R. *South-East Ulster Field Guide* (Cambridge,1986)
McCutcheon,W.A. *Industrial Archaeology of Northern Ireland* (Belfast,1980)
McKibbin,J. *Memories under the Chestnut Tree* (Dundonald,1978)
McKibbin,J. *Dundonald in the new Environment* (Dundonald,1979)
McKibbin,J. *History of Dundonald Presbyterian Congregation* (Dundonald,1980)
McNeill,T.E. *Anglo-Norman Ulster* (Edinburgh,1980)
MacNiocaill,G. *Ireland before the Viking* (Dublin,1972)
McQuitty,Rev.J.A. *Historical Sketch of Dundonald Presbyterian Congregation 1645–*

1932 (Dundonald,1932)

M'Skimmin,S. *Annals of Ulster* (Belfast,1849)

Madden,R.R. *Antrim and Down in 1798* (Dublin,1860)

Manning,*et al Geology of Belfast & the Lagan Valley* (H.M.S.O.,1970)

Marshall, J.J. *Stormont Castle's past* (Bel.Tel.,Nov 17,1932)

Maxwell,C *Irish History from Contemporary Sources* (London,1925)

Miller,H.C.]i[The Church on the Stye Brae (Belfast,1987)

Mitchell,F. *The Irish Landscape* (Collins,1976)

Moody,T.W. & Martin,F.X.*The Course of Irish History* (Cork,1967)

Muff,H.B. *Memoirs of the Geological Survey of Ireland* (Dublin,1904)

Nelson,I. *The Year of Delusion* (Belfast,1861)

O'Byrne,C. *As I Roved Out* (Belfast,1946)

O'Corrain,D. *Ireland before the Normans* (Dublin,1972)

O'Donovan,J. *The Book of Rights* (1847)

O'Laverty,Rev.J. *The Diocese of Down and Connor* (Dublin,1880)

O'Laverty,Rev.J. *History of the Parish of Holywood* (Belfast,c.1878)

Orpen,G.H. *Ireland under the Normans* (Oxford,1920)

Otway-Ruthven,A.J. *A History of Medieval Ireland* (London,1968)

Owen,D.J. *History of Belfast* (Belfast,1917)

Packenham,T. *The Year of Liberty* (London,1968)

Page,R. *Decline of an English Village* (London,1974)

Parker,R. *The Common Stream* (London,1975)

Parliamentary Gazetteer of Ireland 1844–5 (Dublin,1846)

Pender,S.(ed) *Census of Ireland of c.1659* (Dublin,1939)

Perceval-Maxwell,M. *Scottish Migration to Ulster* (London,1973)

Praeger,R.L. *B&CDR Official Guide to Co. Down* (Belfast,1900)

P.H.S.I. *History of Congregations* (Belfast,1982) Proudfoot,V.B. *Settlement & Economy in County Down* (unp.thesis Q.U.B., 1957)

Raftery,J. *Prehistoric Ireland* (London,1951)

Reeves,Rev.W. *Ecclesiastical Antiquities* (Dublin,1867)

Reid,J.S. *History of the Presbyterian Church in Ireland* (Belfast,1867)

Riddell,J.H. *Berna Boyle: A Love Story of the County Down* (London,1884)

Robinson,P.S. *The Plantation of Ulster* (Dublin,1984)

Roebuck,P. *Plantation to Partition* (Belfast,1981)

Royal Automobile Club *N.I. County Road Map and Gazetteer* (Belfast,1937)

Simpson,N *The Belfast Bank 1827–1970* (Belfast,1975)

Stephens,N & Glasscock,R.E.(eds) *Irish Geographical Studies* (Belfast,1970)

Stevenson,J. *Two Centuries of life in Down* (Belfast,1920)

Stewart,Rev.A. *History of the Church in Ireland since the Scots were Naturalised* (in Killen,W.D., Belfast,1886)

Taylor & Skinner *Maps of the Roads of Ireland* (1777)

Teeling,C.H. *The Irish Rebellion of 1798 & Sequel* (Shannon,1972)

Tizdall,W. *The Conduct of Dissenters* (Dublin,1712)

Toye,J. *Brief Memorials of the Rev. Thomas Toye* (Belfast,1873)

Weir,A. *Early Ireland: a Field Guide* (Belfast,1980)

Weir,Rev.J. *The Ulster Awakening* (London,1860)

White,A.R. *Gape Row* (Belfast,1934)

White,A.R. *Mrs Murphy buries the Hatchet* (London,1936)

Whittrow,J.B. *Geology and Scenery in Ireland* (London,1970)

Wilson,H.E. *The Regional Geology of N.I.* (H.M.S.O.,1972)

Woodman,P.C. *The Mesolithic in Ireland* (B.A.R.,1978)

Woodman,P.C. *Excavations at Mount Sandel 1973–77* (H.M.S.O.,1985)
Young,R.M. *Historical Notices of Old Belfast and its Vicinity* (Belfast,1896)

2 Articles

Abbreviations: B.N.F.C. Belfast Naturalist's Field Club; B.N.H.&P.S. Belfast Natural History and Philosophical Society; D,B.&P.W.C Dundonald Business & Professional Woman's Club; J.B.H.S. Journal of the Bangor Historical Society; J.E.B.H.S. Journal of the East Belfast Historical Society; J.R.S.A.I. Journal of the Royal Society of Antiquaries of Ireland; P.H.S.I. Presbyterian Historical Society of Ireland; P.R.I.A. Proceedings of the Royal Irish Academy; U.J.A. Ulster Journal of Archaeology; Ul.Tat. Ulster Tatler.

Baker,R. *Dundonald old and new* (Ul.Tat.,1970)
Belfast Telegraph Cuttings File, Central Library, Belfast;*Shots at Stormont* 20.6.22;*Description of Stormont* 17.11.32.
Boal,F.W. & Moffitt,M.K. *A partly destroyed rath in Killarn townland, Newtownards, Co. Down* (U.J.A.,Vol.22,107–11,1959)
Case,H. *Settlement-patterns in the north Irish Neolithic* (U.J.A.,Vol.32,3–23,1969)
Charlesworth,J.K. *Some observations on the glaciation of north-east Ireland* (P.R.I.A.,45B,255–95,1939)
Carr,P.A. *An Early Mesolithic site near Dundonald, Co. Down* (U.J.A.,Vol.48,122–3,1985)
Carr,P.A. *An Early Mesolithic site near Comber, Co. Down* (U.J.A.,Vol.50,1987)
Carson,J.T. *Irish Presbyterian Communion Tokens* (P.H.S.I.,1980)
Chart,D.A. *The break up of the estate of Con O'Neill* (P.R.I.A.,Vol.48,1942)
Collins,A.E.P. *Settlement in Ulster 0–1100AD* (U.J.A.,Vol.31,53–8,1968)
Cordner,W.S. *Holy wells* (U.J.A.,Vol.5,90–95,1942)
Curl,J.S. *Mausolea in Ulster* (Belfast,1978)
Excursion to Dundonald and neighbourhood (B.N.F.C.,Vol.1,pt.5,301–9,1879)
Davies,O & Quinn,D.B. *Irish Pipe Roll 1211–2* (U.J.A.,Vol.4,1941)
Garner,M.A.K. *N. Down as displayed in the Clanbrassil Lease & Rent Book* (B.N.H.&P.S.,Vol.8,1965)
Geological Survey 1904, *Belfast sheet memoir*
Gillespie,R *Thomas Raven and the mapping of the Claneboy Estates* (J.B.H.S.,Vol.1,1981)
George,A.H. & Davies,O. *Norman Graveslabs from Co.Down* (U.J.A.,Vol.9,37–44,1946)
Gray,W. *Cromlechs in Down and Antrim* (J.R.S.A.I.,Vol.6,354–67,1883–4)
Greeves,J.R.H. *North Down at the end of the 16th century* (B.N.H.&P.S.,Vol.5,5–15,1960)
Griffith,E.M. *From Dundonald to Comber* (Ul.Tat.,73–4,Nov.1974)
Hill,A.R. & Prior,D.B. *Directions of ice movement in north-east Ireland* (P.R.I.A.,66B,71–84,1968)
The Kempe Stones (*Dublin Penny Journal*,293,1834)
Latimer,Rev.T.W. *The old session book of the Presbyterian congregation at Dundonald, Co. Down* (U.J.A..,2nd Ser.,Vol.3,227–32;Vol.4,33–6,1897)
Lawlor,H.C. *Mote & Mote & Bailey Castles in de Courcy's Principality of Ulster* (U.J.A.,Vol.2,1939)
Lawlor,H.C.*Some notes on the dwelling places of prehistoric man in N.E. Ireland* (B.N.H.&P.S.,53,1915–16)

Lawlor,H.C. *Vassals of the Earls of Ulster* (U.J.A.,Vol.3,16–26,1940,Vol.4,23–7,1941)

McAughtry,S. *Comber – the perfect town* (Ir.Times,15 Sept.,1981)

MacNamee,P *The history of Holywood*(Holywood)

Mallory,J.P. *The Long Stone, Ballybeen, Dundonald, Co. Down* (U.J.A.,Vol.47,1–4,1984)

Marshall,J.J. Stormont Castle's past (Bel.Tel.,Nov.17,1932)

Milligan,A. *The Ancient Road to Newtown* (U.J.A.,Vol.2,43–5,1939)

Newtownards Chronicle *Dundonald Pars*

N.I.C.R.C. *Flight: Population Movement in Belfast during Aug. 1981* (1971)

The Ralph Will Case (anon,1834)

Patterson,W.H. *Remarks on ancient grave slabs near Dundonald* (B.N.F.C-.,Vol.3,pt.4,185–7,1891)

Phoenix,E. *Dundonald Graveyard* (Ul.Tat.,Dec.1984)

Rose-Cleland,A. *Urn found in Co. Down* (U.J.A.,1st Ser.,255,1895)

St. Elizabeth's Year Book (Dundonald,1961)

The story of our village (D.B.&P.W.C.,1970)

Scott-Pearson,A.F. *The Origins of Presbyterianism in Co. Down* (Belfast,1948)

Templeton,W *Carn-Gaireah, or Grave Carns* (Collectanea de rebus Hibernica,ed.Vallancey,Vol.6,1804)

Ulster Folklife (Vol.3,pt1,1957,Vol.25,Vol.5,No.1,1979;Vol6,No.2,1981;Vol.8-,No.1,1982;Vol.9,No.20,1985,No.21,1985,No.22,1986)

Vernon,P. *Drumlins and Pleistocene ice flow over the Ards peninsula/Strangford Lough area, Co. Down* (J.Glaciology,6,pt45,401–9,1966)

Wilson,J. *The Clelands of Stormont* (J.E.B.H.S.Vol.1,No.4,1984)

3 Primary Sources

Abbreviations: I.S.P.O. Irish State Paper Office; P.H.S.I. Presbyterian Historical Society of Ireland; P.R.O.N.I. Public Record Office of Northern Ireland.

Church of Ireland:Dundonald Vestry Minute Book 1808–1923, Marriage Register 1811–44, Baptismal Register 1811–45; 1846–78, Burial Register 1823–81; P.R.O.N.I.:D310/2,T2438

Cleland family:P.R.O.N.I.:D495,D654/E2/11,D671/C/142,D1684,D1759,D2929/1/15, T804/36,T1347,T2242/1–3; Telford letter,Stott letter:Greeves Ms Collection, Linenhall Library, Belfast.

Cumming family:P.R.O.N.I.:D509,D1905/2/276B,D2064/1–23,T1418

Galway family:P.R.O.N.I.:D3791

Gordon\family:P.R.O.N.I.:D618/324/VII,D1430/B/5,D1759/3A/6,D1905/12/37A,D2229/1–3

Lambert/Annesley leases:P.R.O.N.I.

Land:Alec Robb's notebook (c.1941) ex.John Robb; P.R.O.N.I.: D438/95,D654/R2/1,Y1/9,D776 p67–9,D778,D1759/3A/1,D1905/2/18/5,276B, DoD778/76,FIN5A/131,FIN5B/2/106,MIC6/140,MIC6A/34,MIC19/8,T776,T784/6,T1009/114,T2253,VAL1B/137,VAL2B/3/17A-B,VAL12B/17/8A-G,VAL12B/23/5A-F;News Letter;Camperdown leases; Ballyhanwood leases

Land war:I.S.P.O.:Outrage Papers,Down1849/26,43,Down1850/396; Banner of Ulster

McClean family:P.R.O.N.I.:D1905/2/145

McDowell family:McDowell geneology & notes (c.1940) ex.Norah McDowell

McRoberts family:Mary McRoberts' family history (c.1920) ex.Norah Gardiner

Mills:News Letter; P.R.O.N.I.:VAL1A/3/5,VAL1B/137,VAL2B/3/17A-B,VAL12B/

17/8A-G,Val12B/23/5A-F

Maps:P.R.O.N.I.:D616,D654/M70/13,D662/6,D2287,DoD662/6,T870,T1244/
  22,T1493/44,T1451,T1763/2,T2158,VAL1A/3/5

Mining:P.R.O.N.I.:D654/P/1

Normans:C.D.I.Vol.I 708,833,1015,2600,2663

Plantation & after:P.R.O.N.I.:D1759/3C/1,D1854/1/1–23:DA106/27;DOD623/1–
  8;T307,T370,T371,T458,T497,T563,T808,T1056

Presbyterian Church:P.R.O.N.I.:T808/15307; P.H.S.I.:Session Book of ye Paroch of
  Kirkdonnel 1678; Records of the Synod of Ulster 1691–1720 Vol.1; Minutes of the
  Presbytery of Down 1707–45 1798 Rebellion: P.R.O.N.I.: D714,D1494/4/31,5/
  3,MIC19/46,T2286; I.S.P.O.Rebellion Papers:620/2/15/22,4/41,15/36,15/43,15/50;
  The Northern Star, Linenhall Library, Belfast.

Roads; P.R.O.N.I.:D671/C/142/1–8; News Letter

Robb family: P.R.O.N.I.:T1454,T1469

School:P.R.O.N.I.:EDI/15 p160–1,SCH127/1/1

Society:Census 1841–1971; Poor Inquiry (Ireland),PP,Vol.32,1836,Supp to app.E,326;
  James Stitt's notebook (c.1890) ex.Richard Morrow;P.R.O.N.I.:E30,T765/1p156,

Stormont:P.R.O.N.I.: CAB 4/1,5,7,10,14,15,16,22,24,25,30,34,52,69,72,80,85,91,93–
  5,126,144–5,152,154,156,161,195,204,205,262,284,303,311,381,427,429,438,476,48-
  0,482,484. FIN 19/ 2/347,4/122,6/13,10/1,120,11/12,52,13/47,16/19,17/34,17/59,19/
  54,63,146,20/44,21/2,23/3,24/77; Hansard 1st ser,I,44,57–9,177,259; Senate Ser,I,57;
  B558/41 Photos: CWPB 1

Toll war: P.R.O.N.I.:D289,D795

Index

Adair, Rev. 74
Afghanistan 147
Agricola 43
Ailsa Craig microgranite 16
Albert Bridge 23
Allen family 157
Alliance Party 152, 226
Alluvium 17, 18
Allybrook, bog of 96; House 195
America, north of 88, 101, 102, 104, 106,
   120, 130, 180, 186, 200, 214, 226
Andrews family 100, 117, 118, 122, 124
Annesley family 91, 93, 115
Antrim 77, 101; county 23, 31, 74, 96, 136;
   plateau 13, 131
Archy's Brae (bray) 96
Ardara Avenue 163, 195
Ardbrin trumpet 42
Ardcarn estate 198, 200, 211, 212, 221, 225;
   Boot Boys 204
Ards peninsula 10, 73; the 54, 55, 56, 66, 67
Armagh 95; museum 35
Atherton, Col. 106
Atkinson 91

B&CDR 39, 125-7, 193
Ballyalton 13, 100
Ballybarnes 52, 100, 101
Ballybeen 13, 39, 40, 65, 74, 75, 101, 109,
   120, 126, 208, 210; estate 14, 24, 26, 37,
   204, 213, 214-215, 217, 219-225, 230;
   House 142, 143; Riot Squad 224
Ballycloghan 65, 70, 72, 85
Ballydavey 72
Ballyhackamore 17, 65 126, 181
Ballyhalbert 68, 184
Ballyhanwood 13, 34, 52, 65, 68, 83, 88, 106,
   116, 134, 151, 152-4, 198, 202, 220, 226;
   House 75, 146; Hanwood House 145,
   146; vill in 59
Ballyhenry 65
Ballykeel 198, 203
Ballylisbredan 53, 65, 75, 91, 95, 208
Ballyloghan 34, 65
Ballymacarrett 138, 161
Ballymagan 17, 55, 60, 68
Ballymaglaff 23-26, 52, 65, 83, 100, 101
Ballymagreehan 65
Ballymena 100
Ballymenoch 198
Ballymiscaw 50, 51, 54, 65, 75, 81, 129, 137,
   155, 160, 161, 175, 217
Ballymorran 57
Ballynahinch 105

Ballyoran 13, 46, 49, 51, 54, 65, 75, 90, 93,
   96, 97, 117, 139, 143–45, 150, 156,
   166–7, 196, 202, 217
Ballyrainey 13, 16, 35, 42, 43, 65, 71, 75, 95,
   100, 101, 127; Road 19
Ballyregan 16, 42, 70, 75, 95, 134, 160, 172,
   197, 198, 211
Ballyrogan 35, 65, 100, 101, 122, 129, 186,
   198, 203
Ballyrussell 52, 54, 59, 65, 75, 80, 93, 95,
   100, 101, 111, 122-3
Ballysallagh 143
Ballyskeagh 65, 100
Ballystockart 52, 65, 129, 176, 183, 208, 217
Ballywalter 68
Bangor 15, 49, 65, 68, 77, 88, 90, 106, 126,
   143, 148, 171, 193, 205, 226
Bann flake 22
Barnett family 98
Barr 145
Barrow, Capt. 66
Basalt 13, 29, 37, 65
Battletown 73
Beeches, the 143, 181, 206, 212
Belfast 28, 50, 64, 67, 77, 82, 83, 85, 86, 95,
   96, 99, 100–106, 109, 113, 116, 118–21,
   123, 131–33, 136, 137, 139, 145, 148,
   154, 156, 160, 162–3, 175, 177, 181, 186,
   196, 198, 201, 202, 226; Castle 177;
   expansion of 96, 126, 162, 204, 211, 214;
   Lake 17; Lough 12, 17, 22, 25, 131;
   Theatre Royal 142; Urban Area Plan
   216, 228, 230
Bell, Granny 170-1, 184
Bellavista 53
Belmont (Campbell College) 84, 111, 141
Belvoir Park 177
Benn, George 28, 37, 56
Berckelay, Sir John 68
Berkshire International 220
Bessmount 116, 160, 184-5
Bethesda Mission Hall 139, 142, 160-1, 167,
   184
Betsy Gray 106
Bigger, F.J. 60
Bingham, James 160, 171-2, 177, 183
Blacksmiths 115, 131, 153, 163, 175, 198, 202
Blathmac, the Ui/Hy 48, 49, 54
Bloomfield 17, 126
Blow, Daniel 89, 103, 114, 213
Borlase 31
Book of Rights 49
Bordes, Lt. 116
Bowman, Hugh 172

Boyd, John 195
Boyd family (of Gape Row) 191
Boy's Brigade, 43rd 184, 199, 208
Boys High School 201, 217, 221
Breda 49, 64, 81, 84
Brice, Lambert 106
Bricru 42, 43
Britain 12, 31
Brookeborough, Lord 180
Browne, Capt. 66
Bullets, 96
Burton, Dr. 177, 183, 195; Avenue 195, 199

Cairn Hill 33, 106, 198, 202; Carngaver 33, 34
Caldwell, James 89
Camperdown 116, 127, 198, 199, 203
Canada 12, 13, 143, 200
Carlton, Minnie 204
Carmody, Rev. 46, 84
Carrickfergus 55, 59, 67, 73, 79, 129
Carrowreagh 10, 11, 42, 46, 48, 50, 65, 75, 97, 101, 103, 122, 150-1, 155, 157, 196, 198, 202, 220, 229; Road 46; Gardens 99
Carson, Samuel 122, 125
Castle Espie 11, 22, 154
Castlebeg 22, 65, 71, 75, 91, 100-101; chapel 47; vill at 59, 62
Castlehill 84, 122, 150
Castlereagh 55, 64, 65–8, 79, 103, 110, 120, 122, 137, 138, 214, 227; Council 199, 211, 220, 226; Hills 9–12, 16, 17, 25; Lord 104, 110, 111
Catholics 76, 87, 90, 137, 138, 155, 181, 205, 220-222
Cavan 69, 155
Cave Glen 54
Cave Hill 62
Celts/ celtic 40, 44
Cemetery 70, 162
Chapel Field 48; Hill 46
Chancellor family 143
Chartists 123
Cherryhill 211
Cherryvalley 184
Chert 10
Church of Ireland 70, 74, 76, 79, 84, 107–9, 146, 155, 158–9, 177, 211, 219; church 50, 88, 108, 112, 130, 148, 158, 206; cemetery 72, 144, 206; school 127–9; Vestry 88, 89, 107–9, 148, 159; St Molua's 219; St Mary's 219
Clachan 71
Clannaboy/Clandeboy 63-8, 73
Cleland family 52, 110–113, 114, 115, 116, 118, 123, 132–6, 146–8, 158–9, 169, 180; mausoleum 112–3, 130

Cobham, Thos 80, 82, 92
Cooke, Henry 120, 139
Cooper's Corner 19, 71; farm 100
Cooper Hill 99
Comber 11, 18, 24, 34, 39, 47, 49, 50, 57, 67-69, 71, 73, 81, 83, 88, 90, 95, 99, 105, 106, 115, 117, 118, 124-6, 138, 148, 151, 157, 184, 190, 214; Road 34, 39, 47, 59, 85, 116, 126, 127, 131, 151, 160, 162, 164, 195, 198, 199, 203, 210, 206, 222; Cummer Annie 172-3 Commodore, the 102,
Conlig 34, 106
Conochobar 42
Connacht 61, 74
Connswater river 22, 202
Cordner, Joe 193, 205
Cork 9, 160, 186
Cornwallis 106
Coronation Park 98, 203, 211
Cotter, John 147, 183, 202
Craig, Sir James 177-9
Craigavad 15, 68, 72
Craigantlet 65, 83, 100, 122, 129, 134, 137, 160-1, 198, 222-4
Craiglea 54
Crawfordsburn 106, 125
Cregagh 213
Creighton's Green 129
Cricky Field 183, 191
Crossgar 65
Cruise, John 206
Crustaceans 9
Cruthin 48
Cuchulainn 42
Cuddy, Hugh 107, 108
Culross Drive 18, 165
Cultra 175
Cumberland estate 18, 20, 69, 71, 211, 215
Cumming family 89, 91-3, 104, 115
Cunningburn 22, 80
Curl, J.S. 112
Cuthbertson, Sally 213

D.U.P. 224-226, 228
Dairmid (& Grianne) 28
Dal-Araidhe (Dalaradia) 45, 48
Dal-Fiatach 48, 49
Dal Riata 48
De Burgh 61
De Courcy 55, 57, 59
De Dundoenald, Richard & Reinard 57
De Lacy 57, 59, 60
De Marisco 59, 60
De Ridelsford, Emeline 61
De Rossal 59
De Weldebuef 59

Deall, Will 77
Delaney, Mrs 84
Dempster, Jean 77; Psyche 193, 208
Derry 15, 61, 63, 67, 79, 81, 139, 145, 155
Derry-Ceite 54
Dickson family 145-6, 202
Dickie, Mary 72
Dickson, Sander 70
Dobbs, Francis 101
Dolerite 13, 19
Donaghadee 37, 43, 65, 69, 75, 80, 86, 88,
    103, 115, 126, 131, 161, 196 Donegal 15.
    155
Donegore Hill 31
Downpatrick 41, 55, 56, 57, 81, 90, 126, 206
Dromore 80
Drumbo 65
Drumlins 17, 18, 19, 51, 55, 70, 97, 229
Dublin 15, 57, 62, 91, 101, 102, 109, 159,
    177, 186,; Castle 101; *Penny Journal* 28
Dufferin 55, 64
Duncrue 59
Dundonald, the 157-8; elephant 110; House
    70, 113, 213, 220, 222; International Ice
    Bowl 145, 226-228
Dundrum 57
Dungannon 102
Dunlady 11, 16, 50, 59, 62, 65, 75, 89, 90,
    93, 96, 101, 103, 109, 116, 123, 129, 143,
    144, 146, 150, 174, 185, 202, 229; House
    10, 57, 90, 130; Road 86, 90
Dun Rogan 25

East Link Road 39
Echlin, bishop 70
Edirsgal (Edresgall) 49, 59; vill of 59, 62
Egilshame, Jane 79
Eliot, George 125
Elizabeth I 66, 67
Elk (Central) Inn 116, 151, 162, 173, 184,
    186, 206, 222
Embroidery 156
Emigration 88, 96, 143, 156
England 35, 43, 44, 57, 66, 68, 102, 133, 148,
    200
Esker (the Rank) 19, 45; House 144
Essex, Earl of 67
Estyn Evans, E. 29, 33, 34, 42

Fairies 52, 56; field 47; forts 52; graveyard
    42; mound 42; rings 42, 47, 48
Farrar, Shirley 84
Farrell, Arthur 128, 140, 159
Faulkner, Brian 180, 222
Ferguson, Sir Samuel 62
Fergusons (of Dunlady) 123
Fergusons (of Ballyregan) 197-8

Fergusons (of Ballyrogan) 186
Fermanagh 155
Fhindich, bishop 45
Finiston, Joseph 79
Finlay, Rev. 114-20
Finnian, St. 46
Fisher Body 220
Fisher family 146
Flat Island 70
Fleming & James 187, 193, 205
Florida Manor 113
Forest 9, 11, 14, 21-3, 25, 27, 35, 44
Fort Road 52
France 25, 41, 60, 80, 102, 203, 106, 132-34,
    136, 146-8, 186
Frizelle, Thomas 211

Gallowgh 65
Galways (of Ballymiscaw) 201; Fort 51
Galway family (of Millmount) 98, 120, 137,
    139-42, 143, 164-5, 172, 176
Galway Park 195
Garnet, Matthew 87
Gape Row (White Row) 114, 148, 149, 168,
    171, 172, 174, 181, 185, 191, 193, 194;
    the novel 169, 208
Gaws Wall 22
Gentry 49, 69, 89-93, 139-48
Germany 133
Gerrard, Sir Thomas 66
Gettysburg 143
Ghosts 89, 167, 197
Giant's Ring 42
Gibson, James 169
Gilnahirk 45, 52, 65, 106, 129, 152, 154
Givan, Rev. 137, 138
Glasgow 157
Glen Hill 60, 97
Gobelin tapestries 136
Goldring, Dr. 206
Gordon family 113-116, 123, 125, 127, 146,
    158, 159, 162
Gortgrib 45, 46, 52, 65
Gourley family 176, 199, 217
Graham, William 119, 120
Grahamsbridge 72, 85, 116, 127, 156, 173,
    207
Grainne 28
Grand Prix Park 184
Gransha 161; Road 94, 187, 195, 210
Graphite 10
Grapholite 9
Grattan 102
Gravel 9, 16, 17, 18, 20
Green Belt Association 229, 230
Greengraves 13, 19, 28, 35, 37, 46, 54, 72,
    83, 129, 198; Road 19, 139;

Ballycloughtogal 28
Greenland 12
Green, the 69, 128, 138, 148, 156, 170, 171, 177, 184, 190, 199, 208, 211, 217
Greeves family 140, 210
Greeves, J.R.H. 66
Grey, Thompson 175, 176
Grey, William 29
Greyabbey 10, 65, 90
Greywacke 9, 10
Griffith, Ted 24
Groomsport 81

Haggerston Castle 136, 146, 147
Halstatt 41
Hamilton, Sir James 69, 70, 73
Hamilton, James 74
Hanna, Sandy 119, 160
Harefield, the 192 Harpur, Reggie 210
Harris, W. 64, 65, 85, 90
Hawthorne, Capts. 157
Hazlett, James 87, 88
Henry, Dr. 190
Henryville 127, 154, 164
Herron, Dr. 116, 146
Hewett, Lord 81
Hill, Alan 18
Hillsborough 124
Holy Well (Ballyoran) 140
Holywood 10, 48, 49, 57, 65, 67, 72, 74, 77, 110, 119, 124, 126, 129, 131, 138, 192; Hills 9, 10, 11, 12, 16, 17, 32, 81, 116, 153, 202
Home Rule 144, 151, 152, 154, 174-5
Hooks Club, the 205
Housing 118, 148–9, 194–5, 206–7,
Hui-Dearca-Chein 45
Hunter, Capt. Henry 80, 81
Hunter, William 82
Hutchinson, Francis 84

Iberian peninsula 41
Iceland 12
Icenci 43
Ikkerin, Lady 84, 89
India 86
Inishowen 61
Inler river 22, 23, 37, 97
Island Hill 22
Isle of Man 21
Itinerants 79-80, 109, 172-4, 196

Jacobites 80, 81
Jacobs, Mabel 195, 196, 201, 205
Jenkins, Rev. 218
John, King 57, 58, 59, 111, 211
Johnston of Ballykilbeg 175

Johnston family 175, 189, 205
Jonesboro' 95
Joyce family 111

Kame 20
Kane family 148, 172, 202, 205, 208
Keats, John 115
Keevett, Thomas 71
Kempe Stone 28-31, 34, 35, 112, 198
Kildownie Moat 50
Killarn 37, 38, 46, 48, 52, 53, 54, 60, 83, 98, 101, 122, 174, 196
Killeen 129, 134
Killinchy 49, 57, 73, 113, 118
Killops family 143, 146, 157, 174
Killyleagh 81
Kintyre, Mull of 21
Kirkdonnell (Curdonnell) 71, 72, 79, 96, 97, 100, 101, 104; well 85
Kirkholme, James 72
Kircubbin 10, 184
Kirkwood family 143, 184, 204
Knock 34, 55, 72, 81, 84, 85, 111, 126, 127, 145, 160, 161, 174, 186, 190, 219
Knock Golf Club 18, 85, 113, 162, 180-2, 184, 199, 200, 203, 208
Knockbreda 49, 65, 70, 84, 110, 115, 137
Kynier, John 70

Lagan, river 22, 67, 131; valley 10, 11, 17, 122
Lake, General 104, 106
Lambert family 89-91, 95, 96, 98
Land 70-1, 77, 79, 93, 116, 141, 149, 151, 152-5, 176, 197-8, 199; field boundaries 71, 93, 116, 150, 165; disturbances on 121-5, 130
Laud, archbishop 70
Larne 61
Lawlor 57, 59
Lecale 59
Leinster (Martyrology of) 45
Leslie, Edmund 84
Leslie & Swanzy 159
Lewis 116
Legoniel 184
Lisburn 10, 73, 85
Lizst, Franz 115, 148
Long Stone Park farm 96
London 136, 146, 147
Londonderry's, the 115, 118, 124, 125, 134
Longford 10
Longstone, the 22, 37-40, 43, 104
Lords, Irish House of 87
Lough Neagh 64
Loughbrickland 42
Loughgall 218

Louth, Co. 94
Lowthian, John 70
Lyttle, W.G. 106

MacDonlevy, Rory 55
McAughtry, Sam 181, 215, 222, 225
McBride, Ben 120-1
McClean family 116, 139, 140
McClements, Hugh 145
McConnell family 169, 171, 181, 191, 192,
    199, 200, 201, 204
McCullough, Peter 42
McDonald, Capt. 116, 131
MacDonlevy, Rory 55
M'Dowell, John (of Ballyhanwood) 88
McFadden, Sgt. 184, 192
MacFirbis, D. 44, 49
McGimpseys 87
McIlwaine, Andrew 99
McKeag family (of Gape Row) 189
McKee's dam 156, 207
McKelvey family 207-8
McKeown, Joe 197,199
McKibbin family 148, 163; Jack 172, 191
McLeroth, Col. Robert 103
MacMalwawg, Nellanus 64
McMillan family 202, 207
McNall, John 107 M'Nall, Minnie (Comber
    Road) 193, 202
M'Nall, Minnie (Gape Row) 169, 170-1
McNeill family 169, 172, 204
McRoberts family 96, 104, 107, 143, 144-5,
    165-7, 176, 197, 207, 210
M'Skimmin 103, 105
McTier, Mrs 90
McVeagh, Grace 123, 130
McQuitty, James 183, 189, 208, 218

Magee, Rev. Roy 219, 228
Magheralin 77
Mahee Island 22
Malone 141
Maroney, Lough 17, 25
Marsh 23, 27, 35, 38, 44, 56, 70, 85, 99, 116,
    134
Marshall, J.J. 50, 51, 55, 57
Martin, E.T. 120, 128, 144, 154, 160
Marvell, Andrew 102
Matheys, George 71
Matthews Stop Line 217
May, Queen of the 185
Meetin' Street 149, 172
Mesolithic 21-26; axe 22, 24; blades 22, 23;
    microliths 22; midden 22
Methodists 161, 184; church 19
Metro cinema 209
Midleton, Anne Lady 84

Millbank 99, 125
Miller's Forge 208, 217
Millisle 161, 196
Millmount (Co farm) 45, 100, 120, 137,
    139-42, 164-5, 184, 190, 197, 202
Mills 71, 97-100, 115, 157
Milltown 120, 160, 165
Mining 90
Moat/motte 19, 50, 55-8, 61, 112, 149, 164,
    189, 191, 200
Moat Inn 51, 57, 114, 115, 169, 191, 205,
    Moat Park 20, 71, 87, 220
Moat players 208
Moatview estate 70, 210, 211, 212
Montgomeries, the 46, 68, 73, 75, 76, 103;
    Manuscripts 73
Moody, Mr & Mrs 108, 131, 148
Morfie, Hew 77
Morrow family 94, 134, 152-4, 228
Morveen Park 144, 215
Motorman, Operation 222
Mountstewart 22, 34, 35, 73, 96
Mourne mountains 13, 80, 152
Movilla 46
Mudstone 9, 10
Muff, H.B. 18
Mullacrew 94
Munro 73
Munster 41, 74
Murder Bridge 86
Murdough, Miss 132, 135, 136
Mussolini 189

Navvy Row 162, 184, 185, 199, 200, 207, 212
Neagh, Lough 14, 15
Newry 81
Newtownards 10, 14, 17, 24, 62, 71, 73, 74,
    77, 80, 83, 85, 86, 87, 88, 95, 96, 99,
    103, 105, 106, 110, 118, 122, 124, 126,
    130, 131, 138, 145, 148, 177, 189, 222,
    223; Fault 10; Road 114, 133, 165, 190,
    204, 215, 219, 222; Nova Villa de
    Blathwic 56, 61
Newtownbreda 123
Nicknames 193
Normans 44, 46, 49, 51, 54, 58, 62, 63
Northern Bank 105
Nugent, General 106

O'Byrne, Cathal 111
O'Donovan, John 56, 116
O'Dornans (Sleught Durnings) 68
O'Gilmore, Thomas 72
O'Laverty, James 37, 45, 46, 47, 63, 64, 65,
    68
Old Dundonald Road 72, 85, 193, 195, 220
O'Neills (of the Clan Aedh Buidhe) 62, 63-8

Onassis family 135
Orange Order 151, 154, 172, 174-5, 208, 210, 225; Hall 127, 159, 174, 184, 191, 209, 217; Independent 174-5
Orangefield 177
Ormeau Park 22

Paisley, Ian 224, 225
Parliament Irish 102, 103
Patterson, William 28
Peartree hill 20
Peebles, Thomas 73-4
Pella Cottage 144, 151, 169
Pipe Roll 57
Pippard, Roger 57
Police barrack 121, 131, 190, 191
Polo Field 199, 201
Poor money 79, 109
Portadown 218
Portaferry 106, 115
Portavogie 10
Portpatrick 69
Portrush 205
Pottery, Neolithic 27, 30, 31; Bronze Age 34, 35, 39; Iron Age 46, 53
Praegar 13, 52
Presbyterians 73, 74, 76-81, 82, 83, 103, 124, 130, 137-9, 146, 155, 160-1, 167, 171-2, 177, 211, 217-8, 219; Communion tokens 83; manse 157, 160; meeting house 73, 80, 131, 138, 172, 201; New Light 89, 103; pewter 82; Presbytery 80, 83, 89; school 127-9; Session Book 76-8, 109; stables 192, 200; Unitarianism 119
Pringle, Francis 106

Quarriar, St. 46
Quarry Corner 10, 17, 19, 25, 38, 60, 61, 71, 100, 111, 156, 165, 187, 189, 191, 197, 228
Quarrying 95, 157
Quarry Lane 193, 195

Rank Road 19
Rankin, James 78
Rath 49, 53
Rathfriland 138
Raven, Thomas 69, 71, 97, 150
Ravera, Island 70
Ray, William 88
Reagh Ialand 22, 65
Reaville Park 70, 195
Reeves, William 49, 64
Reid J.S. 74, 80, 81
Reid, Sgt. 192
Revival, the 120, 136-9
Riddell, Mrs J.H. 118, 129-32, 172

Ring barrow 42, 46
Ringneill 22, 27
Roads 21, 71, 84-7, 115, 186, 189, 220
Robb family 107, 142-44, 181, 184, 199, 210, 219; Robb's Corner 176, 202; Road 142, 192, 204; farm 197, 202
Robinson (miller) 100
Robinson, Peter 226
Rockfield 58, 71, 137, 139-40
Roger of Chester 59
Rolls Royce 220, 223
Romans 43
Ross family 74, 75, 91, 93, 115
Rough Island 22
Russel, Joseph 114

Saintfield 105, 106
Sally river 97
Sand 9, 18, 20
Sandown (food vessel) 34
Sandstone 9, 11, 12, 13
Saunders, Col. 123
Savage, Robert 62
Schomberg 81
Schools 127-9, 137, 168, 175, 183-3, 214, 217
Scotland 15, 16, 17, 18, 21, 28, 43, 58, 61, 62, 65, 67, 68, 69, 72, 80, 92, 117, 131, 132, 143, 197, 217
Scots-Irish 15, 44, 74, 76, 80, 82
Scrabo 11, 13, 16, 36, 41, 99, 131, 136
Shale 9, 10, 11
Shaw, James 140
Shaw, Robert 165
Shawcross, Neil 112
Shucktown 94
Siltstone 9, 10
Sleught Durnings 65, 68
Sleught Owen-M'Quinn 65, 68
Sleught Kellies 65
Slieve Croob 12
Sliocht Aedh Breac 65, 68
Sloane's map 84, 85
Slowan, Edward 71
Smith, Adam 96
Smith, Sir Thomas 66, 67, 68
Solitude 45, 143
Somme, the 176
Sour Brae 99
Souterrain 49, 51, 54
Spar, the 69
Speech, local 72 169
Standing stones 36-40
Star Flute Band 191
State, Secretaries of 181, 225
Steel, Heart of 88, 89, 91
Stewart, James 82, 83, 89
Stewart, Rev. Andrew 69

Stevenson, John 96
Stitt 99
Stoney Road 57, 184, 198, 200, 221
Stormont 9, 10, 16, 20, 28, 70, 84, 110, 111,
   113, 116, 132-6, 147, 148, 150, 155, 157,
   162, 197, 198, 199, 202-3, 216;
   Parliament Buildings at 52, 111, 177-81,
   224, 225; Castle 180, 222
Stott, Thomas 111, 112, 132
Strangford Lough 10, 11, 14, 16, 22, 25, 27,
   80, 153
St. Andrews 65
St. Molioba 45
St. Patrick 45, 48
St. Patrick's College 45, 52
Summerfield 113, 162
Summerhill 45, 116, 189
Swain's Hill 198, 203
Symington family 140, 161; Band 161, 190,
   191, 199, 208-9

Tacitus 43
Tallagh (Martyrology of) 45
Tate, Ninian (also see Lambert family) 74
Taylor-Nobbs, R. 183, 213
Telford, Barney 132-6, 150
Temple Midden 22
Templeton, William 34, 35
Thames, river 10
Thompson, Hamilton 96, 104, 107, 114
Thornhill 111
Timbertown 127, 195
Tintown 127, 195
Tizdall, William
Toll war (and Fund) 109-10, 120
Tourist Trophy, the 186-9, 192
Toye, Thomas 120, 137, 142
Trevor, Arthur 84
Trollope, Anthony 84
Troubles, the 181, 215, 221-6
Tullycarnet 42, 52, 65, 68, 100, 103, 126,
   129, 137, 193, 217; estate 214, 215-6,
   217, 219, 221, 222, 223, 225
Tullycavy 90
Tyrone, Co. 15, 27, 63, 67, 155, 223

Ulster 14, 16, 43, 49, 54, 136, 220, 226; Earl
   of 55, 59, 60, 61, 62; Earldom of 62, 63,
   64: Museum 60, 66; custom 122;
   Farmers Union 152; Volunteer Force
   175; Tenant Right Association 121, 124,
   125; Defence Association 222, 224;
   Worker's Council strike 222-5; Journal
   of Archaeology 25, 35, 60; Cycle 43;
   Hospital 18, 25, 186, 207, 212, 220
Unicarval 16, 65, 71, 89, 91, 92, 104, 157
Union, Act of 111

Unionist Association 209
United Irishmen 103-6, 124, 213

Vikings 44, 48
Village players 208
Volunteers 102, 103

Wales 10, 44; Prince of 178, 179
Walker, Johnny 165, 176
Wanstead estate 211
Ward, William 228
Waterworth, Miss 169
Weir, Mr. 169, 182
Wellington, Duke of 84
Wellworths 20, 69, 206, 214
Westminister 60
Whinney Hill 20, 162
White, Agnes Romilly 115, 168, 169-71, 174,
   208; Rev. 159, 208
White Pillar 22
Whiteman's Row (Daisybank Terrace) 162,
   193, 195, 202
Williamite Wars 149
Williamson's map 81
Williamson, Thomas 109
Wilson, Capt. 102
Wilson, Joyce 134
Woodman, Peter 21
World War One 127, 162, 169, 175-7, 178
World War Two 20, 198-203
Wright, Dr. 205, 206
Wright, Stanley 182-3, 200

Yellow Island 76
York Fencibles 105
Young R.M. 64
Young, Thetford 108

Postscript

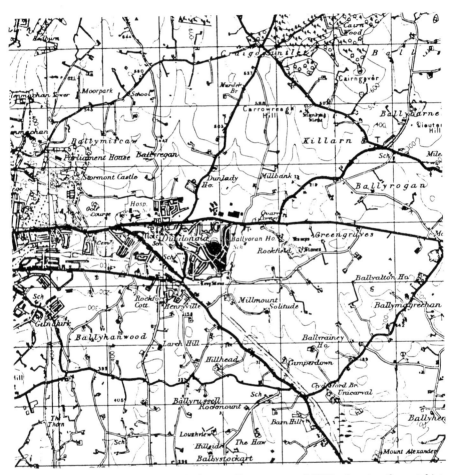

Dundonald as represented in the Ordnance Survey map of 1976, showing the outskirts of Belfast to the left. (Crown copyright; scale: one inch to the mile)